Persons and Bodies

What is a human person, and what is the relation between a person and his or her body? In her third book on the philosophy of mind, Lynne Rudder Baker investigates what she terms the person/body problem and offers a detailed account of the relation between human persons and their bodies. According to the solution Baker offers, a human person is constituted by a human body, but a human person is not identical to the body that constitutes him or her.

Baker's argument is based on a perfectly general view of material objects: the Constitution View. Applied to human persons, the Constitution View aims to show what distinguishes persons from all other beings and to show how we can be fully material beings without being identical to our bodies. The Constitution View yields answers to the questions "What am I most fundamentally?", "What is a person?", and "What is the relation between human persons and their bodies?" Baker argues that the complex mental property of first-person perspective enables one to conceive of one's body and mental states as one's own. She provides a convincing alternative to the competing viewpoints of Immaterialism and Animalism.

This book will be of interest to professional philosophers and graduate students, and will also appeal to psychologists and cognitive scientists interested in the philosophy of mind.

Lynne Rudder Baker is Professor of Philosophy at the University of Massachusetts, Amherst. She is the author of *Explaining Attitudes: A Practical Approach to the Mind* (1995).

Persons and Bodies

A Constitution View

LYNNE RUDDER BAKER

The University of Massachusetts at Amherst

CAMBRIDGE
UNIVERSITY PRESS

PUBLISHED BY THE PRESS SYNDICATE OF THE UNIVERSITY OF CAMBRIDGE
The Pitt Building, Trumpington Street, Cambridge, United Kingdom

CAMBRIDGE UNIVERSITY PRESS
The Edinburgh Building, Cambridge CB2 2RU, UK   http://www.cup.cam.ac.uk
40 West 20th Street, New York, NY 10011-4211, USA   http://www.cup.org
10 Stamford Road, Oakleigh, Melbourne 3166, Australia
Ruiz de Alarcón 13, 28014 Madrid, Spain

First published 2000

Printed in the United States of America

Typeface Bembo 10.5/13 pt.   *System* DeskTopPro$_{/UX}$® [BV]

A catalog record for this book is available from the British Library.

Library of Congress Cataloging-in-Publication Data
Baker, Lynne Rudder, 1944–
Persons and bodies : a constitution view / Lynne Rudder Baker.
p.   cm. – (Cambridge studies in philosophy)
Includes bibliographical references.
ISBN 0 521 59263 1 hb. – ISBN 0 521 59719 6 pb
1. Body, Human (Philosophy)   2. Personalism   I. Title.
II. Series.
B105.B64B35   2000
128'.6 – dc21   99-24024
                                            CIP

ISBN 0 521 59263 1   hardback
ISBN 0 521 59719 6   paperback

For Kate Sonderegger,
a perfect friend

Contents

Preface

In my earlier books, I developed a critique of the dominant view of the mind, according to which attitudes like beliefs are in the first instance brain states, and I offered an alternative, more pragmatic, approach. See *Saving Belief: A Critique of Physicalism* (Princeton, NJ: Princeton University Press, 1987) and *Explaining Attitudes: A Practical Approach to the Mind* (Cambridge: Cambridge University Press, 1995). On my alternative, attitudes – like believing, desiring, and intending – should be understood not primarily as brain states but as states of whole persons. Such a view raises the questions What is a person? and What is the relation between a person and her body? These are the questions that I hope to answer in this book. The answers require a very rich and detailed theory that I call the 'Constitution View.' In this book, I set out the Constitution View and defend it against criticism and rival views.

I have tried out much of the theory and argument that appears here at departmental colloquia and at conferences where I have given papers recently: Yale University, Notre Dame University, York University (Ontario), Texas Tech, Texas A&M, University of Oklahoma, University of California (Santa Barbara), Whittier College, Utrecht University (Holland), Conference on Lynne Baker's Theory of the Attitudes (Tilburg University, Nijmegen University, Dutch Research School in Philosophy [the Netherlands]), American Philosophical Association (Central Division), the Twentieth World Congress of Philosophy, the Conference on Naturalism (Humboldt University [Berlin]), and the Conference on Epistemology and Naturalism (University of Stirling [Scotland]).

Many philosophers contributed helpful criticism and suggestions along the way. These include J. C. Beall, W. R. Carter, Vere Chappell, Max Cresswell, Kevin Corcoran, Joe Cruz, Michael della Rocca, Edmund Gettier III, Anil Gupta, Robert Hanna, Pat Manfredi, Monica Meijsing, Eleonore Stump, Amie Thomasson, Judith Jarvis Thomson, Peter van Inwagen, Albert Visser, Ted Warfield, Dean Zimmerman, and members of my graduate seminar at the University of Massachusetts on Person and Body. Above all, I would like to thank Gareth B. Matthews and Katherine A. Sonderegger, for their never-failing help and encouragement.

Earlier versions of points presented here appear elsewhere: "The First-Person Perspective: A Test for Naturalism," *American Philosophical Quarterly* 35 (1998): 327–48; "What Am I?" *Philosophy and Phenomenological Research* 59 (1999), 151–9, and "Unity Without Identity: A New Look at Material Constitution," *New Directions in Philosophy: Midwest Studies in Philosophy*, Volume 23, Howard Wettstein, ed. (Malden, MA: Blackwell Publishers, 1999). I thank the publishers of these articles for permission to use materials from them. I also thank the University of Massachusetts at Amherst for granting me a University Faculty Fellowship in 1996–7 and a sabbatical leave in fall 1998, during which I worked on this project.

Finally, I wish to thank my husband, Tom Baker, for support and solace throughout this project.

Part One

The Metaphysical Background

1

Persons in the Material World

"But what, then, am I?" Descartes famously asked in the *Meditations*. Descartes then set the philosophical stage for the next few hundred years with his equally famous answer: "A thing that thinks. What is that? A thing that doubts, understands, affirms, denies, wills, refuses and which also imagines and senses."[1] But what kind of thing is a thing that thinks? Descartes's own answer – that a thinking thing is an immaterial mind – has lost ground over the centuries. Today neoCartesian materialists typically take the thinking thing to be the brain and then go on to try to determine how particular neural states can be the mental states involved in thinking (e.g., beliefs, desires, and intentions).[2] But the thinker – the thing that thinks, that has an inner life – is neither an immaterial mind nor a material brain: it is the person. My brain is the organ by which I think; but I, a person embedded in a material world, am the thinker. So, where traditional Cartesians see a mind/body problem and neo-Cartesians see a mental-state/brain-state problem, I see a person/body problem: What is a human person, and what is the relation between a person and her body? This is the problem that I shall investigate here.

According to the solution that I shall offer, a human person is constituted by a human body. But a human person is not identical to the body that constitutes her. Although I am not the only contemporary philoso-

---

1 René Descartes, *Meditations on First Philosophy*, II, trans. Donald A. Cress (Indianapolis: Hackett Publishing Company, 1979):19.

2 I have critically explored this project in *Explaining Attitudes: A Practical Approach to the Mind* (Cambridge: Cambridge University Press, 1995). See also my "What Is This Thing Called 'Commonsense Psychology'?" *Philosophical Explorations, 2* (1999): 3–19, and "Are Beliefs Brain States?" in *Explaining Beliefs: Lynne Baker's Theory of the Attitudes*, Anthonie Meijers, ed., forthcoming.

3

pher who takes persons to be constituted by bodies with which they are not identical, I shall appropriate the label the 'Constitution View' as a matter of convenience and use it for the account of persons and bodies that I shall offer.[3] The aim of the Constitution View is to show what distinguishes persons from all other beings and how we can be fully material beings without being identical to our bodies.

The Constitution View holds that something is a person in virtue of having a capacity for what I shall call a 'first-person perspective.' Something is a *human* person in virtue of being a person constituted by a body that is an organism of a certain kind – a human animal. Minds are not what distinguish persons from other things. The fact that persons have mental or conscious states provides no boundary between persons and nonpersons, according to the Constitution View. Many mammals have mental states of belief and desire; many mammals have conscious states. What marks persons off from everything else in the world, I shall argue, is that a person has a complex mental property: a first-person perspective that enables one to conceive of one's body and mental states as one's own. We human persons are animals in that we are constituted by animals, but, having first-person perspectives, we are not "just animals." We are persons.

THREE QUESTIONS

My attempt to solve the person/body problem will yield answers to three questions:

(1) What am I most fundamentally?
(2) What is a person?
(3) What is the relation between human persons and their bodies?

The first question is Descartes's "What am I?" This question is an ontological question. Any answer to this question has implications about conditions under which I exist and under which I persist over time. (Following Descartes, I invite each reader to engage in thinking about himself or herself in the first person.) Traditionally, there have seemed to be two major alternative answers to the question "What am I?": an

---

3   For example, Sydney Shoemaker long ago considered the possibility that persons are constituted by bodies to which they are not identical. See his "Personal Identity: A Materialist's Account" in *Personal Identity* by Sydney Shoemaker and Richard Swinburne (Oxford: Basil Blackwell, 1984): 112–14.

immaterialistic answer (in line with Descartes), according to which what I am most fundamentally is an immaterial mind, an independent substance contingently connected to a body[4]; and a materialistic answer (in line with Aristotle), according to which what I am most fundamentally is a material animal. Although Immaterialism and what I shall call 'Animalism' do not exhaust the ontological alternatives that have been proposed, they are two of the leading views to which I shall offer a competitor.[5] Thomas Aquinas may be thought to offer a third alternative. On his view, following Aristotle, the soul is the form of the body (an animal); but departing from Aristotle, Aquinas held that the soul is immaterial, is separated from the body at death, and exists apart from the body until it is reunited with it at the general Resurrection. Even though Aquinas did not identify himself (or any other human person) with a soul, the fact that he took the soul to be capable of existing independently of all bodies aligns him with the immaterialistic camp.[6]

All of these major competitors – Immaterialism, Animalism, and my own Constitution View – are competing ontological answers to the question "What am I?" They are ontological answers because each competitor purports to say what most fundamentally I am (and you are) and to give conditions under which I (and you) continue to exist. For example, if Immaterialism is correct, then what I am most fundamentally is an immaterial soul or mind; and I continue to exist as long as a particular immaterial soul or mind exists. If Animalism is correct, then what I am most fundamentally is an organism; and I would cease to exist if a particular organism ceased to exist. If the Constitution View is correct, then what I am most fundamentally is a person, a being with a

---

4   Following Descartes himself (at least in the *Meditations*), contemporary dualists include Richard Swinburne, *The Evolution of the Soul*, rev. ed. (Oxford: Clarendon Press, 1997), and John Foster, *The Immaterial Self: A Defence of the Cartesian Dualist Conception of the Mind* (London: Routledge, 1991).

5   One approach that I shall not discuss extensively (but see the brief discussion in Chapter 5) takes me to be identical to a certain human brain. See Thomas Nagel, *The View from Nowhere* (New York: Oxford University Press, 1986): Ch. 3. The term 'Animalist' comes from P. F. Snowden, one of the proponents of the Animalist View. Animalists include Peter van Inwagen, *Material Beings* (Ithaca, NY: Cornell University Press, 1990); Eric T. Olson, *The Human Animal: Personal Identity Without Psychology* (Oxford: Oxford University Press, 1997); and P. F. Snowden, "Persons, Animals and Ourselves," in *The Person and the Human Mind*, Christopher Gill, ed. (Oxford: Clarendon Press, 1990): 83–107.

6   For a thought-provoking interpretation of Aquinas that indicates that "the battle lines between dualism and materialism are misdrawn," see Eleonore Stump, "Non-Cartesian Substance Dualism and Materialism Without Reductionism," *Faith and Philosophy* 12 (1995): 505–31.

first-person perspective; and I would cease to exist if that first-person perspective were no longer exemplified. As a human person, according to the Constitution View, I am constituted by a human body; even so, my continued existence depends on the continuation of my first-person perspective.

In addition to Descartes's question "What am I?" – my question (1) posed earlier – there is another important question whose answer is to be woven into this discussion: John Locke asked, "What is a person?" My question (2) is Locke's question. It is important to see that these two questions – "What am I?" and "What is a person?" – are distinct questions.[7] Even so, I propose to offer an account that integrates their answers. To Descartes's question, "What am I?" I shall give an explicitly ontological but nonCartesian answer: What I am most fundamentally is a person. This answer to Descartes's question leads straight to Locke's question, "What is a person?" To Locke's question I shall give an answer that is quasi-Lockean in that it takes the defining property of a person to be something mental: A person, as I have said, is a being with a first-person perspective. But the kind of person that I am is a human person, necessarily embodied. If one is necessarily embodied, then one could not exist without having some body or other; but it does not follow that one must have the body that she in fact has. But at all times of her existence, she does have some body or other. So, on the Constitution View, human persons are material beings with first-person perspectives.

Even as I reject Descartes's immaterialist answer to the question "But what, then, am I?," I am convinced that Descartes asked the right question. It is important to see that Descartes's question is essentially first-personal; it could not be posed in the grammatical third person. Descartes's concern was to discover what *he* was; Descartes did not ask, "What is a human being?" or even "What is Descartes?" Answers to these questions would provide no purchase on "What am I?" This latter question, unlike the third-person questions, could not occur to any being that lacked a first-person perspective. So, persons are the only beings with the ability to ask the question "What am I?" Is our ability to ask this question just an accident? I shall say no: Our being able to ask this question indicates a deep fact about us. It is part of our nature to be able to ask "What am I?" Not only is a first-person perspective

---

7 Failure to distinguish these questions leads Animalists to suppose that an Animalist answer to the first question is a theory of *personal* identity. See, for example, Olson, *The Human Animal.*

required in order to raise that question; but also, for beings who have first-person perspectives, the question "What am I?" is a natural and even pressing one to ask. We are puzzles to ourselves in a way that no other kinds of beings are.

One natural answer to the question "What am I?" is that I am a human being. Although no one is likely to take exception to this answer (except for those who think that we are immaterial minds, or monads), it is far from clear how this answer should be interpreted. Some philosophers use 'human being' simply to mean 'human organism.' For example, John Perry says: "By 'human being,' I shall mean merely 'live human body.' It is a purely biological notion."[8] Other philosophers use 'human being' in a richer sense. For example, Mark Johnston says: "[H]uman being' names a partly psychological kind, whereas 'human organism' . . . names a purely biological kind."[9] So, 'I am a human being' requires interpretation, which the Constitution View will provide. On the Constitution View, 'I am a human being' is true because I, who am most fundamentally a person, am constituted by a human organism that has reached a certain level of development.

In ordinary language, 'human being' and 'man' are used more or less interchangeably with 'person.' Although I shall generally avoid the term 'human being,' as well as 'man,' it is worthwhile to mention my own view of the term. First of all, not every human organism is a human being. Exactly when a human organism becomes a human being I leave to biologists to say. (Thomas Aquinas taught that a human fetus became a human being when it began to have a rational soul – at the time of "quickening," around twelve weeks.) I want to point out that it is highly misleading to use 'human organism' and 'human being' interchangeably.

Even if 'human being' is used to denote organisms that have reached a certain stage of development, there is still a conceptual difference between 'human being' and 'human person.' (Biologists themselves distinguish between organisms and persons when they speak, for example, of "the biological substratum of personhood."[10]) It may be that we

8 John Perry, "The Importance of Being Identical," in *The Identities of Persons*, Amelie Oksenberg Rorty, ed. (Berkeley: University of California Press, 1976): 67–90, here p. 70.
9 Mark Johnston, "Human Beings," *Journal of Philosophy* 84 (1987): 59–83, here p. 64.
10 Clifford Brobstein (a member of the American Academy of Sciences), "A Biological Perspective on the Origin of Human Life and Personhood," in *Defining Human Life: Medical, Legal and Ethical Implications*, ed. Margery W. Shaw and A. Edward Doudera, eds. (Ann Arbor, MI: AUPHA Press, 1983): 11.

reserve 'human being' for human animals that support first-person perspectives, in which case all human beings are (i.e., constitute) persons.
But even so, 'human person' is a psychological/moral term. Whether or
not x is a human being depends on biological facts about x; whether or
not x is a human person depends additionally on psychological facts
about x – namely, on the Constitution View, on whether or not x has
a capacity for a first-person perspective. I shall retain Locke's insight that
person is a moral category. As we shall see in Chapter 6, only persons
can be held accountable for what they do. Locke was right: 'person' is a
forensic term – not *merely* a forensic term, but a forensic term nonetheless. "Wherever a man finds what he calls himself, there, I think, another
may say is the same person. It is a forensic term appropriating actions
and their merit; and so belongs only to intelligent agents capable of a
law, and happiness and misery."[11]

Locke also distinguished between a "man" and a person. The "idea
in our minds of which the sound 'man' in our mouths is the sign,"
Locke said, "is nothing else but of an animal of such a certain form: . . .
[W]hoever should see a creature of his own shape and make, though it
had no more reason . . . than a cat or a parrot, would call him still a
man."[12] The identity of an animal consists in "a participation of the same
continued life, by constantly fleeting particles of matter, in succession
vitally united to the same organized body."[13] By contrast, according to
Locke, "what *Person* stands for . . . is a thinking intelligent Being, that
has reason and reflection, and can consider itself as itself, the same
thinking thing in different times and places; which it does only by that
consciousness, which is inseparable from thinking, and as it seems to me
essential to it: It being impossible for any one to perceive, without
perceiving, that he does perceive."[14] Locke's discussion of persons, unlike his discussion of 'man' (i.e., human animal) is couched entirely in
mentalistic terms. It is true that Locke is not entirely consistent in his
use of 'man'; sometimes he takes 'man' to signify a composite of body
and soul. Although I shall depart from Locke in many respects, I shall
follow him in distinguishing between person and animal and in supposing that what is distinctive about persons is something mental.

---

11 John Locke, *An Essay Concerning Human Understanding*, abridged and edited by A. S.
Pringle-Pattison (Oxford: Clarendon Press, 1924): Book II, Ch. xxvii, 26.

12 *Essay* II, xxvii, 8.

13 *Essay* II, xxvii, 6.

14 *Essay* II, xxvii, 9. As we shall see in Chapter 3, on my view, nonhuman animals perceive
without perceiving that they perceive.

On this much – that a person is "a thinking intelligent being that has reason and reflection and can consider itself as itself, the same thinking thing in different times and places," and that a man (human being) is a kind of animal – I agree with Locke. But Locke went further and distinguished a person from a thinking substance (material or immaterial). According to Locke, persons (whose identity consists in the continuity of consciousness) are not basic substances.[15] The term 'substance' in philosophy has a tortured history; in an attempt to avoid the murkiness surrounding 'substance,' let me just say this: If we understand 'basic substance' to apply to those things that must be included in a complete inventory of the world, then I take persons to be basic substances. A description that mentioned material atoms, or even animals, but omitted mention of persons (and omitted mention of properties that could not be instantiated in a world without persons) would be seriously incomplete as a description of the world as it is today. On the view that I shall defend, persons must be mentioned in any complete inventory of what there is.

The third of my three questions is this: What is the relation between human persons and their bodies? On the Constitution View, a human person is constituted by a human body but is not identical to the constituting body. The relation between you and your body – constitution – is the same relation as the relation between Michelangelo's *David* and the piece of marble that constitutes it. As I have argued elsewhere,[16] *David* is not identical to that piece of marble, nor is *David* that piece of marble plus something else. Constitution is a ubiquitous relation, and in Chapter 2, I shall offer a detailed account of 'constitution' in general, with no reference to persons.

The idea of a person, as we use it, is relatively recent. It was not available to Aristotle in his vast studies of "man."[17] The term 'person,'

---

15   See William P. Alston and Jonathan Bennett, "Locke on People and Subtances," *Philosophical Review* 97 (1988): 25–46. However, there are disagreements about how to understand Locke's positive view about what is the alternative to holding persons to be basic substances. According to Vere Chappell, Locke understood persons to be compounded substances (since they are made up of various constituents or parts). See Vere Chappell, "Locke on the Ontology of Matter, Living Things and Persons," *Philosophical Studies* 60 (1990): 19–32. According to E. J. Lowe, Locke took persons to be psychological modes, not substances at all. See E. J. Lowe, "Real Selves: Persons as a Substantial Kind," in *Human Beings* (Supplement to Philosophy), David Cockburn, ed. (Cambridge: Cambridge University Press, 1991): 87–107.

16   "Why Constitution Is Not Identity," *Journal of Philosophy* 94 (1997): 599–621.

17   On Aristotle's view, only males were fully human beings; females were lesser beings. I shall simply ignore this aspect of Aristotle's thought.

as is well known, comes from the Latin word 'persona,' meaning mask. The term first came to prominence in something like the way that we use it today in Christian theology. Although 'Person' is still used for the Christian Trinity, it has come to apply more broadly to beings like us. By the seventeenth century, 'person' had become what Locke called a "forensic" term, one that connoted legal and moral status.[18] So, the concept of a person is relatively recent. But persons have been around since the dawn of history. There were persons long before there was a concept of a person.

Some see an ambiguity in the term 'person' when applied to individuals.[19] Fred Feldman, for example, suggests that people conflate 'psychological persons' and 'biological persons.' He takes biological persons to be simply members of the species *Homo sapiens*; he takes psychological persons to be organisms with psychological capacities such as self-consciousness and the ability to engage in purposeful action.[20] He holds that one can cease to be a psychological person without ceasing to exist, but that one cannot cease to be a biological person without ceasing to exist. Let me emphasize that I do not think that there is any such ambiguity regarding 'person.' First, there do not seem to be the two concepts of personality to which Feldman appeals. What Feldman calls 'the biological concept of personality' is not a concept of *personality* at all; a "biological person," as Feldman uses the term, is simply a member of the species *Homo sapiens;* it may have no personality whatever. Second, the (putative) ambiguity itself is theory-laden in a way that begs the question against the Constitution View. Embedded in the claim that one can cease to be a psychological person without ceasing to exist, but that one cannot cease to be a biological person without ceasing to exist, is a controversial presupposition. The presupposition is that we are to be identified with what Feldman calls 'biological persons' that can exist without ever having any psychological properties at all. This presupposition is an extreme version of the Animalist View that I have already questioned and will challenge further. So, the presupposition required

18 For more on the history of the idea of a person – although with a quite a different aim from mine – see Ross Poole, "On Being a Person," *Australasian Journal of Philosophy* 74 (1996): 38–57.

19 I say 'individuals' in order to exclude from consideration extraneous uses of 'person' – as in "The corporation is a [legal] person."

20 Fred Feldman, *Confrontations with the Reaper: A Philosophical Study of the Nature and Value of Death* (New York: Oxford University Press, 1992): 101. Feldman further distinguishes concepts of moral and legal persons.

to make Feldman's point is a metaphysical thesis that begs the question against the Constitution View. We would do well to begin our inquiry by using 'person' in a less theory-laden way that does not render the Constitution View false before we start.

Pretheoretically, I take the term 'person' to apply to entities like you and me. The domain that I wish to explore includes Elizabeth I, Genghis Khan, Albert Schweitzer, Mother Theresa, Joseph Stalin – the kinds of things capable, for example, of planning their futures. The *theory* that I shall present will identify the first-person perspective as the person-making property and will take human persons to be persons constituted by human bodies. Furthermore, according to the theory, a human person could cease to be human (by gradual replacement of organic by inorganic parts) and yet continue to exist. But a human person could not cease to be a person and continue to exist. Unlike 'adolescent,' 'person' is not a phase sortal: Being an adolescent is a property that an individual has during part of his or her existence, but the same individual who is now an adolescent can (and typically, will) lose the property of being an adolescent without ceasing to exist – simply by growing older. By contrast, on the Constitution View, the same individual who is now a person could not lose the property of being a person without ceasing to exist. If a person died and ceased to be a person, then the entity that had been a person would cease to exist. On the Constitution View – the theory to be developed and defended – *person* is an ontological kind.

Finally, let me defend my use of the plural 'persons' instead of 'people.' Judith Jarvis Thomson has complained, "[P]hilosophers do not use 'person' as a mere innocuous singular for 'people': 'person' in the hands of philosopher trails clouds of philosophy."[21] Well, this *is* philosophy. My aim here is theoretical; I am not trying to sketch out ordinary usage. Rather, beginning with 'person' pretheoretically as referring to things like you and me, I want to give an account of those things. I begin with Descartes's question "What am I?", and I answer that I am a person. Since you, the reader, are also a person, there are at least two of us persons; of course, we are people. But since 'people' suggests a collective and I want the theory to apply to you and me individually, 'persons' seems a better term for us than 'people.' The theory applies to each person and, therefore, to persons (or people) distributively, not collectively. 'A theory of people' sounds collective in a way that 'a theory of

---

21 Judith Jarvis Thomson, "People and Their Bodies," in *Reading Parfit,* Jonathan Dancy, ed. (Oxford: Basil Blackwell, 1997): 202.

persons' does not. So, I shall stick with 'persons' and hope that by the end, the philosophy-trailing 'person' will not be too cloudy.

I began this section by setting out three questions that I intend to answer in this book. One further question that is conspicuous by its absence is this: "What is the relation between the mind and the brain, or between mental states and neural states?" Since the question of the mind/brain relation has occupied many philosophers in recent decades, let me explain why I say so little about it. In brief, I do not discuss "the" relation between minds and brains because I doubt that there is a single relation for a philosopher to detect (such as identity or constitution).[22] Rather, I think that the question of the (probably numerous) relations between brain states and mental states is an empirical issue to be investigated piecemeal by neuroscientists. The brain is implicated in all aspects of human life, but to describe just how is beyond the reach of philosophy. Acknowledging both the brain's importance for mental life and our ignorance of the details of the relations between particular brain states and particular mental states (such as Fay's feeling that she has been treated unfairly by her supervisor or Hank's jealousy of the new employee), I shall rest content to say that the brain *sustains* mental states without hazarding details. So, instead of asking, "How do minds fit into the material world?" I shall ask, "How do persons fit into the material world?" I shall be satisfied to answer the three questions posed at the beginning of this section and to put questions about the relations between mental states and brain states aside. And the answer that I shall give is that persons are constituted by bodies in the sense that I shall explain in detail.

BEYOND BIOLOGY

We persons are human animals, organisms, with a long evolutionary history. As similar as we are in some ways to other species, we are undeniably unique: We are not only the products of evolution, we are also the discoverers of evolution and interveners in evolutionary processes, for good or ill. We clone mammals, protect endangered species, devise medical treatments, stop epidemics, produce medications, use birth control methods, engage in genetic engineering, and so on. And only the human species has philosophy, science, art, architecture, and

22 See my "What Is This Thing Called 'Commonsense Psychology'?" and "Are Beliefs Brain States?"

recorded history. However, with the ascendancy of what might be called 'metaphysical Darwinism' (as opposed to scientific Darwinism), it is unpopular to claim any special status for ourselves.

Many philosophers find it overwhelmingly plausible to hold that, ontologically speaking, we are animals, period. I want to offer motivation for an alternative that recognizes our animal nature without taking us to be identical to animals. Philosophers impressed with a certain interpretation of Darwin hold that if evolutionary biology is correct, then human organisms (like all organisms) are merely "survival machines."[23] But one may agree that human organisms (qua organisms) are merely survival machines while disagreeing that human persons are merely survival machines, all things considered. All that follows from conjoining the view that human organisms are merely survival machines with the view that human persons are not merely survival machines is, as the Constitution View holds, that human persons are not identical to human organisms.

But this is not to deny that we have animal natures, nor is it to deny that as far as our animal natures are concerned, all values may well derive from the values of survival and reproduction: "A Darwinian would say that ultimately organisms have only two [goals]: to survive and to reproduce."[24] But the same Darwinian – the evolutionary psychologist, Steven Pinker – who made this observation attributes to us values that do not derive from survival and reproduction. For example, he says, "If the genes don't get propagated, it's because we are smarter than they are."[25] This cannot be right if we are nothing but organisms, whose only goals ultimately are survival and reproduction. For such organisms are in no position to reject nature's built-in goals, except by malfunction – certainly not by being smarter than their genes. Or again: Pinker points out that he himself is "voluntarily childless" and comments, "I am happy to be that way, and if my genes don't like it, they can go jump in the lake."[26] On the assumption that we are nothing but organisms, I do not see how Pinker can reconcile these extrabiological values with his affirmation that "ultimately organisms have only two [goals]: to survive and to reproduce."

23 Richard Dawkins, *The Selfish Gene* (Oxford: Oxford University Press, 1976): 1. Also see Daniel C. Dennett, *Darwin's Dangerous Idea* (New York: Simon & Schuster, 1995).
24 Steven Pinker, *How the Mind Works* (New York: W. W. Norton and Company, 1997): 541.
25 Pinker, *How the Mind Works*, p. 44.
26 Pinker, *How the Mind Works*, p. 52.

My point is not just an ad hominem, however. Rather, I want to offer motivation for looking beyond Darwin in order to understand human persons. If we are nothing but animals, then either goals that people die for – for example, extending the rule of Allah, furthering the cause of democracy, or something else – should be shown to promote survival and reproduction or those people who pursue such goals should be deemed to be malfunctioning. Neither seems plausible. I have heard Darwinians speak as if altruism were the last hurdle for an exhaustive Darwinian explanation of what we are. But altruism is only the first hurdle. For altruism, understood as doing things that benefit others at the cost of harm to oneself, is not even unique to human animals. So even a fully adequate Darwinian explanation of altruism[27] would not begin to explain uniquely human goals that seem neither to promote survival and reproduction nor to result from biological malfunction. Pinker points out that "happiness and virtue have nothing to do with what natural selection designed us to accomplish in the ancestral environment."[28] But no one, I think, would suggest that our pursuit of happiness and virtue should be chalked up to biological malfunction. Considerations like these suggest that there is more to us than we shall discover from Darwinism (at least on one widespread interpretation).

The first-person perspective allows us, at least to some extent, to be self-conscious about our goals and to decide which ones to pursue and how to pursue them. We are not limited to goals derived from those of survival and reproduction. This partial control is quite compatible with our being unaware of much of what motivates us; it is even compatible with determinism. The point is that animals have no control over their goals; but that we, unlike the rest of the animal kingdom, have a certain control over (some of) our goals, including those of survival and reproduction. Even if our control over our goals is limited and even if our ability to assess and change our goals is itself a product of natural selection, it is precisely such control that biologists like E. O. Wilson appeal to when they say that we must preserve biological diversity. To think of us as being subject to such appeals is to think of us as being significantly different from the rest of the animal kingdom.

I can make this point in another way. Many biologists and psychologists today hold that a person's character and habits are largely deter-

---

27 For a recent study, see Elliott Sober and David Sloan Wilson, *Unto Others: The Evolution and Psychology of Unselfish Behavior* (Cambridge, MA: Harvard University Press, 1998).

28 Pinker, *How the Mind Works*, p. 52.

mined by her genetic endowment. Assuming that such biologists and psychologists are right, consider the difference between persons and other animals, equally genetically determined. Only a being with a first-person perspective can have a grip on the fact that she even has a character or that she has habits at all. Only a being with a first-person perspective can evaluate herself, find herself wanting, and try to change herself in various ways.[29] Nothing lacking a first-person perspective (e.g., a nonhuman animal) can have any beliefs about her own character and habits. The fact, if it is a fact, that one's character and habits are largely determined by one's genetic endowment does not mitigate the consequence of having a first-person perspective. Even if one's character and habits are determined by one's genes, a first-person perspective still allows one to come to know various things about one's character, and to assess them, and to try to change them.[30]

It is a plain fact that people sometimes try to change themselves. Such attempts presuppose that they have first-person perspectives. Otherwise, they would have no conception of themselves as having one kind of character rather than another, and hence they would have no purchase on what or how to change. A person who is dissatisfied with the kind of person that she is and who tries to change herself differs from every nonpersonal animal in having a first-person perspective.

I can imagine an objection like this: "Why don't you save yourself a lot of trouble? You hold that what makes something a person is a first-person perspective. You could simply say that persons are just animals with first-person perspectives. We are animals and nothing but animals; but human animals are special in just the way that you say that persons are. A human animal naturally develops a first-person perspective. You can still say that a first-person perspective is the mark of a person; but you don't have to draw a line between persons and animals. Having a first-person perspective (and hence being a person) is just a property of some human animals during a part of their existence."

Although I agree that human animals normally develop the capacity

---

29 On Harry Frankfurt's view, a person has what he calls "second-order volitions": She can desire to be moved by certain desires. Second-order volitions presuppose the first-person perspective, which I take to be more fundamental. See Harry Frankfurt, "Freedom of the Will and the Concept of a Person," *Journal of Philosophy* 68 (1971): 5–20.

30 This is a denial of a certain kind of determinism that is taken for granted in popular science books, but it is not a denial of determinism *tout court*. For it leaves open the possibility that our attempts to change our characters or habits themselves may be determined.

to support first-person perspectives, it seems obvious (to me, anyway) that anything capable of having a first-person perspective is basically different from anything incapable of having one. (I shall argue for this point, especially in Chapters 6 and 9.) But Darwin's message is that human animals are not basically different from nonhuman animals.

Those who take us to be essentially like nonhuman animals want to describe and explain our traits in terms of general biological traits shared by other species. But the first-person perspective, whether selected for or not, is a biological surd in this respect. As I shall argue, it is utterly distinctive and simply cannot be assimilated to traits of animals that do not constitute persons. It is impossible for even the most lovable dog, having no first-person perspective, to be dissatisfied with his personality, or to wonder how he will die, or to cogitate about what kind of thing he is. (As we shall see, animals have many mental states – including beliefs, desires, and intentions – but, lacking first-person perspectives, they are incapable of having many kinds of mental states that we have.) So, if one takes a person to be identical to an animal, then one must posit a break in the animal kingdom between animals with first-person perspectives (only us) and animals without them (all others). On the other hand, if one takes a human person to be constituted by an animal, as I advocate, one can regard the animal kingdom as unified. Moreover, if we are constituted by animals, there is a clear sense in which we still are part of the animal kingdom.

Whether or not an entity is a person depends on its having a first-person perspective (or a capacity for one, where 'capacity' will be narrowly delineated).[31] And for human persons, the capacity for a first-person perspective depends on the causal powers of the brain. The brain, it is (almost) universally agreed, is a product of evolution. Biologists often point out that "we share most of our DNA with chimpanzees, and that small changes can have big effects."[32] So, the change in brain structure that enabled human brains to support first-person perspectives may well be insignificant from a purely biological point of view. But, as I shall argue throughout, the difference that a first-person perspective makes in what there is in the universe cannot be overestimated. So, if biologists find the differences between nonhuman animals and us to be

---

31 Subsequently, I shall usually omit mention of this qualification. I shall discuss the qualification in detail in Chapter 4.
32 Pinker, *How the Mind Work*, pp. 40–1.

biologically insignificant, then we must look beyond biology to understand ourselves.

If I am right, with the development of first-person perspectives, a new kind of entity emerged – perhaps not a new kind of biological entity, but a new kind of psychological entity. Regardless of its *biological* significance, a first-person perspective makes an important *ontological* difference. Although it would be reckless to ignore the findings of biology, the kinds of entities recognized by biologists need not determine all the kinds of entities that there are. The possibility that there are nonhuman persons – beings with first-person perspectives without human bodies – should make us wary of thinking of persons solely in biological terms. Biology does not dictate ontology. Put the other way, ontology need not recapitulate biology.

Now with respect to the question of whether we are identical to animals, there are three alternatives that seem plausible today. (I omit the logical possibility that we are not animals at all.) Are we nothing but animals?

If Yes, then: Either

(a) Say that we are nothing but animals, and deny the significance of data such as these: We alone among animals have the capacity to modify our goals, to own up to what we do, to hold each other responsible for what we do. We alone are moral agents. (The list could go on indefinitely.) or

(b) Say that we are nothing but animals, but affirm a biological break or gap between human organisms (that are able to modify their goals, own up to what they do, etc.) and nonhuman organisms.

If No, then:

(c) Say that the animal kingdom is unified, and distinguish between persons and human organisms without denying the animal nature of human persons.

Option (a) is unacceptable. For Option (a) simply denies the manifest discontinuity between us – with our culture, governments, wars, art, science, religion, and technology – and nonhuman animals. Likewise, Option (b) is unacceptable. For although Option (b) admits the manifest discontinuity between us and nonhuman animals, it locates the discontinuity *within* the domain of biology. That is, on Option (b), human animals are not biologically continuous with nonhuman animals. But from a biological point of view, human animals (regardless of their first-person perspective) are biologically continuous with nonhuman animals.

So, Option (b) posits a biologically unmotivated gap within the animal kingdom.

Option (c), under which the Constitution View falls, is the only option remaining: Option (c) leaves the domain of biology unified. All organisms, including those that constitute us, are in the domain of biology. Perhaps there will even be a biological explanation of the development of first-person perspectives. Whether there is a biological explanation or not, on the Constitution View the difference between a human person and an organism that lacks a first-person perspective is an ontological difference. The Constitution View does not stand or fall according to whether this ontological difference is reflected in a biological difference.

I expect biologists and biochemists to inform us fully about organic life: the formation of amino acids and proteins, replication of cells, inheritance of certain traits, and so on. But in addition to life considered at those levels, there is personal life, the life that is your biography. Our personal lives are made possible by our organic lives, but they are not exhausted or even fully explained by the facts that professional biologists traffic in. (I say 'professional biologists' because there is a kind of fantasy biology that philosophers engage in.) To say that our personal lives, the stuff of biographies (including but not limited to medical histories), cannot be completely described or explained in wholly biological terms is perfectly compatible with saying that our ability to have personal lives is a product of natural selection. To suppose that any product of natural selection must be understandable in wholly biological terms is to commit what used to be called the 'genetic fallacy': the fallacy of assuming that where something came from determines what it is. I am interested here in what we are, not in where we came from. And what we most fundamentally are, I believe, are persons.

What I am calling a person's 'personal life' encompasses her organic life: There are not two different lives, but one integrated personal life.[33]

---

33 Some philosophers have entertained the idea of life that is not organic or biological at all. For example, in their influential article "Eternity" (*Journal of Philosophy* 78 [1981]: 429–58), Eleonore Stump and Norman Kretzmann say that "anything that is eternal has life" (p. 431). And some materialists at least countenance the possibility of conscious life without biological properties. Richard Boyd says that "there seems to be no barrier to the functionalist materialist's asserting that any particular actual world mental event, state, or process could be – in some other possible world – nonphysically realized." Moreover, Boyd suggests the "possibility that certain kinds of actual world token mental events,

The connection between an injury to one's organs and one's resulting dread of a long convalescence is a causal connection *within* a personal life. (So, the distinction that I am drawing between personal life and organic life is nothing like the distinction between mind and body or between psychological states and physical states.) When an organism comes to constitute a person, an organic life becomes incorporated into a personal life. So, a human person has a single life that has an organic aspect (consisting of the activities of organs and their cells). Although a human person has a single life that incorporates organic life, it is metaphysically possible to "precipitate out" an organic life that is not personal and a personal life that is not organic.

Here is an example of precipitating out an organic life from a personal life: Suppose that a person suffered irreversible brain damage that resulted in the organism's being in a persistent vegetative state, with no hope of regaining consciousness. In this case, the organism would persist but the person would not.[34] Here is the converse example: Suppose that a person slowly had her organs replaced by nonorganic parts, to the point where there was no longer metabolism, circulation, digestion, and so on, but the higher brain functions remained and the person's sense of herself was uninterrupted. In this case, the person would persist but the organism would not. The possibility of cases like these rules out identification of a person with the organism that is her body. Yet, a person is not a separate thing from her body. The Constitution View aims to show both how human persons are related to human organisms and what distinguishes organisms that constitute persons from organisms that do not.

On the one hand, we are wholly constituted by human organisms. We are not human organisms plus something else: I am not a person *and* an animal; I am a person *constituted by* an animal. So, we human persons cannot escape our animal natures. On the other hand, there is more to us than our animal natures. But the "more" that we are has nothing to do with anything immaterial; rather, what sets us apart from other animals is the ability that underlies our asking "What am I?" One

states or processes might be realized in some other possible world even if the body of the subject no longer exists." Richard Boyd, "Materialism Without Reductionism: What Physicalism Does Not Entail," in *Readings in the Philosophy of Psychology*, Volume I, Ned Block, ed. (Cambridge, MA: Harvard University Press, 1980): 101.

34 We may continue to have moral obligations to the organism even though it no longer constitutes a person.

who has this ability has what I call the 'first-person perspective.' It is in virtue of having a first-person perspective that an organism comes to constitute a person.

My account of human persons has two elements: the idea of constitution and the idea of a first-person perspective.[35] I shall explain both of these ideas in detail in order to answer the three questions that I asked earlier:

(1) What am I most fundamentally?
(2) What is a person?
(3) What is the relation between human persons and their bodies?

The answer that I shall give to each question leads to an answer to the next question:

> I am most fundamentally a person. →
> A person, human or not, is a being with a capacity for a 'first-person perspective.' →
> A human person is a person wholly constituted by a body that is a human organism, an animal of the species *Homo sapiens*.

So, a human person is a being that (i) has a capacity for a first-person perspective and (ii) is constituted by a human organism. The purpose of this book is to give a detailed presentation of this idea as a coherent view of human persons and to defend it as superior to its competitors.

As we shall see in Chapter 2, constitution, the relation between a human person and her body, is not unique to persons and bodies. Constitution is a pervasive relation, found wherever one turns. The general idea of constitution is this: When various things are in various circumstances, new things – new kinds of things with new kinds of causal powers – come into existence. When a piece of cloth is in certain circumstances, a new thing, a flag, comes into existence. Flags have different kinds of causal powers from pieces of cloth. A flag, because it is a flag and not merely a piece of cloth, can cause a person to fly into a

---

35 For a somewhat different development of an idea of constitution-without-identity, see Johnston, "Human Beings." For another philosopher who emphasizes the importance of the first person, see E. J. Lowe, *Subjects of Experience* (Cambridge: Cambridge University Press, 1996). A person is a "being which can think that *it itself* is thus and so and can identify itself as the unique subject of certain thoughts and experiences and as the unique agent of certain actions" (p. 5).

rage or it can bring tears to the eyes. Constitution is everywhere: Pieces of paper constitute dollar bills; pieces of cloth constitute flags; pieces of bronze constitute statues. And constitution applies not only to artifacts and symbols, but to natural objects as well: strands of DNA constitute genes. (Some philosophers hold that particular brain states constitute beliefs.[36] Although I do not endorse this claim, the idea of constitution is poised to make sense of it.) So, appeal to the idea of constitution in order to understand human persons is no special pleading on behalf of persons.

Consideration of the general nature of constitution can take us only so far in understanding the relation between persons and bodies. For the person/body relation differs from other constitution relations in that a person has an inner aspect – a person can consider, reason about, reflect on herself as herself – that a statue or other nonpersonal object lacks. This inner aspect is, I believe, the defining characteristic of persons. Its basis, to be explored in Chapter 3, is the first-person perspective. With a first-person perspective, not only can one think of one's body in a first-personal way – typically, in English, with the pronouns 'I', 'me,' 'my,' and 'mine' – but also one has a conception of oneself as oneself. A person not only *has* a perspective, she also has a *conception* of herself as being the source of a perspective. Many nonhuman animals have perspectives (determined perhaps by the positions of their sensory organs – e.g., eyes that are the sources of their visual fields), but only persons have a conception of themselves as having such a perspective.[37] Only persons have a conception of themselves from a first-person point of view.

In short, the aim of this book is to work out an account of human persons that gives our animal natures their due while recognizing and investigating what makes us special. The first-person perspective – however it came about, by natural selection, by accident, or otherwise – makes such a difference that there is a difference in kind between beings that have it and beings that do not. This book is an attempt to work out this view in detail. On the one hand, I want to avoid the immaterialism of those who think that an immaterial mind or soul is needed to explain

36 For example, see Boyd, "Materialism Without Reductionism: What Physicalism Does Not Entail," pp. 67–101. Also see Derk Pereboom and Hilary Kornblith, "The Metaphysics of Irreducibility," *Philosophical Studies* 63 (1991): 125–46.
37 Although the "eye" image here comes from Wittgenstein, Wittgenstein would not approve of the use that I make of it, I think. See *Tractatus Logico-Philosophicus*, D. F. Pears and B. F. McGuinness, trans. (London: Routledge and Kegan Paul, 1961).

our specialness. On the other hand, I want to avoid the reductionism of those who think either that persons are not among the fundamental kinds of things that (now) exist or that everything that exists (including persons) can be fully understand in subpersonal terms. So, I want to navigate between the Scylla of Immaterialism and the Charybdis of Animalism.

This conception of a human person is "naturalistic" in a broad sense: It neither invokes nor presupposes the existence of immaterial souls or supernatural beings. The ability to have a first-person perspective is just as likely to be a product of natural selection as is the ability to speak a language. This conception of a human person rests comfortably with materialism about the natural order, and if the natural order is all that there is, then it rests comfortably with materialism *tout court*.

I start with three basic assumptions. First, this world is a wholly material world; hence, human persons are material beings. Second, material beings endure through time; they are not merely sums of temporal parts. Third, identity is strict identity: if x and y can differ in any property whatever, then x is not identical to y. To anyone who rejects one or more of these basic assumptions, I suggest regarding this book as an effort to see how much ground can be covered, and how many problems about persons can be solved, with these assumptions in play.

A PHILOSOPHICAL STANCE

This book is one of metaphysics, but metaphysics of an unusual stripe. For I write here from the standpoint of what I have elsewhere called 'Practical Realism.'[38] Practical Realism is notable for two commitments. First, the Practical Realist holds that metaphysics should not waft free of the rest of human inquiry. Metaphysics should be responsive to reflection on cognitive (and other) practices, scientific and nonscientific. The Practical Realist does not confuse metaphysics with epistemology, but she does connect them for the reason that metaphysics detached from the rest of inquiry is just idle. The second commitment is that the Practical Realist takes the world of common experience as the source of data for philosophical reflection. The world that we live and die in – the world where we do things and where things happen to us – is the arena of what really matters to all of us, from the least to the most reflective among us. The world of ordinary life is populated with

38   Baker, *Explaining Attitudes.*

medium-sized dry goods (in J. L. Austin's phrase) and persons with intentional states. Persons play a prominent part in the world of everyday life. The attempt to understand persons and their bodies, then, may be seen as metaphysics in the vein recommended by Practical Realism: philosophical reflection on what is found in the world that we all live in and that we all care about.

Many philosophers think that, in the long run (perhaps the indefinitely long run), the sciences will explain everything there is to be explained: To be is to be in the domain of some science or to be part of the explanatory apparatus of some science. Although I do not share this scientistic attitude, I have no desire to place persons beyond the reach of the sciences. Rather than pronouncing persons to be wholly within, or partially outside of, the scope of the sciences, we should simply wait and see how disciplines develop and what we count as science. My account here may be seen as "conceptual" or at least prescientific. However, if the views put forward here are correct, then we can predict that any science of persons will have the following two features: (1) It will countenance intentional properties like believing that p, desiring that q, and intending to A, for persons are essentially intentional beings. No intentionality, no persons. Period. (2) It will take as its object of study the whole integrated person, not just a compendium of parts of persons; for a person has essential properties that are not determined by the properties of a person's parts and their interrelations.

Now either there will be an intentional science that quantifies over persons or not. If there turned out to be such a science, then I would take my view of persons to be vindicated (at least (1) and (2) would not be falsified). If not, then either (a) there are no such things as persons, inasmuch as no science would have persons in its domain; or (b) the view here is just wrong about what persons are; perhaps a person is no more than a compendium of parts that are in the domains of various sciences; or (c) there are persons, but they are not fully understandable by science (although a person's organs, cellular structures, and so on are understandable by science). Having pointed out (a)–(c), I'll leave to the reader the choice among them if it turns out that no intentional science quantifies over persons. For my own part, (c) is the best choice, but I'll not argue for (c) here.

This tentativeness toward the sciences comports well with Practical Realism. The approach is practical because it does not rule out of hand the possibility that there will be an empirical science that is a science of persons. It is realistic because it claims to be an accurate picture of the

nature of persons. Constitution is claimed to be an objective (and ubiquitous) relation. Since we do have a strong interest in the kind of beings
we are, we have every reason to speculate about what we are on the
basis of what we know about the rest of the natural world. The outcome
of such speculations can be judged against empirical science whenever
an empirical science claims to be a science of persons. But in the
meanwhile, a priori claims about the nature of science and reality should
not stop us from reflecting philosophically on a matter of great interest:
ourselves.

So, I regard this book as metaphysics in the Practical Realist mode.
One departure from traditional metaphysics will be especially apparent
in what follows. In traditional metaphysics, it is often taken to be a
deliverance of reason that all essential properties of a thing are intrinsic.
But in the world of everyday life, intrinsic properties have no special
authority to determine the nature or identity of things. What a thing is
most fundamentally is as likely to be determined by what it does in
relation to other things as by what it is made of. (In many cases, form
follows function.) The nature and identity of many of the things that
populate the world of everyday life are not always, or even usually,
determined by what they are made of. The identity of a carburetor is
determined by its function. The identity of a dollar bill is determined by
the rights conferred on its bearer by the government. In general, the
Practical Realist focus on what Husserl called the 'life-world' is salutary
in two quite different ways: It keeps attention on things that actually
matter to us, and it counters the metaphysical neglect of relational
properties.

The ideas of constitution and the first-person perspective are theoretical notions tied to judgments about the common world that we all live
in. Our experience of things' going out of existence leads to the conclusion that a statue is not identical to a piece of marble, nor is a stone wall
identical to the stones that make it up, nor are persons identical to their
bodies. But if a statue is not identical to a piece of marble, nor a person
to a body, what is the relation between statue and piece of marble or
between person and body? This query motivates development of the
idea of constitution-without-identity. Our first-person experience of
ourselves leads to the idea of of a first-person perspective. Any plausible
answer to the question "What am I?" must reveal us to be beings who
can ask that question. (A new paradox! An answer to a question that
renders its asking nonsensical!) The notions of a first-person perspective
and of constitution are more like postulated theoretical ideas than like

the outcomes of pure reason. As with other theoretical ideas, the proof of the pudding is in the eating.

My general philosophical stance is one of ontological pluralism. There are many, many kinds of things. The framework for this pluralism is a broad materialism. Nothing in the natural world is constituted by non-physical stuff – whatever that may be. Take away all the physical atoms, and you take away everything in the natural order. Having said that, however, I want to move on. For on my view, the physical atoms are of less ontological significance than the myriad kinds of things that they constitute. If we suppose that the greater a thing's causal powers, the greater its ontological significance, then a constituted thing is ontologically more significant than what constitutes it. If x constitutes y, then y has all the causal powers that x has plus some new kinds of causal powers of its own. Speaking metaphorically, a constituted thing encompasses and surpasses what constitutes it.

My motivation for this undertaking is twofold. First, I want to take seriously the apparent diversity of the things around us. Persons are one kind of thing; human bodies are another. Statues are yet a different kind of thing; lumps of clay are a further kind of thing, and so on. Whereas reductive approaches flatten out reality to a single kind of property bearer (fundamental particles), I want to do justice to the almost infinite variety of things to be found in the world. If I am right, then, on the one hand, every particular individual in the natural world is wholly constituted by one or more aggregates of material particles, without being identical to the aggregates that constitute it.[39] And on the other hand, the familiar objects of everyday life (constituted by aggregates of particles) are bearers of different kinds of properties from the properties countenanced by fundamental physics. As we shall see, the view of human persons that I shall defend – nonreductive but materialistic – is consonant with this larger picture.

The second part of my motivation stems from considering the relation between persons and bodies. The candidates that have been on offer for that relation seem to me to be all unsatisfactory: (a) I am necessarily identical to my body in that, metaphysically, I could not exist apart from

---

39 I say "constituted by one *or more* aggregates" because I take it that an aggregate of particles cannot gain or lose particles without ceasing to exist. But many constituted things – e.g., a human body, a ship – persist through replacement of particles. At each moment of its existence, a material thing is constituted by an aggregate of particles, although at different moments it may be constituted by different aggregates.

it; (b) I am contingently identical to my body; although, metaphysically, I could exist apart from my body, I in fact do not and will not exist apart from it; (c) I am distinct from my body; I am either an immaterial being or I am a combination of material body and immaterial mind. As for (a), its most plausible version is the Animalist View, which I have begun to criticize in this chapter, and which I shall continue to criticize in Chapters 5 and 9. As for (b), I have argued elsewhere against the coherence of the idea of contingent identity, the idea that x and y, although in fact identical, might not have been identical.[40] As for (c), I shall show in Chapters 5 and 9 how the Constitution View in fact delivers much of what the immaterialist wants without the burden of needing to find a place for the immaterial in the natural world. I hope that the accumulation of detail in the Constitution View will add up to a convincing alternative to all three.

In what follows, I shall lay out in great detail the general notions from which the Constitution View of human persons is constructed: *constitution* (Chapter 2) and the *first-person perspective* (Chapter 3). (These chapters, especially Chapter 2, are rather technical, and anyone who is satisfied with an intuitive understanding of these ideas may skip these chapters without loss; however, I think that the basic ideas of constitution-without-identity and of the first-person perspective are of general interest and great significance even apart from their use in the Constitution View.) Then, using these notions in Chapter 4, I shall present the Constitution View of human persons. Chapter 5 will discuss the vexing question of personal identity over time and compare the Constitution View with other theories. Chapter 6 will investigate ways in which persons differ from nonpersons, with the aim of buttressing the claim that human persons, although animals, are not just animals. The remainder of the book deepens the account of persons and bodies by mounting an extended defense of the basic idea of constitution-without-identity (Chapter 7) and of the Constitution View of human persons (Chapter 8) from a host of objections. Chapter 9 attempts to show the superiority of the Constitution View to its competitors.

---

40   See Baker, "Why Constitution Is Not Identity," pp. 611–15.

2

The Very Idea of Constitution

The relation between a person and his or her body, I shall argue, is simply an instance of a very general relation: constitution. Constitution is a fundamental relation that is ubiquitous. It is the relation that obtains between an octagonal piece of metal and a Stop sign, between strands of DNA molecules and genes, between pieces of paper and dollar bills, between stones and monument; between lumps of clay and statues – the list is endless. So, apart from the light that it sheds on human persons, the idea of constitution holds philosophical interest in its own right. In this chapter, I shall give a very general and technical account of this important idea.

There are additional reasons to be explicit about the idea of constitution. First, as I have argued elsewhere, I think that constitution cannot be understood as identity.[1] But if constitution is not identity, what exactly is it? In this chapter, I am going to try to say. Constitution has been caricatured by those who cannot imagine a relation of unity that is intermediate between identity and separate existence. The idea of such an intermediate position strikes many philosophers as incoherent.[2] Nothing but a detailed exposition of the idea of constitution will absolve it of the charge of incoherence or obscurity. Second, I start with assumptions

---

1 See Lynne Rudder Baker, "Why Constitution Is Not Identity," *Journal of Philosophy* 94 (1997): 599–621.

2 However, anyone who believes in the Christian Trinity is committed to there being a relation (besides proper parthood) between strict identity and separateness. So, an orthodox Christian believer is in no position to declare the claim that there is an intermediate relation between identity and separateness to be incoherent. An orthodox Christian believer should look for fault in my specific account of constitution, not in the general idea of a constitution relation that is not identity.

that are different from those of other writers on constitution. Philosophers typically treat constitution as a matter of relations between things and their parts.[3] But that approach seems plausible only if one overlooks things (like artworks) that have nonintrinsic properties essentially.[4] To understand a thing whose identity is not determined by the identity of its parts and the parts' relations to each other, we need to look beyond mereology. So, I take a different tack and focus on relations between kinds of familiar, medium-sized objects. Third and finally, on my view, constitution is a relation of genuine unity. As I shall develop it, the idea of constitution is not just a recapitulation of the notion, discussed by a number of philosophers, that two distinct entities can be spatially coincident.[5]

To make the idea of constitution perspicuous, I want to set out and defend an explicit account, in full generality, of what it is for an object x to constitute an object y at time t. According to this account, if x constitutes y at any time, then x is not identical to y.[6] Constitution is a relation in many ways similar to identity, but it is not the same relation as identity, understood in a strict, or Leibnizian, sense.[7] We need consti-

---

3 What worries many philosophers is that some things seem more tightly tied to their parts than do others: An ordinary thing (like your car or my house) seems to be able to gain and lose parts and change size, while its "constituting matter" cannot survive similar material change. Mark Johnston uses the term 'constituting matter' in "Constitution Is Not Identity," *Mind* 101 (1992): 89–105. See Chapter 7, second section, for a critique of a mereological approach.

4 See my "Why Constitution Is Not Identity." The argument there entails: $\exists x \exists y \forall z[(z$ is a part of $x \leftrightarrow z$ is a part of $y)$ & $x \neq y]$. Where things (like statues) have relational properties essentially, mereological considerations cannot answer questions about constitution.

5 In *Material Constitution: A Reader* (Lanham, MD: Rowman & Littlefield Publishers, 1997) the editor, Michael C. Rea, has handily collected some of the most important papers on coincident entities: David Wiggins's "On Being in the Same Place at the Same Time," pp. 3–9; Frederick C. Doepke's "Spatially Coinciding Objects," pp. 10–24; Judith Jarvis Thomson's "Parthood and Identity Across Time," pp. 25–43; Mark Johnston's "Constitution Is Not Identity," pp. 44–62; and Ernest Sosa's "Subjects Among Other Things," pp. 63–89.

6 In this chapter, I am only trying to work out the general idea of constitution. One can endorse this account without endorsing the range of application that I claim for it. In particular, one may agree with me about the nonidentity of an artifact with, say, a hunk of metal while disagreeing about the nonidentity of a person and her body.

7 I take identity to be strict, or Leibnizian, identity – not so-called contingent identity, or relative identity, or any other kind of faux identity. Many who use the term 'contingent identity' do distinguish that relation from genuine identity, which is construed (rightly, I think) as a necessary relation. For example, see Stephen Yablo, who uses the term 'contingent identity' to refer to things that are "distinct *by nature*, but the same *in the circumstances*" (p. 296). See his "Identity, Essence, and Indiscernibility," *Journal of Philosophy* 84 (1987):

tution to be similar to identity in order to account for the fact that if x constitutes y, then x and y are spatially coincident and share many properties; but we also need constitution to differ from identity in order to account for the fact that if x constitutes y, then x and y are of different kinds and can survive different sorts of changes. Since a large part of my task is to distinguish constitution from identity, I will be emphasizing ways in which x and y are distinct if x constitutes y. But too much emphasis on their distinctness would be misleading: for, as we see in the examples of, say, a statue and the lump of clay that forms it, x and y are not separate, independently existing individuals. Again: I want to make sense of constitution as a third category, intermediate between identity and separate existence.[8]

A DESCRIPTION OF CONSTITUTION

Since constitution is a very general relation, I do not want to explain it just as a relation between persons and bodies. To avoid loading the dice in favor of my view of persons, then, I shall explicate 'constitution' in terms of a statue and the piece of marble that constitutes it. For purposes of illustration, consider Michelangelo's *David* – which I take to be a three-dimensional object that has endured for almost 500 years. *David* is a magnificent statue constituted by a certain piece of marble; call that piece of marble 'Piece.'[9] But *David* (the piece of sculpture, the artwork)

293–314. I think that it is misleading to insist that 'contingent identity' names a relation that is not identity.

8 Denial of the identity of the statue and the piece of marble does not by itself commit one to constitution. An alternative to constitution is to construe objects as four-dimensional space-time worms that have temporal parts; then, although the statue and the piece of marble are not identical, they have current temporal "stages" that are identical. I cannot discuss this alternative here. See David Lewis, "Postscripts to 'Survival and Identity,'" in *Philosophical Papers*, Volume I (New York: Oxford University Press, 1983): 76–7. For a critique of the temporal-parts view, see Judith Jarvis Thomson, "Parthood and Identity Across Time," *The Journal of Philosophy* 80 (1983): 201–20.

9 I am assuming that the piece of marble that now constitutes *David* is the same piece of marble as one of a different shape that was once in a quarry. If you think that shape is essential to pieces of marble, then change the example to the one I used in "Why Constitution Is Not Identity," where the statue, *Discobolus*, comes into existence at the same time as the piece of bronze that constitutes it.

Also, here I am following Allan Gibbard, who takes it that clay statues and lumps of clay "can be designated with proper names." Gibbard, "Contingent Identity," *Journal of Philosophical Logic* IV (1975): 190. It is admittedly odd to name a piece of marble. The oddness stems from what we might call the 'convention of naming:' If x constitutes y and y constitutes nothing else, then a name of the composite object is a name of y. We name

is not identical to Piece. If *David* and Piece were identical, then, by a version of Leibniz's Law, there would be no property borne by Piece but not borne by *David* and no property borne by *David* but not borne by Piece.[10] However, Piece (that very piece of marble) could exist in a world without art. Although I do not know how to specify conditions for individuating pieces of marble, I am confident that they do not include a relation to an artwork.[11] Piece could have existed in a world without art, in which case Piece would not have had the property of being a statue. By contrast, *David* could not exist without being a statue. So, *David* has a property – the property of being a statue wherever it exists – that Piece lacks. But if *David* were identical to Piece, then it would be impossible for "one" to have a property that "the other" lacked – even an unusual modal property like *being a statue wherever and whenever it exists*. Since *David* is essentially a statue but Piece is not, *David* has a property that Piece lacks. Therefore, 'constitution' is not to be defined as identity.

The reasoning leading to the conclusion that *David* is not identical to Piece is controversial, and I have defended it elsewhere.[12] At this point, I am only trying to illustrate the intuitions behind the notion of consti-

statues, not pieces of marble; monuments (the Vietnam Memorial), not pieces of granite; persons, not bodies. Of course, we can give a name to anything we want. And for the purpose at hand, it is useful to name the piece of marble; but I recognize that this is not what we ordinarily do.

10 According to Robert C. Sleigh, Jr., Leibniz meant his "law" to be understood like this: "if individual x is distinct from individual y then there is some intrinsic, non-relational property F that x has and y lacks, or vice versa" ("Identity of Indiscernibles" in *A Companion to Metaphysics*, Jaegwon Kim and Ernest Sosa, eds. [Oxford: Basil Blackwell, 1995]: 234). I am not claiming that there is any *intrinsic, nonrelational* property F that *David* has but Piece lacks, or vice versa. I am claiming, rather, that *being a statue* is an essential property of *David* but not of Piece – even though *being a statue* is a relational property, inasmuch as whether or not something is a statue depends on its relation to an artwork or to an artist. I depart from the tradition in holding that not all essential properties are intrinsic.

11 This consideration leads straight to a counterexample to the conviction that "If y is a paradigm F and x is intrinsically exactly like y, then x is an F." Using sophisticated metaphysical arguments, Mark Johnston aims to undermine this principle in "Constitution Is Not Identity"; Harold Noonan aims to rebut Johnston in "Constitution Is Identity," *Mind* 102 (1993): 133–46. I think that the principle is undermined merely by considering statues, without any fancy arguments: Suppose that something – call it '*a*' – with a microstructure exactly like *David*'s spontaneously coalesced in outer space, light years away from any comparable mass. Now *David* is a paradigmatic statue and *a* is intrinsically exactly like *David*; but *a* is not a statue.

12 Baker, "Why Constitution Is Not Identity."

tution. The basic intuition is that, as a relation between objects, identity is necessary: if $x = y$, then necessarily $x = y$.[13] If $x = y$, then x cannot differ from y in any respect, including respects in which x might have been, or might become, different from the way x is now. That is, if $x = y$, then x and y share their so-called modal properties – properties of being possibly such and such or of being necessarily such and such. I agree with Kripke when he says, "Where [F] is any property at all, including a property involving modal operators, and if x and y are the same object and x had a certain property F, then y has to have the same property F."[14] So, again, since Piece could exist in a world without art, but *David* could not, they differ in their (modal) properties and hence are not identical.[15] Consequently, the correct account of the relation between *David* and Piece will have to be more complicated than simple identity.

On the other hand, as I think everyone would agree, *David* and Piece are not just two independent individuals. For one thing, many of *David*'s aesthetic properties depend on Piece's physical properties: *David*'s pent-up energy depends on, among other things, the way that the marble is shaped to distribute the weight. Another indication that *David* and Piece are not just two independent individuals is that they are spatially coincident. Not only have they been located at exactly the same places at the same times since 1504, but also they are alike in many other ways as well: They have the same size, weight, color, smell, and so on. And their similarity is no accident, for *David* does not exist separately from Piece. Nor does *David* have Piece as a proper part. For, pretty clearly, *David* is not identical to Piece plus some other thing. *David* is neither

13 Cf. Ruth Barcan Marcus, "Modalities and Intensional Languages," in *Modalities: Philosophical Essays* (New York: Oxford University Press, 1993): 3–23, first published in *Synthese* 13 (1961): 303–22. So, I don't take what is called 'contingent identity' to be identity, and I am unsure whether what is called 'relative identity' is coherent. In any case, I am not committed to relative identity. For a defense of relative identity, see Peter Geach, "Identity," in *Logic Matters* (Oxford: Basil Blackwell, 1972): 238–49. For criticisms of relative identity, see John Perry, "The Same F," *Philosophical Review* 79 (1970): 181–200, and David Wiggins, *Sameness and Substance* (Oxford: Basil Blackwell, 1980).

14 Saul A. Kripke, "Identity and Necessity," in *Identity and Individuation*, Milton K. Munitz, ed. (New York: New York University Press, 1971): 137. Kripke continues: "And this is so even if the property F is itself of the form of necessarily having some other property G, in particular that of necessarily being identical to a certain object."

15 My commitment to the necessity of identity as a relation between objects does not imply that I have to deny either the truth or the contingency of statements of the form 'the F is the G.'

identical to nor independent of Piece. The relation between *David* and Piece is, rather, one of constitution.[16]

If I am right, then instances of constitution abound: A particular school is constituted by a certain building, which in turn is constituted by an aggregate of bricks. (The same high school could have been constituted by a different building; the same building that in fact constituted the high school could have constituted an office building.[17]) There are, of course, limits on what can constitute what, and the limits differ depending on the kind of thing in question. Not just anything could have constituted *David*: If Michelangelo had carved a twelve-centimeter male nude out of jade and named it 'David,' it would not have been *David*; it would not have been the same statue that *we* call 'David.' To take other examples, my car could not have been constituted by a soap bubble; nor could Kripke's lectern have been constituted by a block of ice.[18] A soap bubble is too ephemeral to constitute a car, and a block of ice, which melts fairly quickly, is unsuited to play a "lectern role" in our climate. Further, some things – ships, but perhaps not statues – may be constituted by different things at different times.

As I mentioned earlier, the basic idea behind the notion of constitution is this: When certain things with certain properties are in certain circumstances, new things with new properties come into existence. For example, when a combination of chemicals occurs in a certain environment, a new thing comes into existence: an organism. Or, when a large stone is placed in certain circumstances, it acquires new properties, and

16 Constitution, as I am construing it, differs in important ways from Dean W. Zimmerman's construal in "Theories of Masses and Problems of Constitution," *Philosophical Review* 104 (1995): 53–110. Zimmerman takes the relata of constitution to be masses of kinds of stuff. He also permits *x* and *y* to constitute one another (p. 74), whereas I require asymmetry. In any case, Zimmerman finds the alleged differences between coincidents ungrounded and concludes that "coincident physical objects are not to be countenanced" (p. 90). I believe that my account of having properties derivatively (which I shall set out in the next section), together with my rejection of the thesis that all essential properties are intrinsic, dissolves the difficulties that Zimmerman sees.

17 This intuition receives support from David Hume, who says that a stone church that fell to ruin may be rebuilt out of different materials and with a different form; yet its relation to the members of the parish "is sufficient to make us denominate them the same." *A Treatise of Human Nature*, L. A. Selby-Bigge, ed. (Oxford: Oxford University Press, 1968): 258.

18 I agree with the Kripkean point that the lectern could not have been constituted by a block of ice, but not for the Kripkean reason that a thing's origins are essential properties of the thing. It is not because the lectern had a non-ice origin that it cannot be constituted by a block of ice, but rather because nothing constituted by a block of ice could serve the purposes of a lectern (at least in normal environments).

a new thing – a monument to those who died in battle – comes into being. And the constituted thing (the stone monument) has effects in virtue of having properties that the constituting thing (the stone) would not have had if it had not constituted a monument. The monument attracts speakers and small crowds on patriotic holidays; it brings tears to people's eyes; it arouses protests. Had it not constituted a monument, the large stone would have had none of these effects. When stones first came to constitute monuments, a new kind of thing with new properties – properties that are causally efficacious – came into being.

Pretheoretically, I take constitution to be an asymmetric relation. Piece constitutes *David; David* does not constitute Piece. This asymmetry induces a kind of ontological hierarchy – a hierarchy that reverses the usual reductive hierarchy. When Piece comes to constitute *David*, something new, with new causal powers, comes into existence. Since the coming-into-existence of *David* brings into being new causal powers that Piece would not have had if Piece had not constituted anything, *David* has greater ontological significance than does Piece. If x constitutes y at a certain place and time, then there is a unified individual at that place at that time, and the identity of that individual is determined by y. The object (y) that is constituted by something (x) but that constitutes nothing else is ontologically more significant than the thing (x) that constitutes it. The identity of the constituting thing is submerged in the identity of what it constitutes. As long as x constitutes y, y encompasses or subsumes x. In what follows, I shall try to make good on these metaphors.

Constitution is a contingent relation between individual things. First, constitution is a relation between *individual* things.[19] The relata of the

19 In "The Statue and the Clay" (*Noûs* 32 [1998]: 149–73), Judith Jarvis Thomson also sets out to define 'constitution' for artifacts, but she takes constitution to be a relation between an artifact and some portion of matter. This is not my conception for two reasons.

(1) The identity conditions for portions of matter don't seem to fit my intuitions about constitution. Suppose that I have a cotton dress, and suppose that it is constituted at t_1 by a certain portion of cotton, P_1. Now suppose that I cut a tiny swatch from an inside seam as a color sample that I'll use to match shoes. I take it that anything large enough to be a color sample is itself a portion; hence, after I cut my swatch, P_1 no longer exists at t_2. In that case, my dress is constituted at t_2 by a different portion of cotton, P_2. On the contrary, I have a strong intuition (!) that my dress is constituted by the same thing at t_1 and at t_2. So, I don't think that what constitutes my dress is a portion of cotton, but rather a piece of cotton (which can survive loss of a swatch).

(2) I do not think that portions of matter are ontologically significant. I do not quantify over portions of matter. I see no need for an intermediate level between, e.g., pieces of cloth (things) and bunches of molecules. (The persistence condition for a bunch

constitution relation are not properties (e.g., the property of having an atomic number of 79); so, constitution must be distinguished sharply from supervenience.[20] Nor is "stuff" (e.g., gold) a relatum of the constitution relation. As I am using the term 'constitution,' *David* is constituted by a *piece* of marble, not by marble as stuff.[21] Of course, *David* is made of marble, but the relation between a constituted thing and some stuff is not what I am calling constitution. What enters into the constitution relation is a marble thing (that I have named 'Piece'), not mere stuff. Second, constitution is a *contingent* relation: Piece could have existed and yet failed to constitute anything at all. If x constitutes y at some time, then the existence of x at that time does not by itself entail the existence of y.[22]

Many of the relational properties that make something the thing that it is are intentional. For example, as we have seen, nothing would be *David* that failed to be a statue, and nothing could be a statue except in relation to an artworld, or an artist's intention, or something else that resists nonintentional description. Let us say that a property H is intentional if and only if H could not be exemplified in a world in which no one had ever had a belief, desire, intention, hope, expectation, fear, or other propositional attitude. And let us say that a particular thing, x, is an intentional object if and only if x could not exist in a world in which no one had ever had a belief, desire, intention, hope, expectation, fear, or other propositional attitudes. ('Intentional relation' and 'intentional phenomenon' may be defined similarly.) Then artifacts and artworks, as

of molecules is simply that the bunch persists for as long as all the molecules in the bunch persist, whatever their spatial locations. I use 'bunch' because as far as I know, it's not used in the literature with some meaning that I don't intend.) Things are significant, and bunches of molecules are significant; but, on my view, portions are not. So, appeal to pieces (and other F's that constitute things) is not, I think, susceptible to the charge of duplication.

20 Failure to distinguish between supervenience and constitution has caused a great deal of confusion in the philosophy of mind. See my *Explaining Attitudes: A Practical Approach to the Mind* (Cambridge: Cambridge University Press, 1995): 132. For detailed discussions of supervenience, see Jaegwon Kim's *Supervenience and Mind* (Cambridge: Cambridge University Press, 1993).

21 For an interesting discussion of stuff and things, see Vere Chappell, "Matter," *Journal of Philosophy* 70 (1973): 679–96.

22 In many cases (although not, perhaps, in *David's* case), the converse also holds: y constitutes x & x could have been constituted by something other than y. Although I do not endorse Kripke's doctrine of the necessity of origin as a general thesis, I would agree that in some cases a thing has its origin essentially. See *Naming and Necessity* (Cambridge, MA: Harvard University Press, 1980).

well as persons and passports, are intentional objects.[23] Indeed, many familiar objects are intentional objects: carburetors, cathedrals, menus, birth certificates, flags, search warrants, trophies, obituaries.[24]

But it is important to recognize that not all constituted things are intentional. Genes are constituted by DNA molecules.[25] Something is a gene only in virtue of its relational properties. An otherwise empty world, in which a few DNA molecules coalesced, would not thereby contain genes. In order for DNA molecules to be genes, they must play a certain role in the reproduction of organisms. Although genes are constituted things, they are paradigmatically not intentional entities in the sense just specified. (Presumably, there were genes before there were any creatures with propositional attitudes.) So, appeal to constitution involves no special pleading on behalf of the intentional. Indeed, a prominent virtue of the notion of constitution is that it yields a single account of both intentional and nonintentional individuals without reducing intentional to nonintentional individuals.

Now I want to turn to a more technical exposition of the idea of constitution. For this exposition, I need a background notion of 'having a property essentially.'

THE ROAD TO ESSENTIALISM

In order to develop my view of constitution, I must appeal to essential properties of things. Many people find the notion of essential properties – or, as I prefer, the notion of having a property essentially – obscure. Let me say first what I mean by 'having a property essentially,' and then I shall defend the assumption that ordinary things do have properties essentially. If x has F essentially (alternatively, if F is an essential property of x), then x necessarily has F. The essential properties of an object x are the properties without which x could not exist. So,

---

23 This is a different use of 'intentional object' from its traditional use, in which it denotes "nonexistent" objects like Pegasus and Santa Claus.

24 A number of philosophers (e.g., Richard Boyd, Hillary Kornblith, and Derk Pereboom) hold that (token) beliefs and other attitudes are constituted by (token) brain states without being identical to the brain states that constitute them. For reasons given in *Explaining Attitudes*, I do not endorse that claim. However, I believe that the view of constitution developed in this chapter could help make clear what it might mean to say that (token) beliefs are constituted by, but not identical to, brain states.

25 For a study of the relation of classical genetics to molecular genetics that is congenial to the idea of constitution, see Philip Kitcher, "1953 and All That: A Tale of Two Sciences," *The Philosophical Review* 93 (1984): 335–73.

x has F essentially if and only if at any possible world and at any time at which *x* exists, *x* has F at that world and at that time.[26]

Elsewhere, I have argued that Michaelangelo's *David* has essentially the property of being related to an artworld.[27] What that means is that in a world without art, *David* could not exist. Even a molecule-for-molecule duplicate would not be *David*. On the other hand, *David*'s being located in the Academy in Florence is not an essential property of *David*'s. For there are possible worlds in which *David* is moved to Paris. *David* would not cease to exist simply because it was moved. So, I think that ordinary things have some of their properties essentially and other of their properties accidentally.

The necessity involved in having properties essentially may be made clearer by contrast with another kind of necessity. For example, being enrolled in an institution of higher learning is not an essential property of college students. It is true that *necessarily*, if *x* is a college student, then *x* is currently enrolled in an institution of higher learning. However, it is not the case that: if *x* is a college student, then *necessarily x* is currently enrolled in an institution of higher learning. For although it is necessary for *x*'s being a college student that he or she be currently enrolled in an institution of higher learning, it is not necessary for *x*'s *existence* that he or she be currently enrolled in an institution of higher learning. That is, the necessity that a college student be currently enrolled in an institution of higher learning is a *de dicto* necessity, not a *de re* necessity. If a college student ceased to be enrolled in an institution of higher learning, he or she would cease to be college student but would not thereby cease to exist. However, if he or she had the property of being a college student essentially, he or she could not exist without being a college student.

How did a pragmatist (like me) wander into the thickets of essentialism? By reflections like these: There are many different kinds of things. Things of different kinds can survive different kinds of changes. For example, your body, because it is of the kind *human organism*, can survive complete replacement of all its cells by different cells. But the Bayeux Tapestry, because it is of the kind *tapestry*, could not survive complete replacement of all its threads by different threads – no matter how similar

26 For refinement, see Gareth B. Matthews, "Aristotelian Essentialism," *Philosophy and Phenomenological Research* 50, Supplement (Fall 1990): 251–62. Also see Ruth Barcan Marcus, "Essential Attribution," *Journal of Philosophy* 68 (1971): 187–202; reprinted in *Modalities: Philosophical Essays* (New York: Oxford University Press, 1993): 53–73.

27 Baker, "Why Constitution Is Not Identity."

the replacement threads were to the original. Even if it could survive replacement of some of its threads, complete replacement of threads would result in a new tapestry. It is not that the Bayeux Tapestry would simply lose some properties and gain others; rather, the Bayeux Tapestry would no longer exist.

So, some things go out of existence altogether; it's not just that they lose this property or that, but rather that they cease to exist. And the conditions under which they cease to exist are determined by the kinds of things that they are. For example, when the combatants in the English civil wars dismantled a certain manor house for its stones, the manor house did not just cease to be a manor house – the way that a student who drops out of school ceases to be a student. Rather, the manor house ceased to exist altogether. There was no individual thing that used to be a manor house but then was a bunch of stones scattered all over the county.[28] The thing that was a manor house did not survive the dismantling.

Indeed, anything that exists at t and is not eternal can (and will) go out of existence. If a thing can go out of existence altogether, and not just cease to be an F (a manor house or whatever), then there are conditions under which it would cease to exist altogether and conditions under which it would persist. That is, it has what I shall call '*de re* persistence conditions.' Since most (if not all) of the things around us will cease to exist sooner or later, most of the things around us have *de re* persistence conditions.[29]

Once we have the notion of *de re* persistence conditions, it is but a short step to the notion of essential properties. For x's *de re* persistence conditions include those in the absence of which x could not exist, and essential properties of x are those in the absence of which x could not exist. So, if staying intact is a *de re* persistence condition of the manor house, then the manor house has staying intact as an essential property. So, anything that exists and is not eternal has essential properties in the previously defined sense: If F is an essential property of x, then x cannot exist without having F.[30]

---

28 See Chapter 7 for a discussion of mereology. On my view, ordinary things often cannot be identified with mereological sums; rather, mereological sums constitute ordinary things.

29 One reason to reject "contingent identity" understood as '$x = y$, but possibly $x \neq y$' is that anything that can go out of existence has *de re* persistence conditions; but x's being "contingently identical" to y is logically incompatible with x's having *de re* persistence conditions. See "Why Constitution Is Not Identity."

30 Note that this construal of essential properties leaves open the possibility, which on my theory is an actuality, that one thing may have F essentially and another thing may have

I am not invoking the occult. Anything that can go out of existence has *de re* persistence conditions; and anything that has *de re* persistence conditions has essential properties. But essential properties are not limited to *de re* persistence conditions. Essential properties should be thought of more generally as "existence conditions." For example, if something is a landscape painting, that thing is necessarily related to an artworld with certain conventions, and if something is a carburetor, then that thing is necessarily related to automobiles and automotive practices.[31] So, being related to an artworld is an essential property of a landscape painting, and being related to automotive practices is an essential property of a carburetor. However, the artworld and the automotive practices could disappear without extinction of landscape paintings and carburetors. The fact that the things that are landscape paintings and carburetors had been related, respectively, to an artworld and to automotive practices is enough for them to continue to exist (as landscape paintings and carburetors) after the demise of the artworld and automotive practices. So, if everyone died of a plague that left all the contents of museums and automobiles intact, Carracci's *Landscape with the Flight into Egypt* would still exist, and so would the carburetor in my car. But neither the carburetor in my car nor Carracci's *Landscape* could have existed in a world that never had automotive practices and an artworld.

A property may be essential to one thing but not to another thing that also has it. For example, having a certain shape may be essential to a certain statue, but if a meteor happened to have that same shape, having that shape would not be an essential property of the meteor. What I have said suggests several important (and perhaps idiosyncratic) features of the kind of essentialism that I am endorsing here:

1. Everything that exists and is not eternal has essential properties.
2. Some things (e.g., artworks and artifacts) have relational properties essentially.
3. Some things (e.g., artworks and artifacts) have intentional properties essentially.
4. Some things (e.g., artworks and artifacts) have properties whose instantiation depends on conventions, on language, or on other aspects of culture essentially.

F nonessentially. A manor house has the property of staying intact essentially, but a bunch of molecules that is currently intact does not.

31 For a discussion of artifacts, see *Explaining Attitudes*. For a discussion of artworks, see "Why Constitution Is Not Identity."

5. One thing may have a certain property essentially, while another thing may have same property contingently.

Where I depart from tradition is in taking certain relational and intentional properties to be essential properties of concrete things. Not everything that exists could exist in total isolation. If there were only one thing in the world, it would not be a national flag, even if it had the characteristic pattern of three bands of red, white, and blue that in our world would constitute a national flag; nor would it be a gene, even if it had the molecular structure of a gene. (And, of course, if there existed only one thing in the world, it would not be a carburetor or a landscape painting.) Thus, I dissent from Allan Gibbard when he says, "If the statue is an entity over and above the piece of clay in that shape, then statues seem to take on a ghostly air."[32] Relational properties are in no way ghostly. (Indeed, this is the lesson of externalism in philosophy of psychology. That the believer is in a certain kind of environment is an essential property of a belief that water is wet.) And it is in virtue of its relational properties that *David* exists. Even if it is also in virtue of its relational properties that Piece exists, there remains this irreducible difference between them: Piece could exist in the absence of an artworld; *David* could not.

Philosophers generally consider this version of essentialism the strongest grade of essentialism. For me, this essentialism is motivated by such down-to-earth considerations as the fact that there are conditions under which a particular manor house, say, would cease to exist. This version of essentialism, stemming as it does from reflection on the everyday lifeworld, seems fully compatible with a basically pragmatic outlook. (In particular, it fits well with the Practical Realism that I espoused in *Explaining Attitudes*.) In the next section, I shall use the idea of *x*'s having a property essentially when I introduce the notions of a primary kind and of primary-kind properties.

A DEFINITION OF 'CONSTITUTION'

The features of constitution may be codified. For codification, I need two ideas: the idea of a primary kind and the idea of what I'll call 'circumstances.' Each concrete individual is fundamentally a member of

---

32   Gibbard, "Contingent Identity," 191.

exactly one kind – call it its 'primary kind.' To answer the question "What most fundamentally is x?" we cite x's primary kind by using a substance noun for: example, 'a horse' or 'a bowl.' x's primary kind is a kind of thing, not just stuff: Piece's primary kind is not just marble, but a piece of marble; the Nile's primary kind is not just water, but a river (of water). Since *David*'s primary kind, for example, is a statue, call the property of being a statue *David*'s 'primary-kind property.' An important feature of primary kinds is this: An individual has the *de re* persistence conditions of its primary kind and hence has its primary-kind property essentially. It cannot cease to have its primary-kind property without ceasing to exist. If *being a horse* is a primary-kind property, then a world just like ours except that it lacked horses would be a world with fewer things in it than our world. Contrast, say, *being a husband*, which is not a primary-kind property: A world like ours except that it lacked the institution of marriage (and hence had no husbands) would not thereby have fewer individuals in it than our world. So, in general, if being an F is x's primary-kind property, then being an F is essential to x: It is impossible for anything that is not an F to be (identical to) x.[33]

It would be useful to have a theory of primary kinds. The general question that a theory of primary kinds would answer is this: Under what conditions does one thing come to constitute a new entity as opposed to simply gaining a property? For example, suppose that I buy an anvil with the intention of using it to hold open the barn door, and that I use it in that capacity for years. Does the anvil now constitute a doorstop? Is the doorstop an entity distinct from the anvil? Well, the anvil does have the property of being a doorstop, but I doubt that many would say that the doorstop is an entity distinct from the anvil. Being a doorstop is just a property that the anvil acquired. A theory of primary kinds would provide a principled way to distinguish between cases (like the anvil/doorstop) in which an object merely acquires a property and cases (like Piece/*David*) in which a new entity comes into existence. Since a theory of primary kinds would be tantamount to a theory of everything, however, it is not surprising (although still regrettable) that

33 As we shall see when I discuss 'having properties derivatively,' it is possible, for some x, y, and H that x has H essentially and y has H nonessentially. For example, *David* has the property of being a statue essentially; Piece borrows the property of being a statue from *David*, and Piece has the property of being a statue contingently. To put it differently, being an F (e.g., being a statue) may be x's (e.g., *David*'s) primary-kind property, and y (e.g., Piece) may have the property of being an F by borrowing that property from x. In that case, being an F is not y's primary-kind property.

I do not have one. And since we are constantly bringing into existence new kinds of things – from airliners to personal computers – there is no saying in advance exactly what the primary kinds will turn out to be.

In the absence of a theory of primary kinds, let me suggest a consideration that would lead us to say whether a case is one of constitution or of mere property acquisition. If x constitutes y, then y has whole classes of causal properties that x would not have had if x had not constituted anything. The anvil acquires the property of being a doorstop by our enlisting a physical property of the anvil – its heaviness – for a special purpose: to hold open the barn door. The use of the anvil as a doorstop does not bring about instantiation of whole classes of properties that anvils per se do not have. On the other hand, *David* has many causal properties of different kinds that Piece would not have had if Piece had not constituted anything. And you and I have uncountably many causal properties that our bodies would not have had if they had not constituted anything – from looking forward to graduation, to reminding a friend to return a book, to serving on a jury, and on and on. So, even without a theory of primary kinds, we have some clear cases of constitution, and we have a characteristic – the constituted thing has different kinds of causal properties than the constituting thing would have had if it had not constituted anything – that marks off constitution from mere property acquisition. In any case, in order to define 'x constitutes y at t,' I need the idea of a primary kind.

Second, in order to define 'x constitutes y at t' in full generality, I need a variable for different answers to the question "In virtue of what is y the kind of thing that it is?" For example, it is in virtue of certain legal conventions that a particular piece of paper constitutes a marriage license; it is in virtue of the arrangement of molecules that something constitutes a block of ice; it is in virtue of its evolutionary history that a particular conglomerate of cells constitutes a human heart.[34] I'll call the various answers 'circumstances.' It is only in certain circumstances – different circumstances for marriage licenses and human hearts – that one thing constitutes another. It is in virtue of one kind of circumstance that the piece of paper constitutes a marriage license, and it is in virtue of an entirely different kind of circumstance that the conglomerate of cells constitutes a human heart. The variable for 'circumstances' ('D') ranges over states of affairs in virtue of which something is the kind of thing that it is.

---

34 At least, this is the view of Ruth Millikan.

41

Many properties can be instantiated only in certain circumstances. For example, the property of being a national flag can be instantiated only in circumstances where there are beings with certain kinds of intentional states, certain kinds of social and political entities, and certain conventions. Such circumstances are essential to national flags: Nothing is a flag without them. For any property of being a G, where G is a primary kind, call the milieu required for something to be a G 'G-favorable circumstances.' G-favorable circumstances entail instantiation of every property, except for primary-kind properties, that must be exemplified for something to be a G. For any particular place and time, the presence of G-favorable circumstances is a necessary, but not a sufficient, condition for the property G to be instantiated then and there.★ The presence of something of a suitable primary kind in G-favorable circumstances is sufficient for G to be instantiated then and there.[35]

An informal idea of material constitution is this: Where *being an F* and *being a G* are distinct primary-kind properties, it is possible that an F exists without there being any spatially coincident G. However, if an F is in G-favorable circumstances, then there is a new entity, a G, that is spatially coincident with the F but not identical to it.

Now let me offer a general schema for 'constitution.' To allow for the possibility that x may constitute y at one time, but not at another, I have a variable for time; but I'll drop the time index later when it does not matter. Let *being an F* be x's primary-kind property, and let *being a G* be y's primary-kind property, where *being an F* $\neq$ *being a G*, and let D be G-favorable circumstances. Let F★ be the property of *having the property of being an F as one's primary-kind property*, and let G★ be the property of *having the property of being a G as one's primary-kind property*.[36] Then:

★The reason for the locution 'at any particular place or time' is illustrated by this: Perhaps the existence of an artworld is required for something to be an artwork. The existence of an artworld by itself may well entail that there are artworks without entailing, for any particular place or time, that the property of being an artwork is instantiated there and then.

35 The reason for the locution 'at any particular place or time' is that perhaps the existence of an artworld is required for something to be an artwork. The existence of an artworld by itself may well entail that there are artworks, without entailing – for any particular place or time – that the property of being an artwork is instantiated there.

36 The reason to distinguish F★ and G★ from F and G is that some x may have the property of *being an F* derivatively, in which case x is an F but *being an F* is not x's primary-kind property. Introduction of F★ restricts the definition of cases to Fs that have the property of *being an F* as their primary-kind property.

Definition of 'Constitution'

(C) x constitutes y at $t =_{df}$

   (a) x and y are spatially coincident at t; and

   (b) x is in D at t; and

   (c) It is necessary that: $\forall z[(F^\star zt \& z$ is in D at $t) \rightarrow \exists u(G^\star ut \& u$ is spatially coincident with z at $t)]$; and

   (d) It is possible that: (x exists at t & $\sim\exists w[G^\star wt \& w$ is spatially coincident with x at $t]$); and

   (e) If y is immaterial, then x is also immaterial.

Let me make two brief comments about (C) before showing how *David* and Piece satisfy it: First, although I ultimately want to use (C) in an account of human persons as material beings, (C) does not rule out there being immaterial things or even immaterial things that are constituted. But (e) requires that if there are immaterial constituted things, they are not constituted by wholly material things. Assuming that human bodies are wholly material, then (e) excludes the possibility that a human body could constitute a Cartesian person, where a Cartesian person is defined as consisting of a human body and an immaterial soul.[37]

Second, the modalities in (c) and (d) – 'it is necessary that' and 'it is possible that' – are context dependent. For any actual situation, there will be relevant alternative situations to be considered. Although relevance will ultimately be determined by the facts of the actual situation, the laws of nature are to be held constant. Moreover, to avoid vacuous satisfaction of (c), the relevant alternatives are always to include some in which the F is in G-favorable circumstances. The examples in the next section will make clearer how to interpret the modalities.

Now let me illustrate (C) by showing how *David* and Piece satisfy it. Let the property of *being an F* be the property of *being a piece of marble* (Piece's primary-kind property). Let the property of *being a G* be the property of *being a statue* (*David's* primary-kind property). Now let D be the circumstance of being presented as a three-dimensional figure in an artworld, given a title, and put on display (or whatever is required by the correct theory of art for something to be a statue). Then,

(a) Piece and *David* are spatially coincident at t; and

(b) Piece is in the circumstance of being presented as a three-dimensional figure in an artworld, given a title, and put on display at t.

---

37 Anil K. Gupta proposed this counterexample to an earlier definition.

(c) It is necessary that: if anything that has being a piece of marble as its primary-kind property is presented as a three-dimensional figure in an artworld, given a title, and put on display at t, then there is something that has being a statue as its primary-kind property that is spatially coincident with the piece of marble at t.

(d) It is possible that: Piece exists at t and that no spatially coincident thing that has being a statue as its primary-kind property exists at t.

(e) Neither *David* nor Piece is immaterial.

David would not exist but for the relational and intentional properties of the piece of marble: On (almost?) every theory of art, something is an artwork in virtue of its relations to something else – the artist, the artworld, the history of the medium.[38] The moral here is that what makes a thing the thing that it is – *David*, for example – may be its relational properties and not always, as tradition has held, its nonrelational properties. Although a number of philosophers have discussed the relation between things like *David* and Piece, they have assumed that something is the thing that it is in virtue of its nonrelational properties.[39] I think that it is time to put aside the long-standing prejudice that what x really is – in itself, in its nature – is determined exclusively by x's nonrelational properties. In many cases – as we have seen with *David* – there is no x to be considered in isolation, apart from everything else: To abstract away from all the relations would be to abstract away from the relatum.

One virtue of (C) is that it yields what I think are the intuitively correct properties of constitution. In particular, constitution is irreflexive, asymmetric, and nontransitive. So, (C) guarantees that constitution is not identity. Constitution is an irreflexive relation: Clause (d) guarantees that nothing constitutes itself. Constitution is an asymmetric relation: If x constitutes y, then y does not constitute x.[40] To see that

---

38 Thus, I dissent from those who take statues to be determined by shape (e.g., "statuesque").

39 A recent example may be found in Michael Della Rocca, "Essentialists and Essentialism," *Journal of Philosophy* 93 (1996): 186–202. In "Why Constitution Is Not Identity," I reply to Della Rocca.

40 The intuitions of philosophers who assume pretheoretically that constitution is symmetrical are foreign to me. See, e.g., Michael Rea in "The Problem of Material Constitution," *The Philosophical Review* 104 (1995): 526. Rea takes symmetry to be a defining characteristic of the target relation, constitution. And Eli Hirsch calls attention to 'constitutive identity,' an allegedly symmetric relation that holds between "two strictly distinct objects [that] occupy the same place at once." Pace such philosophers, it seems pretheoretically obvious to me that the lump of clay constitutes the statue but that the statue does not constitute the lump of clay.

constitution is asymmetric, proceed by cases. Suppose that *a* (with the primary-kind property of *being an F*) constitutes *b* (with the primary-kind property of *being a G*).

Case 1. Necessarily, everything with the primary-kind property of *being a G* is constituted by something with the primary-kind property of *being an F*. In Case 1, it is not possible that a G exists but no spatially coincident F exists. But if *b* also constituted *a*, then by (d) it would be possible that a G exists and no spatially coincident F exists. So, in Case 1, if *a* constitutes *b*, then *b* does not constitute *a* (since (d) is not satisfied for '*b* constitutes *a*').

Case 2. Not necessarily everything with the primary-kind property of *being a G* is constituted by something with the primary-kind property of *being an F*. (Certain G-things that are instances of Case 2 are multiply realizable.) In Case 2, it is not necessary that for every G in F-favorable circumstances, there is a spatially coincident F. (For example, a statue may be in piece-of-marble-favorable circumstances and yet be constituted by a piece of bronze, in which case there is no piece of marble spatially coincident with the statue.) But if *b* also constituted *a*, then by (c) necessarily, for any G in F-favorable circumstances, there would be a spatially coincident F. So, in Case 2, if *a* constitutes *b*, then *b* does not constitute *a* (since (c) is not satisfied for '*b* constitutes *a*').

Case 1 and Case 2 exhaust the possibilities. Therefore, constitution is asymmetric.

Finally, constitution according to (C) is nontransitive. In order to derive '*x* constitutes *z* at *t*' from '*x* constitutes *y* at *t*' and '*y* constitutes *z* at *t*' the H-favorable circumstances (where *being an H* is *z*'s primary-kind property) would have to include the G-favorable circumstances (where *being a G* is *y*'s primary-kind property). But in general, something can be in H-favorable circumstances without being in G-favorable circumstances. To see this, consider an aggregate of H_2O molecules, *a*, that constitutes a block of ice, *b*, at time *t*. Also, suppose that *b* constitutes an ice sculpture, *s*, at *t*. Does it follow that *a* constitutes *s* at *t*? The block-of-ice-favorable circumstance in which *a* constitutes *b* is the spatial proximity of the molecules in *a*; the ice-sculpture-favorable circumstances in which *b* constitutes *s* are the conventions of parties, decorations, and so on. Checking the definition (C), we see that *a* does not constitute *s* at *t*. Clause (c) fails for '*a* constitutes *s* at *t*.' It is not necessary that for any aggregate of H_2O molecules in ice-sculpture-favorable circumstances, there is a spatially coincident ice sculpture. After the ice sculpture has melted, the aggregate of H_2O molecules remains in a liquid pool. At that time, the aggregate is still in ice-sculpture-favorable circumstances, but there is no ice sculpture. Hence, even though a constitutes b at t and b constitutes s at t, clause (c) is not satisfied for 'a constitutes s at t.'

Even though constitution is nontransitive, there are chains of constitutionally related things all the way "down" to fundamental particles. Say that 'x is constitutionally linked to y' if and only if: Either [y constitutes x or $\exists z_1, \ldots z_n(y$ constitutes z_1 & z_1 constitutes z_2 & $\ldots$ & z_n constitutes $x)$] or [x constitutes y or $\exists z_1, \ldots z_m$ (x constitutes z_1 & z_1 constitutes z_2 & $\ldots$ & z_m constitutes $y)$]. With this definition, we can formulate a weak thesis of materialism: Every concrete thing is either a fundamental particle or is constitutionally linked to an aggregate of fundamental particles.[41]

HAVING PROPERTIES DERIVATIVELY

Constitution is, as I have said, a unity relation; it is not mere spatial coincidence. Some critics of constitution speak as if, according to the idea of constitution-without-identity, a particular body and a particular person are two things that just happen to occupy the same space.[42] But these critics seriously misinterpret the idea of constitution-without-identity. For when x constitutes y, there is a unitary thing – y, as constituted by x – which is a single thing in a sense that I shall try to make clear. As long as x constitutes y, x has no independent existence. If x continues to exist after the demise of y, then x comes into its own, existing independently. But during the period that x constitutes y, the identity of "the thing" – y, as constituted by x – is determined by the identity of y. So, what is sitting in front of you when you go to see the dean is a person, constituted by a particular body.[43]

41 For further discussion of materialism, see Chapter 9.
42 Michael B. Burke, "Copper Statues and Pieces of Copper," *Analysis* 52 (1992): 12–17.
43 In "Preserving the Principle of One Object to a Place: A Novel Account of the Relations Among Objects, Sorts, Sortals and Persistence Conditions" (*Philosophy and Phenomenological Research* 54 [1994]: 591–624), Burke offers a view that seems to fit parts of this description. However, I understand it, Burke's account, applied to the relation between persons and bodies, has the following as a consequence: Human body 1 (a fetus, when it is not a person) is not the same human body as Human body 2 (an adult, who is a person spatiotemporally continuous with Human body 1). This consequence seems implausible. Whatever we say about persons and bodies, surely there is only one human body through-

Nevertheless, the dean and his body are not identical, and we can speak of the properties of each. The dean has some of his properties (e.g., being over six feet tall) in virtue of being constituted by the body that constitutes him. The dean's body has some of its properties (e.g., having the right to be at the head of the procession at graduation) in virtue of constituting a particular person who has certain properties. In general, x will have some, but not all, of its properties in virtue of constituting something or of being constituted by something. This important feature of constitution induces a distinction between having a property nonderivatively and having a property derivatively.[44]

Say that x and y are constitutionally related if and only if either x constitutes y or y constitutes x. The basic idea of having a property derivatively is this: x has H at t derivatively if and only if x's having H at t depends wholly on x's being constitutionally related to something that has H at t independently of its being constitutionally related to x. If x constitutes y, then x and y share many properties: The dean is over six feet tall, and so is his body. But since the dean derives the property of being over six feet tall from the body that constitutes him, the dean has that property derivatively. For stylistic reasons, I'll sometimes speak of 'derivative properties,' which I'll use as a synonym for 'having properties derivatively.'

Before developing the account of derivative properties in greater detail, I want to emphasize an important feature of derivative properties that distinguishes my view from others' views. On my view, having properties derivatively goes both ways: If x constitutes y, then *both* x and y have some of their properties derivatively. (The recognition of "downward derivation" as well as "upward derivation" indicates the antireductive thrust of my view.) Many philosophers hold that constituted things derive their properties from what constitutes them, and not vice versa. Calling this view "upward-only derivation" of properties, let me give some counterexamples to it.[45] To simplify, I'll drop reference to times here.

out – from fetus to corpse. My view of persons and bodies allows that that there is a single human body, and at times it constitutes a person and at other times it does not.

44 In "Unity Without Identity: A New Look at Material Constitution," *New Directions in Philosophy: Midwest Studies in Philosophy*, Volume 23, Howard Wettstein, ed. (Malden, MA: Blackwell Publishers, 1999), I use the label 'borrowing properties' for what I am here calling 'having properties derivatively.'

45 For example, with respect to nonessential properties that are such that they may not be rooted outside the times at which they are had (as defined by Chisholm), Chisholm thinks

Here is a simple counterexample to the upward-only-derivation claim. Suppose that it is illegal to burn a U.S. flag. Now consider a particular U.S. flag, constituted by a particular piece of cloth. Its being illegal to burn the flag makes it illegal to burn the constituting cloth. But the flag does not derive the property of *being an x such that it is illegal to burn x* from the piece of cloth that constitutes the flag. Clearly, the direction of fit is the other way. What makes it illegal to burn the piece of cloth is that the piece of cloth constitutes a U.S. flag. Legislators write laws to protect national symbols, not to protect pieces of cloth.

There is two-way derivation of properties for persons and the bodies that constitute them as well. Since the dean's body constitutes the dean, if the dean has a right to be at the head of the procession, so does his body. But the dean's right to be at the head of the procession does not derive from his being constituted by a certain body. On the other hand, the right of the dean's body to be at the head of the procession does derive from the fact that that body constitutes person, the dean, who has that right independently of being constituted by that body. So, here is another example of downward derivation of properties.

Granted, these counterexamples to the upward-only-derivation claim concern relational and intentional properties. But, as I have tried to show elsewhere,[46] recognition of such properties is crucial for understanding reality. So, on my account of constitution, there is two-way derivation of properties: If x constitutes y at t, then x derives some properties from y at t, and y derives some properties from x at t.

To be more precise about the notion of having properties derivatively, we need to define four special classes of properties. (a) Call any property expressed in English by the locutions 'essentially' or 'primary kind' (as in 'has F as its primary-kind property'), or by 'possibly' or 'necessarily' or variants of such terms, 'an alethic property.' (b) Call any property expressed in English by the locutions 'is identical to' or 'constitutes' or 'exists' or variants of such terms 'an "identity/constitution/

---

that ordinary things (like tables) borrow such properties from what constitutes them, and not vice versa. See Roderick Chisholm, *Person and Object: A Study in Metaphysics* (LaSalle, IL: Open Court Publishing Company, 1976): 100–1. The counterexamples that I give to the "bottom-up-borrowing-only" claim in the text all concern nonessential properties, and all conform to Chisholm's definition of properties that are such that they may not be rooted outside the times at which they are had. So, I think that they are counterexamples to Chisholm's view. For detailed discussion, see my "Persons in Metaphysical Perspective" in *The Philosophy of Roderick M. Chisholm* (The Library of Living Philosophers, Volume XXV) (LaSalle, IL: Open Court Publishing Company, 1997): 433–53.

46   Baker, "Why Constitution Is Not Identity."

existence" property.' (c) Call any property such that necessarily, x has it at t only if x exists at some time other than t 'a property rooted outside the times at which it is had.'[47] To illustrate the notion of a property rooted outside the times at which it is had, suppose that Piece was quarried at t and later came to constitute *David* at t'; Piece's property at t' of having been quarried at t is rooted outside times at which it is had. (d) Finally, call any property that is a conjunction of two or more properties that either entail or are entailed by two or more primary-kind properties a 'hybrid property.' For example, the property of being a *cloth flag* – which is a conjunction of properties entailed by the primary-kind property *being a piece of cloth* and the primary-kind property *being a flag* – is a hybrid property.

In order to define the notion of having properties derivatively, I need to define a notion that I shall use in the definition of 'having a property derivatively': the notion of having a property independently of constitution relations. Let H range over properties that are neither alethic properties, nor are identity/constitution/existence properties, nor are properties such that they are rooted outside times at which they are had,[48] nor are hybrid properties. Then,

(I) x has H at t independently of x's constitution relations to y at $t =_{df}$

    (a) x has H at t; and

    (b) Either (1) (i) x constitutes y at t, and

                (ii) x's having H at t (in the given background) does not entail that x constitutes anything at t.

      or (2) (i) y constitutes x at t, and

                (ii) x's having H at t (in the given background) does not entail that x is constituted by something that could have had H at t without constituting anything at t.

---

47   This notion comes from Roderick Chisholm. On Chisholm's definition, a property F is rooted outside times at which it is had if and only if: Necessarily, for any x and for any period of time p, x has the property F throughout p only if x exists at some time before or after p. See *Person and Object*, p. 100. Chisholm goes on to define 'G *may be* rooted outside times at which it is had' like this: 'G is equivalent to a disjunction of two properties, one of which is, and the other of which is not, rooted outside times at which it is had.'

48   To be precise, I should bar H from ranging over properties that *may be* rooted outside the times at which they are had. A disjunctive property like being such that x is or was square *may be*, but need not be, rooted outside the time at which it is had.

The point of (b)(1)(ii) is that, if x has H at t independently of its constitution relations to y at t and if x constitutes y at t, then x could still have had H at t (in the given background) even if x had constituted nothing at t. The point of (b)(2)(ii) is that, if x has H at t independently of its constitution relations to y at t, and if y constitutes x at t, then x could still have had H at t (in the given background) regardless of whether or not what constituted x at t could have had H at t (in the given background) without constituting anything. To put the consequent differently: x's having H at t is compatible with x's being constituted at t by something that could not have had H at t (in the given background) without constituting something at t.

(b)(1)(ii) and (b)(2)(ii) are intended to capture a particular idea of dependence. The idea of dependence here concerns what is logically or metaphysically required for something to have a certain property. For example, suppose that Smith has the genes for blue eyes. On the one hand, Smith's body — call it 'Bs' — does have the property of having genes for blue eyes independently of Bs's constitution relations to Smith. The relevant instances of clauses (a), (b)(1)(i), and (b)(1)(ii) of (I) are satisfied since Bs has genes for blue eyes at t, and Bs constitutes Smith at t, and Bs's having genes for blue eyes at t (in the given background) does not entail that Bs constitutes anything at t. On the other hand, Smith's having genes for blue eyes is not independent of Smith's constitution relations to her body. Check the definition for 'Smith has the property of having genes for blue eyes at t independently of Smith's constitution relations to Bs at t.' Although (a) is satisfied, since Smith does have genes for blue eyes at t, (b) is not satisfied. (b)(1) is not satisfied since Smith does not constitute Bs, but vice versa. (b)(2) is not satisfied since, although Bs constitutes Smith at t, the instance of (b)(2)(ii) is false. Since it would be impossible for Smith to have genes for blue eyes without being constituted by an organism with genes for blue eyes, and since an organism can have genes for blue eyes without constituting anything, it follows that, contrary to (b)(2)(ii): Smith's having genes for blue eyes at t (in the given background) does entail that Smith is constituted by something that could have had genes for blue eyes at t without constituting anything at t.

The sense of 'independence' at issue is not causal. Indeed, x may have H independently of x's constitution relations to y, although in a causal sense, the dependence relation may go the other way. Suppose that two members of the team hoisted Coach Jones to their shoulders. The position of Coach Jones's body — call that body 'Bj' — is causally dependent on Bj's constituting Coach Jones. The team members would not have hoisted Bj to their shoulders if Bj hadn't constituted the coach who led the team to victory, for example. But this causal sense of 'dependence' is not the one at issue. Rather, what makes it the case that Coach Jones is, say, five feet off the ground – regardless of what brought about that state of affairs – is the fact that Coach Jones is constituted by Bj, where Bj has the property of being five feet off the ground independently of Bj's constitution relations (in the relevant noncausal sense). Bj has the property of being five feet off the ground independently of Bj's constitution relations to Coach Jones because Bj has that property at t; Bj constitutes Coach Jones at t; and Bj's being five feet off the ground at t (in the given background or in any other background) does not entail that Bj constitutes anything at t. Although Bj has the property of being five feet off the ground independently of Bj's constitution relations to Coach Jones in the sense of 'independence' captured by definition (I), the causal history of Bj's coming to have that property depends on Bj's constituting Coach Jones.

The idea of having properties derivatively shows how something can have a property in virtue of its constitution relations. Constitution is a unity relation that allows x to have a property in virtue of being constitutionally related to something that has the property independently. If x's having H at t depends on x's constitution relations to some y that has H at t, where y has H at t independently of y's constitution relations at t, then H has x at t derivatively. Again, let H range over properties that are neither alethic, nor are constitution/identity/existence, nor are such that they may be rooted outside times at which they are had, nor are hybrid properties. Then,

(D) x has H at t derivatively = $_{df}$ There is some y such that:
   (a) it is not the case that: x has H at t independently of x's constitution relations to y at t; &
   (b) y has H at t independently of y's constitution relations to x at t.

Note that, because of definition (I) of 'having a property independently of constitution relations,' satisfaction of (b) in (D) guarantees that x and y are constitutionally related at t. So, for any property that x has derivatively, there is some y, to which x is constitutionally related, such that y has H independently of its constitution relations to x. (In Chapter 4, I shall enlarge the definition of 'having a property derivatively' to accommodate hybrid properties, which are explicitly excluded from

(D).[49] For any object x and property F, if x has F but not derivatively, then x has F nonderivatively. If x is constitutionally related to y and x has H derivatively, then it will sometimes be convenient to say that x *borrows* the property H from y. Now let me further illustrate these definitions. Again, for simplicity, I'll drop reference to time.

(I) Consider again the example of Smith's having genes for blue eyes. We have already seen that Smith does not have the genes for blue eyes independently of Smith's constitution relations to her body, Bs, and that Bs does have the genes for blue eyes independently of Bs's constitution relations to Smith. So, it is easy to see that by (D) Smith has the genes for blue eyes derivatively.

(b)(1)(ii) and (b)(2)(ii) are to be interpreted relative to a given background. The particular background has played no role in the examples given so far. But sometimes, as we shall see, we must consider background conditions, where background conditions include relevant conventions – social, political, legal, or economic.

(II) Now, to illustrate the qualification "in the given background," suppose that the queen has the property of being respected in certain ways – for example, when she enters a room, all persons stand.[50] Call this 'the property of being regally respected.' Her body – call it 'Bq' is also regally respected – for example, when Bq enters a room, all persons stand. Here, however, Bq has the property of being regally respected derivatively. Bq's property of being regally respected is not independent of Bq's constitution relations to the queen. Check the relevant instance of (I) for Bq's having the property of being regally respected independently of Bq's constitution relations to the queen: Bq has the property of being regally respected, and Bq constitutes the queen; however,

49 The reason that hybrid properties are excluded from (D) is this: Suppose that we allowed that the slab of granite that constitutes the Vietnam Memorial in Washington, DC, to have the property of being a granite monument derivatively. In that case, by (D) and (I), it would follow that the Vietnam Memorial had the property of being a granite monument independently of its constitution relations. But, clearly, the Vietnam Memorial's being a *granite* monument depends on its being constituted by something that is granite. So, (D) cannot cover hybrid properties like being a granite monument. I defer the modification of (D) to cover hybrid properties until Chapter 4 because I think that further complications at this point would be distracting. In any case, (D) is the root definition of 'having a property derivatively,' and I shall use the notion of 'having a property derivatively,' as defined by (D), to explain hybrid properties and to motivate the modification.

50 Although it is deployed for a different purpose, this example is similar to one that Fred Dretske uses in *Explaining Behavior: Reasons in a World of Causes* (Cambridge, MA: MIT Press/Bradford Press, 1988), p. 43. Dretske credits Susan Feagin for his use of the example.

(b)(1)(ii) is false: Bq's having the property of being regally respected (in the given background) most definitely does entail that Bq constitutes something at *t*. For Bq would not be regally respected (in the given background) if it constituted nothing. On the other hand, the queen does have the property of being regally respected independently of her constitution relations to Bq. Again, (a) is satisfied. (b)(2)(i) is satisfied since Bq constitutes the queen; and (b)(2)(ii) is satisfied since the queen's being regally respected (in the given background) does not entail that the queen is constituted by something that could have been regally respected if it had not constituted anything. It is now easy to see that the relevant instance of (D) is satisfied: (a) Bq does not have the property of being regally respected independently of its constitution relations to the queen; (b) the queen has the property of being regally respected independently of her constitution relations to Bq. Therefore, Bq has the property of being regally respected derivatively.

This example illustrates the qualification "in the given background" because our conventions are part of the given background. On our conventions, queens have the property of being regally respected, but bodies like Bq are not the objects of regal respect per se. Of course, we could have different conventions, and if conventions changed to accord regal respect to bodies per se, then the queen would no longer have the property of being regally respected independently of her constitution relations to Bq, and Bq would no longer have the property of being regally respected derivatively. But in the *given* background, the queen does have the property of being regally respected independently of her constitution relations to Bq, and Bq does have the property of being regally respected derivatively.

(III) Consider an example that illustrates the qualification "in the given background" in a different way. Suppose that there were regulations about what could go up in certain very small aircraft. The regulations bar any object weighing over 300 pounds, and they bar anybody who had no advance reservations from going up in these small planes. Now suppose that Brown had no advance reservations and that Brown's body weighs over 300 pounds. In that case, Brown would be barred from going up independently of his constitution relations (since he had no advance reservations), and Brown's body would be barred from going up (since it is an object weighing over 300 pounds.) So, Brown has the property of being barred from going up, and Brown's body also has that property. But since Brown and Brown's body each has the property of being barred from going up independently of the other, neither Brown nor Brown's body has the property of being barred from going up derivatively.

(IV) Finally, on my view, Piece is a statue, albeit derivatively. *David* has the property of being a statue independently of its constitution relations since *David*'s being a statue does not entail that *David* is constituted by something that could have been a statue without constituting anything. It is not the case that Piece has the property of being a statue independently of its constitution relations since Piece's being a statue does entail that Piece constitutes something. So, Piece has the property of being a statue derivatively. Moreover, whereas *David* is a statue essentially, Piece – which might have remained in the quarry and constituted nothing – is a statue contingently.

To conclude this section, I would like to make several comments about the idea of having properties derivatively.

(i) My point here is metaphysical, not linguistic. I am not postulating an ambiguity in the predicative use of 'is a person.' I take it that '*a* is a person' is true if and only if *a* has the property of being a person, where *a* has that property either derivatively or nonderivatively. For any property, G, if x has G at t, then $\exists y$(y has G at t nonderivatively and either $x = y$ or x is constitutionally related to y at t). For example, 'Michelangelo's *David* is a piece of marble' is true because *David* has the property of being a piece of marble derivatively.

This gives us a way to cash out what I (along with others) have called "the 'is' of constitution."[51] If '*a* is (an) F' should be read as '*a* constitutes (is constituted by) something that is (an) F,' then *a* has the property of being (an) F derivatively. For example, understanding the copula as an 'is' of constitution, 'Michelangelo's *David* is a piece of marble' should be read as 'Michelangelo's *David* is constituted by a piece of marble.' And the latter is true only if *David* has the property of being a piece of marble derivatively.

(ii) Constituted things are unified individuals. It is the unity of constituted things that underwrites the idea of having properties derivatively. If x constitutes y, then y is an individual that encompasses x (while x

---

51   For example, see Sydney Shoemaker, "Personal Identity: A Materialist's Account," in Sydney Shoemaker and Richard Swinburne, *Personal Identity* (London: Basil Blackwell, 1984).

constitutes y). Constitution is as close to identity as a relation can get without being identity. Constitution is close enough to identity so that if x and y are constitutionally related, then certain properties that x could have had without being constitutionally related to y (properties that are neither alethic, nor constitution/identity/existence, nor rooted outside the times they are had, nor are hybrid properties) are properties of y at t derivatively. The fact that y has a property at t derivatively just *is* the fact that at t y is constitutionally related to some x that has the property at t independently of being constitutionally related to y at t. Again, there are two ways to have a property – nonderivatively and derivatively.

For example, a person – Smith, say – may have a blood alcohol level of 1.2 percent. (Indeed, a person's having that property may have important consequences for suspension of his driver's license; so, there is no doubt that this is a property that a person may have.) On the Constitution View, the fact that Smith has a blood alcohol level of 1.2 percent is the same fact as the fact that the person is constituted by a body that has a blood alcohol level of 1.2 percent independently of the fact that the body constitutes a person. The reason that a person's having this property reduces to the fact that he is constituted by a body that has the property independently is this: The constitution relation produces a unity, an individual, a person (who is constituted by a particular body). Because the body constitutes a person, the body's property of having a blood alcohol level of 1.2 percent is ipso facto the person's property of having a blood alcohol level of 1.2 percent. And when a person's property derives exclusively from the fact that he is constituted by a body that has that property, the person has that property derivatively but has the property nonetheless. Such is the unification effected by constitution.

(iii) None of the following properties can ever be had derivatively: the property of being identical to a person, the property of constituting a person, the property of being constituted by a body. This is so, because the definition (I) – of x's having H independently of x's constitution relations – is not defined for such properties. So, none of these properties can be had independently of constitution relations and hence none can satisfy (D). Necessarily: If x has constitution relations to y, and x has one of these noninheritable properties, then x has the property nonderivatively and y does not have it at all, derivatively or nonderivatively. A body does not have the property of being identical to a person derivatively. The thesis that persons are constituted by bodies has as a consequence that a body never has the property of being identical to a person, derivatively or nonderivatively.

The idea of having properties derivatively drives a wedge between certain properties. For example, the property of being *identical* to a person (a property that cannot be had derivatively) must be distinguished from the property of predicatively being a person (a property that can be had derivatively). An object x has the property of being identical to a person if and only if there exists a y such that y is a person nonderivatively and $x = y$. An object x has the property of being a person if and only if there exists some y such that y is a person nonderivatively and *either*: $x = y$ *or* x is constitutionally related to y. Only in the former case is x guaranteed to be a person nonderivatively.

The distinction between having properties derivatively and having properties nonderivatively is analogous to a more familiar distinction. Some philosophers (though not I) suppose that beliefs are fundamentally states of brains. That makes brains the primary bearers of beliefs; a person has a belief that p, on this view, if and only if she has a brain in a certain state. So, on this view, an object x has the property of being a believer if and only if there exists some y such that y is a brain and either: $x = y$ or x has the relation of having-y-as-a-brain to y. On this view, a brain has beliefs (in a way analogous to what I am calling) nonderivatively, but a person has beliefs (in a way analogous to what I am calling) derivatively. Although this is not my view, it is a prevalent one whose coherence is usually taken for granted.

(iv) Not only are there properties, like being over six feet tall, that some things have derivatively and others have nonderivatively, but also there are properties, like being a person or being an animal, that some things have essentially and other things have nonessentially. Looking ahead, whereas Brown is a person essentially, Brown's body – which might have been aborted and constituted nothing – is a person contingently (as well as derivatively). And conversely, whereas Brown's body is an animal essentially, Brown – whose body may be slowly replaced by nonorganic parts – is an animal contingently (as well as derivatively). For any primary-kind property, *being an F*, if any x is an F at all, then either x is an F essentially or x has the property of being an F derivatively.

On my view, *David* is a statue essentially and nonderivatively, and Piece is a statue contingently and derivatively. Some philosophers may accept the idea of having properties derivatively but deny that a thing (e.g., Piece) could have a primary-kind property – like *being a statue* – derivatively.[52] One main reason that I hold that things may have primary-kind properties derivatively is to account for things' having certain of their nonprimary-kind properties derivatively. Consider the (nonprimary-kind) organic properties that a person can have. For example, the property of having a pancreas is a nonprimary-kind property, and Brown has a pancreas derivatively: He has a pancreas in virtue of being constituted by an animal that has a pancreas and that could have had a pancreas without constituting anything. But the property of having a pancreas is proper to animals; only animals have pancreases (in the relevant sense of 'have'). So, Brown's having a pancreas (derivatively) is good reason to hold that Brown is an animal (derivatively). The property of being an animal is a primary-kind property, but it is not Brown's primary-kind property. For Brown's primary-kind property is the property of being a person. Nevertheless, since Brown has organic properties derivatively, he has the property of being an animal derivatively. So, unlike other philosophers, I hold that Brown is an animal and that Piece is a statue. And my definitions accommodate these facts.

I have gone into so much detail about the idea of having properties derivatively for several reasons. First, this idea is one of the features that distinguishes my account of constitution-without-identity from what has been called 'the standard account.'[53] Suppose that 'Copper' is a name for the piece of copper that makes up a copper statue, 'Statue.' According to the standard account, Copper is not (predicatively) a statue.[54] I believe that the standard account construes Copper and Statue as *too* separate. On my view, by contrast, the relation between Copper and Statue is so intimate that, although Copper and Statue are not identical, Copper is, nonetheless, a statue in virtue of the fact that Copper constitutes a statue. As we have just seen, Copper has the property of being a statue derivatively. Second, in Chapters 7 and 8, I shall use the idea of having properties derivatively to defend my account from the charge of incoherence. Third, the account of having properties derivatively shows why, when x constitutes y at t, x and y share so many of their properties

---

52 Michael Della Rocca raised this point in correspondence.
53 Michael B. Burke, "Copper Statues and Pieces of Copper," *Analysis* 52 (1992): 12–17.
54 It is essential to the plausibility of the standard account, according to Burke, that Copper is not a statue. For, Burke says, if Copper were a statue, then Statue would be coextensive with *another* statue. As I shall show, my view does not have this consequence.

at t without being identical. So, constitution, as I construe it, is a genuine third alternative beyond the recognized alternatives of either identity or separate existence.

CONCLUSION

Constitution is a relation of genuine unity that stops short of identity. During the period that x constitutes y, there are not two separate things. If x constitutes y at any time, then y is a unity that encompasses x during the time that x constitutes y. Constitution is as close to identity as a relation can get without being identity. Constitution is close enough to identity so that if x constitutes y at t, then certain properties[55] that x would have had if x had not constituted y are – solely on account of the fact that x constitutes y at t – properties of y at t derivatively. (And vice versa.) And the fact that y has such properties at t is not a different fact from the fact that x has them at t and x constitutes y at t. For any property that y has at t derivatively, the fact that y has it at t derivatively just is the fact that at t, y is constitutionally related to some x that has the property at t independently of being constitutionally related to y.

I have explained the idea of constitution-without-identity in a way that makes it apparent that the relation is not peculiar to persons and bodies. 'Constitution' can be explicitly defined, using familiar logical notions, together with the notions of primary-kind properties and 'circumstances.' Although there remains some vagueness (due mainly to the latter notions), I hope that the idea of constitution in its generality is reasonably clear. And I hope to make the application of the idea of constitution to the relation between persons and bodies quite clear in Chapter 4.[56]

55 Those that are neither alethic, nor constitution/identity/existence, nor rooted outside the times at which they are had, nor hybrid properties.
56 Parts of the sections "A Description of Constitution" and "A Definition of 'Constitution'" appear in "Unity Without Identity: A New Look at Material Constitution."

3

The First-Person Perspective

According to the Constitution View, human persons are constituted by bodies. Constitution, as we have seen, is not identity. But if a person is constituted by a body to which she is not identical, what distinguishes a person from the body that constitutes her? My answer, which I shall explain in this chapter, is that a person has a capacity for a first-person perspective essentially; her constituting body has it contingently. The person/body case is thus analogous to the statue/piece-of-marble case. The statue has the property of being related to an artworld essentially; the constituting piece of marble has that property contingently. Having a capacity for a first-person perspective plays the same role in the human person case that being related to an artworld in such-and-such a way plays in the statue case.

A first-person perspective makes possible an inner life. On the Constitution View, something with a capacity for an inner life is a fundamentally different kind of thing from anything that has no capacity for an inner life. (Thus, I am ontologically closer to a self-conscious Martian than I am to a racehorse or to an early-term fetus.) The body of a human person is (identical to) an animal. An animal, human or not, can exist without any capacity for an inner life; a person cannot. This view is not Cartesian: An inner life does not require an immaterial soul, nor is it independent of the world around us. Our inner lives – although ontologically distinctive – are not conceptually, temporally, or ontologically prior to the rest of the material world.

In the next chapter, I shall use the idea of a first-person perspective, as well as the idea of constitution, to set out the Constitution View of human persons. In this chapter, I want to describe the first-person perspective, and to show that recognition of the first-person perspective is required both for our understanding of reality and, more humbly, for psychological explanation. I shall argue that the first-person perspective underlies all forms of self-consciousness. Finally, I shall look at some recent accounts of self-consciousness to illustrate the indispensability of the first-person perspective. As the idea of constitution turned out to be an interesting relation in its own right, so too does the idea of the first-person perspective. Consideration of the first-person perspective, like consideration of constitution, opens up a metaphysically rich vein to be mined.

FIRST-PERSON PHENOMENA

In recent years, there has been growing attention to the family of concepts traveling under the banner of 'consciousness.' Various concepts of consciousness have been distinguished: phenomenal consciousness, access consciousness, monitoring consciousness, and self-consciousness.[1] Self-consciousness, which I think is the key to being a person, has not been singled out for particular attention. Indeed, one prominent philosopher has declared that self-consciousness "pose[s] no deep metaphysical enigmas."[2] I think that this dismissal of self-consciousness is too quick. For underlying self-consciousness in all its forms, I shall argue, is what I call 'the first-person perspective.'

A conscious being becomes self-conscious on acquiring a first-person perspective – a perspective from which one thinks of oneself as an individual facing a world, as a subject distinct from everything else.[3] All sentient beings are subjects of experience (i.e., are conscious), but not all sentient beings have first-person concepts of themselves. Only those who do – those with first-person perspectives – are fully self-conscious.

---

1 For an overview, see Ned Block, "Consciousness," in *A Companion to the Philosophy of Mind*, Samuel Guttenplan, ed. (Oxford: Basil Blackwell, 1994): 210–19.

2 David Chalmers, *The Conscious Mind: Toward a Fundamental Theory* (Oxford: Oxford University Press, 1996): 24.

3 There have been many discussions of subjectivity and related issues in recent years. One of the most prominent is Thomas Nagel's on the first-person perspective in terms of something that "it is like to be." See Thomas Nagel, "What Is It Like to Be a Bat?" in *Mortal Questions* (Cambridge: Cambridge University Press, 1979): 165–80, and *The View from Nowhere* (New York: Oxford University Press, 1986). I am not going to try to define 'consciousness.' I am inclined to agree with those philosophers who say that no noncircular definition is possible. For example, see John R. Searle, *The Rediscovery of the Mind* (Cambridge, MA: MIT press/Bradford Press, 1992): 83, and Ned Block, "On a Confusion About a Function of Consciousness," *Behavioral and Brain Sciences* 18 (1995): 227–47.

Beginning with nonhuman sentient beings, I shall distinguish two grades of first-person phenomena: weak and strong. Then I shall claim that only those who are subjects of strong first-person phenomena have a first-person perspective.

The weak grade of first-person phenomena is illustrated by problem-solving creatures whose behavior is explainable in terms of practical syllogisms – including how things seem to them. We attribute beliefs and desires (perhaps in the vocabulary of aversions, appetites, and learning states) to nonhuman animals, which seem to be reasoning from a certain perspective. For example, the dog digs there because he saw you bury the bone there, and he wants it. (The fact that he stops digging when he finds the bone is evidence of the correctness of the explanation.) Or a researcher on infants hooks up a light so that it goes on and off when a neonate turns its head twice to the right; when the neonate figures out how to control the light, she soon stops. (She gets bored.) And when the researcher changes the formula for turning on the light, the infant tries new combinations until she hits on the new formula.[4]

Such explanations do not thereby attribute to the dog or to the infant any concept of itself as itself. Rather, they assume only that each organism has a certain perspective on its surroundings with itself as the "origin." The dog does not think of himself as himself or of himself as anything else; rather, we might say, the dog is the center of his own universe. He experiences things from his own egocentric perspective. If the dog could speak, he might say, from his own egocentric perspective, "There's a bone buried there in front of me, and I want it."[5] Two points should be noted about weak first-person phenomena: (i) They are exhibited by sentient organisms, who solve problems by means of perspectival attitudes; these attitudes then explain the problem-solving behavior. (This point is independent of any theory of how, or whether, attitudes are explicitly represented in the brain.) (ii) No first-person concept is needed to bind belief-desire-behavior to a single organism. Since all the organism's psychological states are perspectival with the organism at the origin, the belief, desire, and behavior all belong to the same individual, so to speak, by default. Although such an animal has

---

4 I. G. Bower, *Development in Infants* (San Francisco: W. H. Freeman & Company, 1974). This example is discussed by Gareth B. Matthews, *Thought's Ego in Augustine and Descartes* (Ithaca, NY: Cornell University Press, 1985).

5 This hypothetical remark by the dog is intended to be neutral with respect to what "representations" (if any) may be "tokened" in the dog's brain.

beliefs and desires, he has no conception of belief or desire, or of himself as the subject or bearer of beliefs and desires. He acts from his own perspective without any conception of having a perspective that differs from other perspectives.

The hallmark of a weak first-person phenomenon is that it is perspectival. (John Perry's work on indexicals illuminates this initial level of first-person phenomena. I suspect that those who treat the first-person perspective so dismissively assume that all first-person phenomena can be understood as merely perspectival.[6]) In sum, animals whose behavior is explainable only in terms of their egocentric perspectives exhibit the weak grade of first-person phenomena.

Before turning to the strong grade of first-person phenomena, let me mention Gordon Gallup's well-known research with chimpanzees, which can be taught to recognize their bodies as their own.[7] Chimpanzees' self-recognition seems to fall between weak and strong first-person phenomena. Typically, when a nonhuman animal sees itself in a mirror, it responds as if it were seeing another animal. Gallup exposed young chimpanzees to a full-length mirror for ten days. At first, they made other-directed responses (responses that would typically be made in the presence of other chimpanzees), but within two or three days, they began to display self-directed behavior – grooming parts of their bodies that were visually inaccessible without the mirrors, for example. Then Gallup anesthetized each animal and put red, odorless, nonirritating paint over one eyebrow and the opposite ear. After recovery from the anesthesia, the mirrors were reintroduced, and the chimpanzees began touching and exploring the marked areas at twenty-five times the rate before the mirrors were reintroduced. They smelled and visually examined the fingers that had touched the marked areas. Chimpanzees in the

---

6   For a discussion of (merely) perspectival phenomena, see John Perry, "The Problem of the Essential Indexical," *Noûs* 13 (1979): 3–22. David Lewis and Roderick Chisholm are often mentioned together as both giving accounts of all attitudes in terms of self-ascription. I suspect that there may be an important difference between them. Since Lewis treats all indexical attitudes, first person or not, in the same way, I suspect that for him there is no more to the first-person perspective than perspectivalism (what I'm calling 'weak first-person phenomena'). I think that Chisholm, on the other hand, takes his direct attribution to require what I'm calling 'strong first-person phenomena.' See Roderick Chisholm, *The First Person: An Essay on Reference and Intentionality* (Minneapolis: University of Minnesota Press, 1981), and David Lewis, "Attitudes *De Dicto* and *De Se*," *Philosophical Review* 88 (1979): 513–43.

7   Gordon Gallup, Jr., "Self-Recognition in Primates: A Comparative Approach to Bidirectional Properties of Consciousness," *American Psychologist* 32 (1977): 329–38.

control group, which had not been exposed to mirrors before they were anesthetized and marked, displayed no mark-directed behaviors when mirrors were introduced. (With the exception of orangutans, other primates, such as monkeys displayed no self-directed behavior after much longer exposure to mirrors.[8]) Gallup concluded that chimpanzees have a cognitive capacity that monkeys lack, and that those chimpanzees that engage in self-recognition have rudimentary self-consciousness.[9]

Another sort of intermediate case is illustrated by research on rhesus monkeys. One monkey ('O' for 'operator') was placed in a divided box and taught to secure food by pulling one of two chains when a signal light was on. A second monkey ('SA' for 'stimulus animal') was placed on the other side of the box, on a grid attached to an electric shock source, behind a one-way mirror, so that the O could see the SA but the SA could not see the O. After three days during which the O adapted to the presence of the SA, the circuit was completed, so that when the O pulled one of the chains, the SA received a severe shock. Pulling the other chain when the light was on produced food but no shock to the SA. The experimenters varied the sequences and intervals of the light signals to ascertain the extent to which the O's pulling the shock-producing chain was influenced by the O's perception of the SA's agony. The conclusion was that "a majority of rhesus monkeys will consistently suffer hunger rather than secure food at the expense of electroshock to a conspecific."[10] One possible interpretation of the results is that rhesus monkeys can appreciate the points of view of conspecifics.

Without entering into the dispute over how to interpret Gallup's research or the research on the rhesus monkeys, I want to point out only that, on any reasonable interpretation, these chimpanzees and mon-

---

8   *The New York Times* (April 22, 1997, P. C9) reported that recent research by Marc D. Hauser at Harvard University suggests that certain monkeys – e.g., cotton-top tamarins of South America – also can recognize themselves.

9   It would be very interesting to compare brains of chimpanzees and brains of monkeys that apparently cannot learn self-recognition to see whether there are structural differences that can account for the apparent cognitive difference.

10 Stanley Wechkin, Jules H. Masserman, and William Terris, Jr., "Shock to a Conspecific as an Aversive Stimulus," *Psychonomic Science* 1 (1964): 47–8; and Wechkin et al., " 'Altruistic' Behavior in Rhesus Monkeys," *The Journal of Psychiatry* 121 (1964): 584–5. My description in the text, along with the quotation (p. 215), comes from James Rachels, "Do Animals Have a Right to Liberty?" in *Animal Rights and Human Obligations*, Tom Regan and Peter Singer, eds. (Englewood Cliffs, NJ: Prentice-Hall, 1976): 205–23. The quotation is on p. 215.

keys are still a long way from the self-consciousness enjoyed by humans.[11] So, we must consider a higher grade of first-person phenomena.

A conscious being who exhibits strong first-person phenomena not only is able to recognize herself from a first-person point of view (as Gallup's chimpanzees did), but also is able to think of herself as herself. For strong first-person phenomena, it is not enough to *distinguish* between first person and third person; one must also be able to *conceptualize* the distinction, to conceive of oneself as oneself. To be able to conceive of oneself as oneself is to be able to conceive of oneself independently of a name, or description, or third-person demonstrative. It is to be able to conceptualize the distinction between itself and everything else there is. It is not just to have thoughts expressible by means of 'I,' but also to conceive of oneself as the bearer of those thoughts. Nonhuman animals, which exhibit weak first-person phenomena, have subjective points of view. But merely having a perspective, or a subjective point of view, is not enough for strong first-person phenomena. One must also be able to conceive of oneself as having a perspective, or a subjective point of view.

Let me illustrate the distinction between weak and strong first-person phenomena in terms of grammar. Grammatically, we can distinguish between *making* a first-person reference (as when Smith says, "I am tall") and *attributing* first-person reference (as when Smith says, "Jones wishes that she [herself] were tall"). In the second case, Smith attributes to Jones a wish that Jones would express by saying, "I wish that I were tall." The *attribution* of first-person reference occurs in indirect discourse, in a 'that' clause following a psychological (or linguistic) verb. However – and this is the important point – not only do we attribute first-person reference to others, but also we attribute first-person reference to ourselves – as when Jones says, "I wish that I were tall." A person who thinks, "I am tall" can distinguish himself from others; a person who thinks, "I wish that I were tall" can conceptualize that distinction, can think of herself

---

11 If Gallup's chimpanzees are self-conscious at all, the appearance of their self-consciousness is not part of their normal development. Rather, self-recognition in chimpanzees requires direct intervention by members of another species. Moreover, the chimpanzees' self-consciousness, if that is what it is, is bound to the circumstances in which it was developed; it is not available for integration into a variety of attitudes independent of the situations that originally provided evidence of their self-recognition. Finally, it is not clear to what extent the chimpanzees' self-recognition is a conceptual ability as opposed merely to an ability to discriminate. For these reasons, I do not take chimpanzees with a capacity for self-recognition to have a full-blown first-person perspective.

64

as herself. The former *makes* first-person reference; the latter *attributes* (as well as makes) first-person reference to *herself*. The ability to attribute to oneself first-person reference in indirect discourse ('I wish that I were tall') is a signal of strong first-person phenomena.

Following Hector-Neri Castañeda, I'll put an asterisk pronounced 'star,' beside a pronoun to signal that it is an attribution of a first-person reference.[12] Call a sentence an 'I* sentence' if it is of this form: 'I Φ that I* . . . ,' where 'Φ' is replaced by a linguistic or psychological verb and 'I* . . . ' is replaced by a sentence containing a first-person reference. The use of an I* sentence – for example, 'I think (or hope or fear.) that I* am F'[13] – is an indication that one is entertaining an I* thought. (But it is not an infallible indication; a computer could be programmed to produce I* sentences without having any thoughts at all.) An I* thought is one in which the thinker conceives of himself as himself* without identifying himself by means of any third-person referential device, such as a name, description, or demonstrative. 'I' is not a name for myself; I can use any name competently and still be mistaken about whose name it is. But I am never mistaken about who is picked out by my competent uses of 'I.' If I entertain an I* thought, I do not have to identify the person that I am thinking about; nor can I mistakenly believe that I am thinking about someone else. The ability to entertain I* thoughts – thoughts that attribute to oneself first-person reference in indirect discourse – is the ability to conceive of oneself as oneself*. I shall extend the use of the asterisk to contexts in which the speaker is thinking of himself as himself* even in the absence of an embedded sentence.

In short, S can think of herself as herself* if and only if S can think of herself in a way naturally expressible in the grammatical first person as the bearer of first-person thoughts. 'I am tall' expresses a simple first-person thought. S can express her thought of herself as the bearer of the thought 'I am tall' by saying, 'I am having the thought that I* am tall.' This latter sentence indicates that S is thinking of herself as herself*.

The ability to think of oneself as oneself* brings with it a number of

12 Hector-Neri Castañeda, who did pioneering work on making and attributing first-person reference, used 'he*' to mark the reflexive use of 'he (himself).' See "He: A Study in the Logic of Self-Consciousness," *Ratio* 8 (1966): 130–57 and "Indicators and Quasi-Indicators," *American Philosophical Quarterly* 4 (1967): 85–100. For a study of philosophy from a first-person point of view, see Matthews, *Thought's Ego*.

13. It does not matter what predicate is substituted for 'F.' "I think that I am tall" indicates that the speaker can think of himself as himself* just as well as "I think that I will have nightmares."

related abilities. If one can think of oneself as the bearer of first-person thoughts, then one has the concept of a subject of thought and can think of others as subjects of thought. If one can think of oneself as oneself*, then, in addition to having desires (say), one can reflect on one's desires *as one's own*. (Conversely, without the ability to think of oneself as oneself*, one could not have the attitudes toward one's own desires ['second-order volitions'] that some take to be definitive of being a person.[14]) To be able to think of oneself as oneself* is not just to have a perspective or subjective point of view – dogs have perspectives – but also to be able to think of one's perspective as one's own and to think of others as having different subjective points of view from one's own.

Anyone who has the ability to conceive of herself as herself* has the ability to conceive of other things as different from herself. From a conceptual point of view, it seems that one cannot conceive of oneself as oneself* unless one can conceive of oneself as distinct from other things. And one cannot conceive of oneself as distinct from other things unless one has concepts of things as other. (The ability to conceive of things as distinct from oneself is required in order to doubt that such things exist.) This conceptual point is borne out by – or rather taken for granted by – developmental psychologists, who routinely describe the acquisition of self-concepts in tandem with the acquisition of concepts of other things as different from oneself.[15]

An ability to conceive of oneself as oneself* in the sense just described is both necessary and sufficient for the strong grade of first-person phenomena: An individual who is the locus of strong first-person phenomena can conceive of himself as a bearer of first-person thoughts. He manifests an ability not only to make a first-person reference, but also to attribute to himself a first-person reference. Strong first-person phenomena do not seem reducible to purely non-first-person phenomena. For example, the thought expressed by "I regret that I* had to be the one to break the news of the nonrenewal of your fellowship" is not adequately paraphrased as "L. B. regrets that L. B. had to be the one to break the news . . ." (which substitutes attribution of a third-person reference for the attribution of first-person reference). You may adequately report what I said by "L. B. regrets that she/he*

---

14 See Harry Frankfurt, "Freedom of the Will and the Concept of a Person," *Journal of Philosophy* 68 (1971): 5–20.

15 Daniel N. Stern, *The Interpersonal World of the Infant* (New York: Basic Books, 1985).

had to be the one to break the news . . . ," but that sentence retains the attribution of first-person reference to me by the speaker. If I attribute first-person reference to myself, my sentence cannot be adequately paraphrased by any sentence that fails to attribute first-person reference to me: The attribution of first-person reference to oneself seems to be ineliminable.[16]

We can sum up the grades of first-person phenomena this way: Weak first-person phenomena are exhibited by problem-solving beings whose behavior is explained by attitudes understood perspectivally, from their own points of view. If a dog that exhibits weak first-person phenomena could express its attitudes in English, it would locate things relative to its own spatiotemporal position (e.g., "There's danger over there"). But it would not thereby show that it had any concept of itself or even any ability to recognize itself from a first-person point of view. It simply acts from its own perspective, with itself as the center. All experience of any sentient being is perspectival, had from its own point of view. It is characteristic of weak first-person phenomena that they are perspectival in this way. The dog has conscious states like pain and dispositional states like beliefs and desires about its present environment, but it cannot conceive of itself in the first person as the subject of those states.

On the other hand, strong first-person phenomena require that the subject conceptualize the distinction between himself (and everything else) from a third-person point of view and himself from a first-person point of view. The subject of strong first-person phenomena is not only able to think first-person thoughts (typically, using 'I'), but is also able to attribute to himself first-person thoughts (typically, using 'I*'). Not only can he think of himself, but also he can think of himself as himself*. He can consciously entertain thoughts and conceive of his thoughts as his own*.

Those with the ability to exhibit strong first-person phenomena have a first-person perspective. Although Gallup's chimpanzees have some claim to making a first-person reference, and although the rhesus monkeys in the study described earlier appear to appreciate the perspectives of conspecifics, I shall reserve the term 'first-person perspective' for the subjects of strong first-person phenomena. To have a first-person perspective, then, is not just to have a phenomenological point of view in

16 Lynne Rudder Baker, "Why Computers Can't Act," *American Philosophical Quarterly* 18 (1981): 157–63.

the sense of having mental episodes that "can be directly apprehended in consciousness by virtue of their felt quality."[17] I suspect that certain primates have a phenomenological point of view, but they do not have first-person perspectives in the sense that I am specifying. Again: One has a first-person perspective if and only if one has the ability to conceive of oneself as oneself*, where this ability is signaled by the linguistic ability to attribute (as well as to make) first-person reference to oneself.

In short, to have a first-person perspective is to have a certain *ability*. This ability is manifested typically, but not only, by the use of 'I*' sentences. It is also manifested on occasions when one has a thought that one would express by a non-I* sentence – for example, "Why, it's *me* they're talking about!" To take another example, one manifests a first-person perspective by wondering, "Am I the winner?" For one could not ask this question if one lacked the conceptual resources to think, 'I wonder whether I* am the winner.' So, although a sentence like 'Am I going to die, Doc?' is not an I* sentence, it does indicate that the questioner has a first-person perspective. A first-person perspective is manifested any time that a person has a thought, however it is expressed, that could not be entertained by anyone who lacked the ability to think of oneself as oneself*.

Although, from a first-person perspective, I have the ability to think of myself in a unique way, there is no funny object that is myself-as-myself; there is no entity that is "self" other than the person who I am.[18] The referent of 'I' and of 'I*' is the person: not a body, not a disembodied ego. 'I*' does not denote a spooky entity to which I alone have direct access, "self." When I say, 'I wonder whether I* will still dream of being unprepared for class in ten years,' I refer twice to myself – to the person, L. B., in my embodied concreteness. When I refer to myself by means of 'I*,' *what* I refer to is no different from what you refer to by means of 'L. B.' What is special about 'I*' is that I can conceive of that person in a way that you cannot, from the "inside," so to speak.

---

17 Carol Rovane, *The Bounds of Agency: An Essay in Revisionary Metaphysics* (Princeton, NJ: Princeton University Press, 1998): 20. Rovane emphasizes a first-person point of view, which she construes as the rational point of view of an agent.

18 Strawson was right that states of consciousness are ascribed to the very same things as corporeal characteristics, and that thing is the person. (P. F. Strawson, *Individuals: An Essay in Descriptive Metaphysics* [Garden City, NY: Doubleday Anchor Books, 1963]: 98.) But on my view, a person has corporeal features derivatively and first-person-perspective states nonderivatively.

Descartes's discovery – or rather his rediscovery, after Augustine – of the 'inner' is the real contribution of *Meditations* II.[19] It is Descartes's reification of inwardness that I reject: What is distinctive about being a person does not need to be secured by a logically private entity to which no one has access but me.

So, as used by someone with a first-person perspective, 'I' and 'I*' have the same referent. Do they also express the same concept? Assuming that 'I' and 'I*' express concepts at all, then use of 'I' by a toddler (who does not yet exhibit strong first-person phenomena) does not express the full self-concept that he later expresses with both 'I' and 'I*' after he has acquired a full first-person perspective. For a being without a concept of itself as itself*, 'I' is just a marker of perspective. Acquisition of a first-person perspective brings with it a genuine self-concept – a concept of oneself as oneself*. So, for a being who has come to conceive of itself as itself, 'I' and 'I*' express the same self-concept. But before acquiring a first-person perspective, a being who uses 'I' does not have that full self-concept. Such a toddler has not fully mastered the use of 'I.' Complete mastery of 'I' includes the ability to use 'I*.'

The relation between the first-person perspective and self-consciousness is this: The first-person perspective is a necessary condition for any form of self-consciousness and a sufficient condition for one form of self-consciousness as well. For a conscious being with a first-person perspective can conceive of her thoughts, attitudes, feelings, and sensations as her own*. And the ability to conceive of one's thoughts and so on as one's own* is a form of genuine self-consciousness. Every other form of self-consciousness that I know of presupposes self-consciousness in this basic sense. So, every self-conscious being – 'self-conscious' in any sense whatever – has a first-person perspective.

FEATURES OF THE FIRST-PERSON PERSPECTIVE

There are several unusual features of the first-person perspective. I wish to draw attention to two of them: (1) the fact that the first-person reference is immune to a certain kind of referential error and (2) the fact that the first-person perspective is relational in that it would be impos-

19 Cf. Matthews, *Thought's Ego*.

69

sible for a being truly alone in the universe to have a first-person perspective.

(1) First-person reference is often said to enjoy a kind of immunity to self-referential error.[20] This point is about self-reference and has nothing to do with Descartes's view that his mind was transparent to him. Not only is there something to which 'I' refers every time it is used literally and sincerely, but also, from the first-person perspective, one could never use 'I' literally and take oneself to be referring to someone other than oneself.[21] What I take to be myself *is* myself. First-person pronouns in their typical use are immune to the kind of referential error to which names are susceptible. (This explains why the device for first-person reference does not function simply as a name for the user.[22]) In short, one can unknowingly refer to oneself in the third person; but from a first-person perspective, one cannot fail to realize to whom one is referring. From the first-person perspective, in contrast to the third-person perspective, there is a particular way in which one cannot misidentify oneself. This is so because, from the first-person point of view, one does not identify oneself at all.

I think that this point holds with respect to all genuine first-person reference by someone with a first-person perspective. Wittgenstein distinguished between "the use of 'I' as subject" and "the use of 'I' as object," and some philosophers have taken immunity to referential er-

---

20 See Ludwig Wittgenstein, *The Blue and Brown Books* (Oxford: Oxford University Press, 1958): 66f. Also, see Sydney Shoemaker, "Self-Reference and Self-Awareness," *Journal of Philosophy* 65 (1968): 555–67, and Shoemaker, "Introspection and the Self," in *Studies in the Philosophy of Mind*, Midwest Studies in Philosophy, Vol. X, Peter A. French, Theodore E. Uehling, Jr., and Howard K. Wettstein, eds. (Minneapolis: University of Minnesota Press, 1986): 101–20.

21 Thus, I disagree with J. David Velleman in "Self to Self," *Philosophical Review* 105 (1996): 39–76, who interprets the second occurrence of 'I' in certain uses of 'I imagine that I am Napoleon viewing Austerlitz' to "pick out" Napoleon as the notional subject, who "gets into the act by being thought of as the subject, as the person reflexively presented by the image, and hence as the target of self-reference within the visual scheme of representation" (p. 53). Even if I "inherited" the visual image from Napoleon (and I am unsure about what that would mean), all my sincere and literal uses of 'I' pick out [L.B.], not Napoleon.

22 In "The First Person," in *Metaphysics and the Philosophy of Mind* (Minneapolis: University of Minnesota Press, 1981), G. E. M. Anscombe uses such considerations to argue for this: " 'I' is neither a name nor another kind of expression whose logical role is to make a reference, at all" (p. 32). I agree that 'I' is not a name, and I agree that 'I' does not refer to a body or an immaterial mind; but it does not follow that when I use 'I,' I am not referring to myself.

70

ror to apply only to "the use of 'I' as subject."[23] In 'I have a tooth-ache,' 'I' appears as subject; in 'I have long toenails,' 'I' appears as object. Wittgenstein distinguishes these two categories of uses of 'I' by saying that in the use of 'I' as subject, "there is no question of recognizing a person when I say I have tooth-ache;" but in the use of 'I' as object, "the possibility of error has been provided for."[24] On Wittgenstein's view, I think, I could misidentify the person who has long toenails (when I see several feet, including mine, sticking out from under a blanket and mistake your foot for mine) but not the person who has the toothache. Now I agree that the word 'I' has these two uses, and I agree that I could be mistaken about the person who has long toenails, but my mistake is not that I have made a referential error in my use of 'I.' My mistake is a misattribution of the property of having long toenails, not a referential error at all. I refer to myself when I say 'I,' and I know very well to whom I refer by using 'I'; then I wrongly attribute the property of having long toenails to that person.[25] I know exactly whom I mean – which person – when I (mistakenly) say, "I have long toenails." When I make first-person reference – even in the use of 'I' as object – I make no mistake about which person I mean to refer to (or how I mean to refer to that person). So, the point that I want to make about immunity to referential error in the first person applies to all literal and sincere uses of 'I,' whether as subject or as object.

A corollary of the claim that the first-person perspective is immune to error of a certain sort is this: One cannot sincerely and literally think of anyone other than oneself in the first-person way. One can use 'I' to refer to one's character in a skit, or to refer to someone else when one is role playing, but these uses of 'I' are not literal, sincere uses of 'I.' When one is using 'I' literally and sincerely – even in contexts like 'I imagine that I am Napoleon' – both occurrences of 'I' refer to the speaker. I may imagine that the person to whom I make first-person reference (i.e., L. B.) is Napoleon. But – no matter what I am pretending or how confused I am – the sincere, literal uses of 'I' in my mouth (e.g.,

---

23 See Sydney Shoemaker, "Self-Reference and Self-Awareness," in *Identity, Cause and Mind* (Cambridge: Cambridge University Press, 1984): 6–18.
24 Wittgenstein, *The Blue and Brown Books*, pp. 66–7.
25 After writing this, I came across Andrea Christofidou's "First Person: The Demand for Identification-Free Self-Reference," *The Journal of Philosophy* 92 (1995): 223–34. Christofidou has a similar argument against Carol Rovane.

I am not quoting or acting, etc.) refer to me (L. B.).[26] As a matter of referential fact, I can no more sincerely and literally use 'I' to refer to Napoleon than I can sincerely and literally use 'L. B.' to refer to Napoleon. As a matter of phenomenological fact, I do not think that I am able to imagine Napoleon in the way that Napoleon thought of himself in the first person.

So, 'I' (in its standard, literal use) always refers to the person using or thinking it, and having a first-person perspective, I am never wrong about who I mean to refer to when I use 'I.' My use of 'I' refers to me, the person constituted (at this time) by this body.

(2) The second feature of the first-person perspective that I wish to discuss is more controversial. It is that the first-person perspective is relational in a certain sense. One cannot think of oneself as oneself* without concepts of other things by means of which to distinguish things as being different from oneself; and one cannot have concepts of other things without the presence of other things.[27] It is only over and against other things in the world that one stands as subject with a first-person perspective.[28] Here is a simple argument for the relational character of the first-person perspective:

(1) x has a first-person perspective if and only if x can think of herself as herself*.

(2) x can think of herself as herself* only if x has concepts that can apply to things different from x.

(3) x has concepts that can apply to things different from x only if x has had interactions with things different from x.

Therefore,

(4) If x has a first-person perspective, then x has had interactions with things different from x.

So, x's having a first-person perspective depends upon x's relations to other things. Therefore, the property of having a first-person perspective is, in one sense, a relational property. The claim is that x has a first-

---

26   In "Self to Self," Velleman uses the example of imagining that I am Napoleon to detach metaphysical questions of the identity of persons from referential questions about the "selves" to whom uses of 'I' can refer.

27   For an elaboration of this theme, see Jean-Paul Sartre, *Being and Nothingness* (New York: Washington Square Press, 1966).

28   On this point, I agree with Strawson, *Individuals*, who held that a "condition of the ascription of states of consciousness to oneself is ability to ascribe them to others" (p. viii).

person perspective only if x is embedded in a world of things from which x can distinguish herself as herself*. The argument is valid, but is it sound?

Premise (1) is simply a restatement of the definition of a first-person perspective. Premise (2) is what I argued earlier is a conceptual truth, taken for granted by developmental psychologists. The controversial premise is the anti-Cartesian premise (3). (3) is a strong rejection of internalism in the philosophy of mind, against which I have argued at length elsewhere.[29] Here I'll simply point out the consequence of denying (3). The main consequence is that denial of (3) leaves one with no plausible account of concept acquisition. Descartes, who would deny (3), never questioned whether his own use of concepts in his *Meditations* was at odds with his ontological assumptions. He just assumed that he could bracket his beliefs about things other than himself and still have available his empirical concepts of other things (e.g., 'sitting in front of the fire'), as well as the concepts required to think, 'I am certain that I* exist.' Descartes did not ask himself how, if he were the only finite being, he could have access to the concepts needed to have all these thoughts.

Perhaps, a Cartesian may say, Descartes acquired a concept of 'sitting' and of 'in front of' and of 'fire' from the fact that it *seemed to him that* he was sitting in front of a fire. But this is a nonstarter: If Descartes could reason from the premise that it seemed to him that he was sitting in front of a fire, then he must *already* have had the concept of sitting in front of a fire, and hence the concepts of 'sitting' and of 'in front of' and of 'fire.' But the acquisition of these concepts (of 'sitting' and of 'in front of' and of 'fire') is just what we are wondering about.

Perhaps, a Cartesian may say, all concepts are innate; in that case, Descartes was born with concepts of 'sitting' and of 'in front of' and of 'fire.' But this cannot be right: The innateness hypothesis cannot be taken in so strong a sense. For in this overly strong sense, everybody not only is born with a concept of 'sitting,' and so on, but also with the concept of 'quarks.' But that's false; Descartes was a genius, but he had no concept of quarks. Moreover, the sense (if any) in which Descartes was born with a concept of sitting in front of a fire is not a sense in which it would be available for his use in reasoning. (He could not

---

29 Lynne Rudder Baker, *Saving Belief: A Critique of Physicalism* (Princeton, NJ: Princeton University Press, 1987): 23–105 and *Explaining Attitudes: A Practical Approach to the Mind* (Cambridge: Cambridge University Press, 1995): 42–56.

reason about sitting in front of the fire until years after his birth.) However, it seems partly definitive of having a concept – whether concepts are mental representations, skills, or something else – that it is available for use in reasoning. So, we cannot say that Descartes was born with a concept of sitting in front of a fire (in the relevant sense).[30]

Perhaps, a Cartesian would say, Descartes was born with concept seeds, so to speak, that grew in him (like toenails) without any interactions with finite things other than himself. Or perhaps a Cartesian would say that God put all the relevant concepts in Descartes's mind at the appropriate time. I find such suggestions utterly implausible. A Cartesian may object: "Sure," he may say, "these suggestions are empirically implausible, but still, they are metaphysically possible." I am at a loss about how to respond, except to say this: In virtue of what does someone have a concept of *fire* independently of his interactions with other things (maybe not fires, but lighted cigarettes or electric stoves)? I'm not asking for evidence; I'm asking what would make it the case that, independently of his interactions with other things, a person has one concept and not another? A particular state of a brain or a soul, or a particular mental representation? But the original question won't stay down: What makes it the case, independently of interactions with the environment, that a particular state of a brain or a soul is a concept of 'sitting' or of 'in front of' or of 'fire,' or that a particular mental representation represents any of those things? These questions concern not contingent facts about the acquisition of concepts, but rather (noncontingent) facts about what it is to have empirical concepts. And I see no possible answers to such questions without adverting to the environment.

Perhaps a contemporary Cartesian would even agree that one must also stand in a certain causal relation to certain things in the external world (like fire), and add that in order to have the concept of fire, one must be prepared to make certain inferences from certain sorts of sense experience. But, the Cartesian may continue, in addition to the concept of fire, we may imagine an alternative concept, 'fire$_2$' – a concept that has the same inferential role as 'fire' but that can be possessed without satisfying any externalist causal requirement. In that case, it may be claimed that Descartes did have the concept 'fire$_2$' and, furthermore, that concepts like 'fire$_2$' are the only kinds of concepts needed to satisfy (2) of the argument for the relational character of the first-person per-

---

30 My point here would not be affected by the truth of innateness hypotheses proposed by cognitive scientists, including Chomsky and Fodor.

spective. So, the contemporary Cartesian may conclude, premise (3) is false and the argument is unsound.

Now premise (3) is false only if a person can acquire the concept 'fire$_2$' without any interaction with things different from herself. But the same old question comes up: Under what conditions would a person have the concept 'fire$_2$'? The contemporary Cartesian cannot just help himself to the notion of inferential role.[31] For if a person were the sole occupant of the universe, what would count as inferring that p rather than inferring that q? In virtue of what would something be an inference at all? The contemporary Cartesian cannot advert to its *seeming* to the person that she is inferring that p or inferring anything at all. For not only is it the case that someone's inferring (as opposed to its seeming to her that she is inferring) does not require that she have the concept of inferring, but also its *seeming* to someone that she is inferring does require that she have the concept of inferring, a concept of whose acquisition we have no Cartesian account. Nor can the contemporary Cartesian advert to the tokening of mentalese symbols (or to brain states). For, by hypothesis, *none* of these mentalese symbols (if there are any) is interpreted. The concept of 'fire$_2$' is not like the idea of Hume's missing shade of blue, for which a place has been made, so to speak, by impressions of other colors. If a person were alone in the universe, it would be an implacable mystery what would count as having one concept rather than another.[32] So, pretending that there are alternative concepts like 'fire$_2$' provides no good reason to deny (3).

I do not claim to have refuted those who deny (3), but I do hope to have made plain the difficulty of holding this aspect of Cartesianism. Although I have no theory – Cartesian or nonCartesian – of concepts or of concept acquisition, I would look to Wittgenstein for the former and to developmental psychologists for the latter. Both sources – Wittgenstein and developmental psychologists – rely heavily on interactions with the environment as partly determinative of one's concepts.

31 The assumption that a particular concept may be individuated by inferential role construed solipsistically may rest on a picture like this: A homunculus in my head is watching an internal monitor, where the interpretation of what is on the monitor is determined independently of what the monitor is hooked up to. Such a picture would be totally misleading.

32 Compare: What would count as a solution to an "equation" that consisted of nothing but variables? Or worse: What would count as a certain mark's being a variable, or in virtue of what would the whole string count as being one equation rather than another, or even as being an equation at all?

It is noteworthy that (3) completely defuses the threat of solipsism, understood as the view that nothing but me exists. For (3) shifts the issue of solipsism from the question often asked of beginning students, "What reason is there to reject solipsism?" to a prior question: "Is solipsism conceivably true?" If I can formulate the thesis of solipsism, then I have concepts applicable to other things beside myself. And if I have concepts applicable to other things besides myself, then (given (3)) solipsism is conceptually false; and if solipsism is conceptually false, then no further reason is required to reject it. The argument for the relational character of the first-person perspective implies that Descartes could not even have raised his skeptical question unless he had already been guaranteed a nonskeptical answer.

INDISPENSABILITY OF THE FIRST-PERSON PERSPECTIVE

Two different sorts of considerations suggest that the first-person perspective is indispensable for our theorizing about reality. The first sort (I) concerns language: First-person reference is not eliminable from I* sentences, whether it is eliminable from simple, direct-discourse 'I' sentences or not. The second sort (II) concerns psychological explanation: Certain psychological explanations of behavior require attribution of a first-person perspective to the one whose behavior is to be explained.

(I) Although the first-person perspective does not depend on natural language, it is often manifested, as we have seen, in a person's use of I* sentences. I want to show that I* sentences differ from simple, direct-discourse I sentences in that first-person reference is ineliminable from I* sentences, whether it is eliminable from simple I sentences or not. Consider first-person contexts in which some philosophers have suggested that we might do without the grammatical first person. According to Peter Geach, for example, the pronoun 'I' serves to call attention to the speaker, and in soliloquy, 'I' is "idle, superfluous." If Descartes had said, "I am getting into an awful muddle," Geach said, he could have expressed himself equally well by saying, "This is an awful muddle."[33] Bertrand Russell made a similar point: The premise 'I think' could be rephrased as 'There is thinking' (and hence, said Russell, does

---

33 Peter Geach, *Mental Acts* (New York: Humanities Press, 1957): 118. In "On Beliefs About Oneself," in *Logic Matters* (Oxford: Basil Blackwell, 1972): 128–9, Geach considers the indirect reflexive pronoun in 'believes that he himself is clever.'

not support the conclusion 'I exist,' where 'I' refers to a substantial self).[34]

Russell and Geach give a reason to conjecture that the use of 'I' in simple sentences, together with an inability to use I★ sentences, would be an indication of weak first-person phenomena. Imagine that a dog, which lacks a first-person perspective, could talk. As a subject of weak first-person phenomena, however, the imagined dog may well utter simple first-person sentences like "I see a potential mate." Such an utterance could as well be rendered as "There's a potential mate over there." But lacking a first-person perspective, the dog would not have the ability meaningfully to utter, "I hope that I★ will find a suitable mate." On the basis of the remarks of Russell and Geach, I conjecture that the grammatical first person could be eliminated altogether for beings that enjoyed weak first-person phenomena but lacked a full first-person perspective.

The situation is rather different for beings who have a full first-person perspective and who speak a language like English. For English speakers with first-person perspectives have the capacity meaningfully to utter I★ sentences, from which first-person reference is ineliminable.[35] The thought that one expresses by 'I★' cannot be equally well expressed in a non–first-person way.[36] For example, there is no third-person way to express the Cartesian thought "I am certain that I★ exist." The certainty that Descartes claimed was certainty that *he*★ existed, not certainty that *Descartes* existed. And these states of certainty

34 Bertrand Russell, *A History of Western Philosophy* (New York: Simon & Schuster, 1945): 567. Moritz Schlick attributes substitution of 'There is a thought' ['Es denkt'] for 'I think' to "the wonderful eighteenth-century physicist and philosopher," Lichtenberg. ("Meaning and Verification," *Readings in Philosophical Analysis*, Herbert Feigl and Wilfrid Sellars, eds. [New York: Appleton-Century-Crofts, 1949]: 166.)

35 Lewis's and Chisholm's approach misses the crucial distinction between, e.g., 'I hope that Jones will survive the flight' (said by Jones) and 'I hope that I★ will survive the flight' (also said by Jones). Lewis's and Chisholm's technical use of 'ascribe' renders the distinction invisible, for both are construed as 'Jones ascribes to herself the property of hoping that Jones will enjoy the flight.'

36 If we construe Descartes's premise in the cogito not as 'I think' but as 'I am certain that I★ am thinking,' then it does support the conclusion that I exist. But: (1) given his skeptical assumptions about contingent things apart from himself, Descartes is not entitled to either premise. He cannot just help himself to the concept of thinking. (2) Even if I am a thing that thinks (as I agree that I am), I am not an immaterial soul. (3) 'I' and 'I★' refer to the same thing: me, a person. A person is, in some sense, a substance: an embodied thinking substance with a first-person perspective.

are not equivalent.[37] So, 'I am certain that I* think,' which indicates a first-person perspective, cannot be subjected to the same treatment that Russell proposed for 'I think,' which plausibly may be rendered as, 'There is thinking.' The 'I*' is ineliminable. In sum: Whether or not Geach and Russell were right about the eliminability of 'I' in direct discourse, their point would not apply to the use of 'I' in indirect discourse: First-person reference is ineliminable when 'I' is used as 'I*' in indirect discourse, where such use indicates a first-person perspective.

(II) The second way in which the first-person perspective may be seen to be indispensable is in psychological explanation. Some psychological explanations require a first-person perspective in that they attribute attitudes that would be unavailable to an agent who lacked a first-person perspective. For example, part of the explanation of Oedipus's blinding himself is that he came to realize that he* was the killer of Laius. Oedipus may have expressed this realization without using an I* sentence, by saying, for example, simply, "I killed Laius." But the psychological state that helps explain his self-blinding – the realizing that he* killed Laius – requires that Oedipus have the ability to think of himself as himself*. We can see this in two ways.

(i) Oedipus's realization that he* was the killer of Laius included an understanding that earlier, when he had been looking for the killer, he had not realized that he* was the killer of Laius. We have seen that one's wondering whether she* is the winner requires that she have the conceptual resources to entertain the thought expressible as "I wonder whether I* am the winner." In the same way, Oedipus's coming to realize that he* is the killer of Laius required that he have the conceptual resources to entertain the thought expressible as "Although I did not realize it before, I now realize that I* am the killer of Laius." No one lacking a first-person perspective would have the ability to have that thought. So, whether actually expressed in an I* sentence or not, Oedipus's realization was one that required that he have the ability to conceive of himself as himself*.

(ii) On one reasonable interpretation, in order for Oedipus's realization that he* killed Laius to have motivated him to blind himself, Oedipus had to be thinking of himself as himself*. I am not just remak-

37 Castañeda. "He" and "Indicators and Quasi-Indicators"; Baker, "Why Computers Can't Act." The crucial difference between 'Descartes believes that he* exists' and 'Descartes believes that Descartes exists' is lost on views of attitudes wholly in terms of self-ascriptions, for self-ascription views would render both as instances of 'x self-ascribes.'

ing John Perry's point that action is explained by belief states understood indexically.[38] Indexically characterized belief states (sometimes called 'self-locating beliefs') situate an agent perspectivally in an environment. That self-locating ability, as we saw earlier, is shared by all problem-solving animals (which are subjects of weak first-person phenomena) and does not suffice for a first-person perspective. Nor do mere self-locating beliefs explain Oedipus's blinding himself. For example, the following line of reasoning, which includes self-locating beliefs, would not suffice as an adequate explanation of Oedipus's self-blinding: "Who-ever killed Laius should be blinded; I killed Laius; therefore, I should be blinded." Rather, Oedipus blinded himself because of the horror of the realization that *he himself* had killed Laius. Nothing less than a first-person perspective would do justice to Oedipus's motivation. If this is right, then in order to explain Oedipus's blinding himself, we must suppose that he not only was the subject of weak first-person phenom-ena that would enable him to have first-person self-locating beliefs, but also that he had a conception of himself from a first-person point of view. Since the correct psychological explanation of Oedipus's blinding himself requires that Oedipus had the ability to conceive of himself as himself*, a psychology that aims to be a complete theory of behavior cannot afford to ignore the first-person perspective.

A LOOK AT OTHER VIEWS

The first-person perspective is the key to self-consciousness. Without trying to offer an analysis or a theory of self-consciousness beyond the characterization that I have already given, I now want to show that the first-person perspective causes trouble for recent prominent views on self-consciousness. To see what is at stake, first consider two ways that David Rosenthal's 'higher-order thought' account might be interpreted. Rosenthal builds up what he calls 'introspective consciousness' by a kind of iteration: A "mental state is conscious – non-introspectively conscious – just in case one has a roughly contemporaneous thought to the effect

---

38 Nor does my point concern the semantics of first-person sentences. For example, John Perry would describe the change from third-person to first-person perspective as a change of belief state, not as a change in the proposition believed. Steven Boër and William Lycan have argued that there is no semantic difference between first-and third-person perspectives, only a pragmatic difference. See Perry, "The problem of the Essential Indexical," and Steven E. Boër and William G. Lycan, *Knowing Who* (Cambridge, MA: MIT press/Bradford Press, 1986).

that one is in that very mental state." And the mental state is "introspectively conscious" when the relevant contemporaneous second-order thought is itself conscious. "Since a state's being conscious is its being accompanied by a suitable higher-order thought, introspective consciousness occurs when a mental state is accompanied both by such a second-order thought, and also by a yet higher-order thought that one has that second-order thought."[39] To report that one is in a certain mental state is to express a higher-order thought in virtue of which the first-order mental state is conscious. If Sally says, "I have a headache," she is reporting her headache by expressing a higher-order thought in virtue of which she is conscious of her headache.

Rosenthal puts it this way: "[I]n general, our being conscious of something is just a matter of our having a thought of some sort about it. Accordingly, it is natural to identify a mental state's being conscious with one's having a roughly contemporaneous thought that one is in that mental state."[40] He makes a similar point when he says that "a mental state's being conscious will be the same as one's having the ability to express one's higher-order thought that one is in that mental state."[41] Now how are we to understand 'one' in the "higher-order thought that one is in that mental state"? Is it one★ (oneself as oneself★) or just oneself? Thoughts that simply happen to be about oneself – as Oedipus's thoughts about the killer of Laius before his awful realization – do not require that one have a first-person perspective; thoughts about oneself as oneself★ do require that one have a first-person perspective. So the question "How are we to understand 'one' in the 'higher-order thought that one is in that mental state'?" gives rise to two ways of formulating this account of consciousness in terms of higher-order thought. The first interpretation leaves out the first-person perspective; the second interpretation – Rosenthal's own[42] – requires a first-person perspective. The

---

39 David M. Rosenthal, "Thinking That One Thinks," in *Consciousness: Psychological and Philosophical Essays*, Martin Davies and Glyn W. Humphreys, eds. (Oxford: Basil Blackwell, 1993): 199.

40 David M. Rosenthal, "Two Concepts of Consciousness," in *The Nature of Mind*, David M. Rosenthal, ed. (Oxford: Oxford University Press, 1991): 465.

41 Rosenthal, "Thinking That One Thinks," p. 204.

42 In a footnote, Rosenthal says, "It is not sufficient that the report be about somebody who happens to be oneself. Rather, the report must be about oneself, as such; that is, it must be a report that the being that is in the mental state is oneself" (Rosenthal "Two Concepts of Consciousness," p. 476, n. 12). In other footnotes, Rosenthal mentions some of the relevant literature about the difference between believing of someone who turns out to

point that I want to emphasize by giving two interpretations of Rosenthal's view is the importance of the first-person perspective.

First Interpretation

Mental state M is introspectively conscious if and only if there is some thinker or subject S and some time t such that:

(1) At t, S is in mental state M.
(2) At t, S has a thought that S is in mental state M.
(3) At t, S has a thought that S has a thought that S is in mental state M,

where S's reporting the thought that she had in (2) is sufficient for the truth of (3).

Second Interpretation

Mental state M is introspectively conscious if and only if there is some thinker or subject S and some time t such that:

(1) At t, S is in mental state M.
(2a) At t, S has a thought that she★ is in mental state M.
(3a) At t, S has a thought that she★ has a thought that she★ is in mental state M,

where 'she★' attributes a first-person reference to S and where S's reporting the thought that she has in (2a) is sufficient for the truth of (3a). As we have seen at length, sentences like (3a), which attribute first-person reference, cannot be replaced without loss by any sentences – like (1) or iterations of (1) – that are free of the first person.

Let us begin with the first interpretation, which leaves out the first-person perspective altogether. On the first interpretation, the "higher-order-thought" account is subject to counterexamples. Satisfaction of conditions (1)–(3) does not account for a thinker's being in a mental state of which she is introspectively conscious. Suppose that Jones is being tested on her ability to read position emission tomography (PET) scans and that she is reading a contemporaneous PET scan of her own brain. Although she knows that she is reading a PET scan of an alert subject named 'Jones,' she does not realize that that Jones is herself★.

---

be oneself that he is F, and believing that he★ is F. See, e.g., Rosenthal, "Thinking That One Thinks," p. 216, n. 10.

(She thinks that the Jones whose brain she is watching is in the next room.) Now suppose that the telephone rings in the next room, where she thinks that the subject Jones is located. At *t*, she points to a lit-up portion of the brain on the screen and says to the tester, "Now Jones is hearing the phone." In so saying, Jones is expressing her thought that now Jones is hearing the phone. At the same time, with no conscious inference, Jones thinks to herself, "Jones is having the thought that Jones is hearing the phone."[43]

This story, I believe, satisfies conditions (1)–(3) for Jones to be introspectively conscious of hearing the phone at *t*: Jones hears the phone at *t*, thus satisfying (1); Jones has a thought that Jones hears the phone at *t*, thus satisfying (2); and Jones reports that thought, thereby expressing the third-order thought that Jones has a thought that Jones is hearing that phone and thus satisfying (3). Yet, in the circumstances described, satisfaction of (1)–(3) does not make Jones introspectively conscious of hearing the phone at *t*. Even if we stipulate that Jones is indeed introspectively conscious of hearing the phone at *t*, it is not in virtue of satisfying (1)–(3) that Jones is introspectively conscious of hearing the phone at *t*. For Jones (mistakenly) believes that the person whose hearing of the phone she is talking about is someone other than herself★. In short, Jones's thought that Jones is having the thought that Jones is hearing the phone does not make Jones's hearing the phone introspectively conscious.[44] So, omission of the first-person perspective by the first interpretation of the "higher-order-thought" account, (1)–(3), leads to counterexamples. No non-first-person thought could possibly confer introspective consciousness on a mental state.

Whether or not the second interpretation – (1), (2a), and (3a) – ultimately provides a satisfactory account of introspective consciousness, it does build in the first-person perspective. Note, however, that the second interpretation, whether otherwise satisfactory or not, gives no purchase on a reductive explanation of consciousness. Rosenthal hopes to show "how consciousness can occur in physical things" by "explain-

---

43 Although Rosenthal requires that the associated higher-order thoughts be independent of *conscious* inference, he explicitly allows that "non-conscious inference may well underlie the presence of the higher-order thoughts that make mental states conscious. Such non-conscious inferences are not precluded here, since they would not interfere with the intuitive immediacy of such consciousness" (Rosenthal, "Thinking That One Thinks," p. 219, n. 18).

44 Rosenthal, I believe, would agree since he rejects the non-first-person interpretation of his view. See note 42.

ing the consciousness of mental states in terms of mental states that are not conscious."[45] So, on the second interpretation, the explanation of "the consciousness of mental states in terms of mental states that are not conscious" is that a first-order mental state becomes conscious by being accompanied by a second-order (nonconscious) state. And the accompanying second-order state itself becomes conscious when it is accompanied by a (nonconscious) third-order state that *only a being with a first-person perspective can have.*

This explanation, as it stands, I think, cannot be a fully reductive explanation of consciousness. For the third-order nonconscious states that are to explain introspectively conscious states cannot be understood simply in terms of less complex states; rather, the third-order explanatory states themselves require what the first-order mental states do not – namely, a first-person perspective. So, on Rosenthal's account as developed so far, the first-person perspective would itself remain unexplained and unreduced.

To see this, consider again the mental state of hearing the phone. On the second interpretation of Rosenthal's view, this state becomes conscious when I have the second-order thought expressed by

(a) I am hearing the phone;

and the state of hearing the phone becomes introspectively conscious when I have the third-order thought expressed by

(b) I am having the thought that I★ am hearing the phone.

It may seem that the mental state expressed by (b) can be understood as a mere iteration of the mental state expressed by (a).[46] But, as we have seen, not every being with the capacity to entertain the thought expressed by (a) has the capacity to entertain the thought expressed by (b). All that is required to entertain the thought expressed by (a) is the kind of perspectival consciousness that we attribute to dogs and other problem-solving creatures that are subject to weak first-person phenomena. But in order to entertain the thought expressed by (b), a being must

45 Rosenthal, "Two Concepts of Consciousness," p. 474.
46 Compare the KK thesis in epistemology: If S knows that p, then S knows that she (S? she★?) knows that p. One may suppose that (a) and (b) are related by an analogous principle: If S has the thought that p, then S has the thought that she★ has the thought that p. But this could not be Rosenthal's view since he does not think that all conscious states are introspectively conscious. Moreover, the discussion of the first-person perspective shows that the principle analogous to the KK thesis is false (as is the KK thesis itself).

have a first-person perspective – something that a dog lacks. So, the thought expressed by (b) introduces a new factor – a first-person perspective – that is absent from the lower-order states.

If an explanatory account requires a new factor that is absent from the states to be explained, then the account is not reductive unless the concept of the new factor itself is either part of a reductive apparatus (as, e.g., the concept of molecules is) or the new factor is itself reduced (as, e.g., heat is reduced to molecular motion). The concept of the first-person perspective is not part of a reductive apparatus; so, unless the first-person perspective can be reductively explained, no account in which it figures is fully reductive. This is so even if Rosenthal's account does succeed in (reductively) explaining conscious states in terms of nonconscious states. My point is twofold: (a) the nonconscious states in terms of which the conscious states are to be explained introduce something new, the first-person perspective, and, therefore, (b) the account is not fully reductive unless the first-person perspective itself is reductively explained.[47]

At best, the second interpretation of Rosenthal's view reduces introspectively conscious states to nonconscious states that require a first-person perspective, with no attempt to reduce the first-person perspective. For this reason, I do not think that Rosenthal's view, even if successful as an account of conscious states, provides the kind of reduction that robust naturalists hanker after. For the first-person perspective that is required for the explanation of conscious states is itself left unexplained.

The upshot of this discussion of the "higher-order-thought" account of introspectively conscious states is a dilemma for any reductive account of self-consciousness: On the one hand, if (as on the first interpretation) the account is indifferent to the distinction between conceiving of oneself as oneself* and simply having a point of view that allows one to conceive of oneself in a third-person way, then it leaves out the first-person perspective; and the account is subject to counterexamples. On the other hand, if (as on the second interpretation) the account invokes

---

47 The need for a reductive account of the first-person perspective in order to complete a reductive account of introspective consciousness is obscured by a tendency to construe the introspective consciousness of a mental state M as one's having the thought that one has the thought that one is in M. Formulated in this way, it appears that the third-order mental state is built up from the first-order mental state by some mechanical means like iteration. Thus, it is not surprising that the need for a reductive account of the first-person perspective has gone unnoticed.

the first-person perspective, then it does not succeed in reductively explaining consciousness or self-consciousness; and it is incumbent upon the naturalizer to give a naturalistic account of the distinction in question and our ability to make it.[48]

Let me briefly mention three other prominent approaches to self-consciousness and show how they too falter over the first-person perspective. Consider the accounts of self-consciousness: as self-scanning of internal states, as approachable from a third-person point of view, and as possession of a "narrative self."

(A) Some philosophers, such as D. M. Armstrong, take self-consciousness (or introspection) to be "a self-scanning process in the brain."[49] Perhaps, but self-scanning as it is now understood is not sufficient for self-consciousness. A self-scanner cannot make the distinction that is crucial for self-consciousness: A self-scanner cannot distinguish between acquiring information about something-that-is-in-fact-itself and acquiring information about itself-as-itself. Suppose that S is a system that has a scanner S' of its internal states. S' acquires information about S and feeds it to a device that regulates S's states. In a sense, then, S acquires information about itself. But in the system, there is no place for a distinction between saying "S acquires information about S" and saying "S acquires information about itself as itself." And the *use* made of S's information about S's internal states could be described as well by saying that S regulates S's states as by saying that S regulates its own states. So, the behavioral difference that the first-person perspective makes for self-conscious beings is wholly absent in the case of self-scanning scanners. Since S cannot distinguish between itself-as-S (from the third person) and itself-as-itself, the system makes no distinction between scanning S and scanning itself. And without that distinction, there is no self-consciousness in S. Therefore, self-scanning scanners do not account for self-consciousness.

Let me be more cautious: Perhaps in the future self-scanning scanners will be able to accommodate the crucial distinction between a first-

---

48 To try to accommodate the first-person perspective by hypothesizing that there is a special first-person psychological mode of presentation under which one represents oneself as oneself* is only a relabeling of the distinction from a functionalist point of view. See the comments in the final section.

49 David M. Armstrong, *A Materialist Theory of Mind* (London: Routledge and Kegan Paul, 1968), p. 324; William G. Lycan, *Consciousness* (Cambridge: MIT Press/Bradford Press, 1987), pp. 72–3; cf. William G. Lycan, *Consciousness and Experience* (Cambridge: MIT/Bradford, 1996).

person perspective and a third-person perspective on oneself. I just can't imagine how. The point I want to make here, however, is that writers on the mind have not even tried to accommodate the crucial distinction, and until they do, they have not addressed a feature essential to self-consciousness.

(B) Some philosophers explicitly eschew first-person approaches to consciousness and to self-consciousness. Daniel Dennett, for example, is emphatic: A theory of consciousness "will have to be constructed from the third-person point of view," he says, "since *all* science is constructed from that perspective."[50] Despite his official view, however, Dennett's practice takes advantage of the first-person perspective inasmuch as the study of consciousness utilizes a subject's "heterophenomenology." A heterophenomenology is constructed by videotaping and soundtaping and electroencephelographing a subject, preparing a transcript from the soundtape, and interpreting the resulting text as a record of speech acts (i.e., treating the subject as a rational agent). The resulting text is the subject's "heterophenomenological world."[51] Then, to determine the accuracy of the subjects' reports, the investigator checks the " 'defining' properties of the items that populate [the subjects'] heterophenomenological worlds" against the "real goings-on in people's brains."[52] Brain events are presumed to be "the real referents of the beliefs we express in our introspective reports."[53]

What is of interest here is that the heterophenomenology cannot have broken free of the first-person perspective. For, presumably, the original soundtape from which the heterophenomenology was prepared contained numerous I⋆ sentences by which the subject attributes first-person attitudes to herself⋆. The first-person perspective is not left behind by a heterophenomenological text that renders Jane's words "I wish that I⋆ could have seen John once more," for example, as "Jane wishes that she⋆ could have seen John once more." The way to avoid recognizing a first-person perspective would be to render Jane's words as "Jane wishes that Jane could have seen John once more"; but, as we have seen repeatedly, a genuinely third-person rendition of Jane's utter-

---

50 Daniel C. Dennett, *Consciousness Explained* (Boston: Little, Brown, and Company, 1991): 71.

51 Dennett, *Consciousness Explained*, pp. 74–81.

52 Dennett, *Consciousness Explained*, p. 85.

53 Dennett, *Consciousness Explained*, p. 85. Disregard the fact that Dennett's views on consciousness seem quite at odds with his views on intentionality.

ance would not be accurate.[54] On the other hand, if Dennett were to accept attributions of the first-person perspective to Jane as being consistent with his insistence on the third-person perspective, then he, too, would need a reductive account of the first-person perspective.

(C) Finally, there is another angle on self-consciousness – this one associated with Dennett as well. We can think of a very sophisticated kind of self-consciousness as the construction of a narrative self. When philosophers speak of a self – as Dennett's self as the center of narrative gravity or as Owen Flanagan's self as an emergent set of models – they are considering a much thicker concept than what I mean by the 'first-person perspective.'[55] Indeed, they tend to skip over the first-person perspective altogether. Flanagan, for example, distinguishes a weak sort of self-consciousness enjoyed by any beings, even infants, that are subjects of experience, from a strong sort of self-consciousness that requires a temporally extended soliloquy or dialogue. We "are self-conscious in a deep way, for example, when we are engaged in figuring out who we are and where we are going with our lives." This sort of self-consciousness involves, Flanagan says, "thinking about one's model of one's self, or as I shall say for simplicity, the self."[56] Clearly, "thinking about one's model of one's self" must be understood as thinking about one's model of oneself as oneself, and not just as thinking of a model of someone-who-is-in-fact-oneself.[57] The point again is that a view of self-consciousness is demonstrably false unless it presupposes the first-person perspective.

The idea of a self is much richer than the idea of a first-person perspective. A self is the locus of personal integrity and coherence, but

---

54 For what it's worth, I think that heterophenomenology is an excellent way to study consciousness. I just wouldn't claim that it avoided the first-person perspective. Nor would I try to map "items that populate heterophenomenological worlds" onto items in the brain.

55 Dennett, *Consciousness Explained*, and Owen Flanagan, *Consciousness Reconsidered* (Cambridge, MA: MIT Press/Bradford Press, 1992).

56 Flanagan, *Consciousness Reconsidered*, pp. 194–5.

57 A number of prominent philosophers take self-consciousness to be access to a self-model. As David Chalmers put it, self-consciousness is "our ability to think about ourselves, our awareness of our existence as individuals and of our distinctness from others. My self-consciousness might be analyzed in terms of my access to a self-model or my possession of a certain sort of representation that is associated in some way with myself." (Chalmers, *The Conscious Mind: Toward a Fundamental Theory* [Oxford: Oxford University Press, 1996]: 27.) For reasons that I have rehearsed several times, "my access to a self-model" cannot simply be my access to a model of myself from a third-person point of view, but also of myself as myself* from a first-person point of view.

such a self is not required for a first-person perspective. A. R. Luria wrote about a soldier, Zasetsky, who suffered a brain wound in World War II and who desperately tried to recover his self, his source of identity.[58] What Zasetsky had lost was a coherent and comprehensive story of his life, of which he was the subject; but he had not lost his first-person perspective. Indeed, his quest to find out who he was pre-supposed a first-person perspective. For a first-person perspective is required in order to be in the position of searching for who one* is. A first-person perspective is necessary, but not sufficient, for an idea of a self in the sense that Zasetsky lost.

On each of these views, either a first-person perspective is presupposed without being explicitly discussed or it is genuinely left out. If it is genuinely left out, as I have tried to show, then the view is subject to counterexamples. So, I think that there is no way for an adequate account of self-consciousness to avoid the first-person perspective.

CONCLUSION

In this chapter, I hope to have shown several things: what the first-person perspective is and how those with a first-person perspective differ from merely sentient beings; that the first-person perspective has a nonCartesian feature of being relational in a certain sense; that the idea of a first-person perspective is indispensable for a comprehensive theory of reality; and how theories of self-consciousness overlook the first-person perspective at their peril.

In the next chapter, I shall show that what distinguishes persons from nonpersons is a capacity for a first-person perspective, the idea of which, as I have argued in this chapter, is indispensable for a comprehensive understanding of reality. So, persons are ineliminable from a comprehensive understanding of reality.[59]

58 A. R. Luria, *The Man With a Shattered World* (New York: Basic Books, 1972).
59 Much of this chapter appeared in "The First-Person Perspective: A Test for Naturalism," *American Philosophical Quarterly* 35 (1998): 327–48. A translation of an earlier version of part of this essay appears in German in a volume of proceedings of a conference on Naturalism at Humboldt University in Berlin (February 1997) as "Die Perspektive der Ersten Person: Ein Test fuer den Naturalismus," in *Naturalismus. Philosophische Beitrage*, Geert Keil and Herbert Schnädelbach, eds. (Frankfurt am Main: Suhrkamp Verlag, 1999).

Part Two

The Constitution View Explained

4

The Constitution View of Human Persons

In ordinary discourse, we speak of people as *having* bodies without making much fuss about just what this 'having' relation is. What does it mean to say that I have a body? The Constitution View offers an answer: For a person to have a body is for the person to be constituted by a body (in the sense of 'constitution' explicated in Chapter 2). A person is not a separate thing from the constituting body, any more than a statue is a separate thing from the constituting block of marble. Nor is a person identical to the constituting body. The nonidentity of person and body, on the Constitution View, is guaranteed by the fact that any body could exist without a first-person perspective, but no person could exist without a capacity for first-person perspective (in the sense of 'first-person perspective' explicated in Chapter 3). Now I shall try to spell out in detail just how human persons are related to their bodies.

WHAT A HUMAN PERSON IS

On the Constitution View, what makes a human person a *person* is the capacity to have a first-person perspective. What makes a human person a *human* is being constituted by a human organism.

A first-person perspective is a defining characteristic of all persons, human or not. From a first-person point of view, one can think about oneself as oneself and think about one's thoughts as one's own. In English, we not only use first-person pronouns to refer to ourselves "from the inside," so to speak (e.g., "I'm happy"), but also to attribute to ourselves first-person reference (e.g., "I wonder whether I'll be happy in ten years"). The first occurrence of 'I' in "I wonder whether I'll be happy in ten years" directs attention to the person per se, without recourse to any name, description, or other third-person referential device to identify who is being thought about. The second occurrence of 'I' in "I wonder whether I'll be happy in ten years" shows that the speaker has a concept of herself as herself*. The first-person perspective opens up a distinction between thinking of oneself in the first person (not just having thoughts expressible by 'I' but conceiving of oneself as having such thoughts) and thinking of oneself in the third person. Once someone can make this distinction, she can think of herself as a subject in a world of things different from herself.

In order to have a first-person perspective, one must be the subject of numerous intentional states of various kinds – believing, desiring, intending, hoping, fearing, wondering, and so on. But there are many intentional states that humans and other animals can have without being able to conceive of themselves in the first person. So having intentional states is a necessary but not a sufficient condition for being a person. To be a person – whether God, an angel, a human person, or a Martian person – one must have the capacity for a first-person perspective. Person is a genus, of which there may be several species: human, divine, bionic, Martian, and so on. It is in virtue of the capacity to have a first-person perspective that a person is a person.

I have already explained what I mean by a 'first-person perspective.' It remains to say what a *capacity* for a first-person perspective is. Although the term 'capacity' is extremely elastic, I can give a necessary and sufficient condition for the capacity for a first-person perspective, as I intend it: An object x has the capacity for a first-person perspective at t if and only if x has all the structural properties at t required for a first-person perspective and either (i) x has manifested a first-person perspective at some time before t or (ii) x is in an environment at t conducive to the development and maintenance of a first-person perspective. Given this condition, a person can go into a coma without ceasing to exist, and a normal newborn human is (i.e., constitutes) a person.[1] In general, a

---

1 "Infants begin to experience a sense of an emergent self from birth. . . . They never experience a period of total self/other undifferentiation." Daniel N. Stern, *The Interpersonal World of the Infant: A View from Psychoanalysis and Developmental Psychology* (New York: Basic Books, 1985): 10. Stern also notes that infants do not recognize their reflections in mirrors as themselves until about eighteen months of age (p. 165). By about twenty-seven months of age, however, a child seems to be aware of what he is doing and makes sophisticated self-descriptive utterances using the first-person pronoun. (Jerome Kagan, *Unstable Ideas: Temperament, Cognition, and Self* [Cambridge MA: Harvard University Press, 1989]: 233.) So, from birth, development of a first-person perspective is underway.

normal birth is the entrance of a new being into the world. (That's why we observe birthdays, and why Christians celebrate the Incarnation at the Nativity and not at the Annunciation.)

A human person – who, like all persons, has the capacity for a first-person perspective – is distinguished from other kinds of persons in that a human person is constituted by a human body that is (or will be, in the normal course of things) the object of his first-person reference. A human person is constituted by a biological entity – an organism, a member of the species *Homo sapiens* – that is physically able to support first-person intentional states.[2] (It is up to neurophysiologists, not philosophers, to determine the conditions under which a human organism is able to support first-person intentional states.) As a human person, Smith, say, must have a biological body that he can think about in a first-person way. Smith can think of a biological body in the first-person way if he can entertain thoughts about that body without the aid of a name or description or third-person pronoun.

If Smith wonders whether he has cancer, he is wondering about his body from a first-person point of view. He is not wondering whether there is a malignant tumor in some particular body identified by a third-person demonstrative pronoun or description; he is wondering whether there is a malignant tumor in his own body, considered as himself. This is different from wondering about a material possession, say. If Smith wonders whether his car will run, he wonders about a particular car, which he identifies by a description or a third-person demonstrative reference. Without a third-person way to think about the car, he could not wonder about its battery. But if Smith is wondering how he will die, he can think of his body as his own without recourse to any name or description or second- or third-person demonstrative pronoun. And conceiving of oneself without recourse to the familiar third-person devices is the mark of first-person reference.

To put it differently, Smith thinks of a biological body in the first-

2 Unlike Wiggins, if I understand him correctly, I do not distinguish between an animal and an animal body. In *Sameness and Substance* (Oxford: Basil Blackwell, 1980: 187), Wiggins says, "[M]y claim is that by *person* we mean *a certain sort of animal.*" Then he distinguishes the animal (that I supposedly am) from the body (that supposedly constitutes it). On the other hand, I think that an animal *is* (identical to) a body of a special self-sustaining and self-organizing sort, and I distinguish the animal/body from the person. Also, I take an animal to be a member of its species whether it is alive or dead. How could an animal lose species membership on dying? It simply becomes a dead member of its species. Cf. Fred Feldman, *Confrontations with the Reaper* (New York: Oxford University Press, 1992): 104.

person way if he conceives of its properties as his own. For example, even if he is totally paralyzed, Smith has a first-person relation to his body if he can entertain the thought "I wonder if I'll ever be able to move my legs again." Or again: Smith's thoughts about how photogenic he (himself) is, or his worries about his (own) state of health – thoughts that he would express with first-person pronouns – make first-person reference to his body as his own. As we have seen, constitution is a very intimate relation. Since a human person is constituted by a body, a first-person reference to one's body is ipso facto a first-person reference to oneself.

So, what makes a particular body Smith's, rather than someone else's, is that it is the body that Smith can think of and refer to in a first-person way "from the inside." The body to which Smith has a first-person relation is the body some of whose parts he (normally) can move without moving anything else, the body that he tends when he is in pain, and the body that expresses intentional states and character traits that are his. Posture, countenance, bearing, sounds, and all manner of bodily motions express states like pain, longing, sadness, hope, fear, frustration, worry, effort, and joy, as well as states like believing, desiring, and intending. Likewise, a person's character traits may be apparent in her body. Political cartoonists indicate the politician's corruption by portraying the politician's doughy face and "power jowls." In a drawing of John More (father of Thomas More, the "man for all seasons"), Hans Holbein the Younger "sketched the lineaments of a full and awakened life. . . . [T]he study of John More has none of the remoteness and diffidence which appear in the portrait of his son [Thomas More]."[3]

The body that expresses a person's states and character traits is the body to which the person has a first-person relation. Smith's first-person relation to his body at t does not imply that Smith is actually thinking of his body at t; indeed, Smith may believe at t that he is disembodied. The body to which Smith has a first-person relation is the body whose sweaty hands would manifest the fact that Smith is nervous, and whose knotted stomach would express the fact that Smith is frightened, or the body that would move if Smith carried out his decision to leave the room. Smith's body at time t distinguishes Smith from all other persons at t. What distinguishes me now from all other coexisting persons – even physical and psychological replicas of me, if there are any – is that at this time, I have a first-person relation to this body and to no other;

3 Peter Ackroyd, *The Life of Thomas More* (New York: Nan A. Talese/Doubleday, 1998), p. 65.

and any replica of me at this time has a first-person relation to some other body, not to this one.

Smith's body is a human body in virtue of being a member of the species *Homo sapiens*. What makes something a human body are its biological properties, in particular its DNA; its career may be followed from beginning to end without respect to whether or not it is any person's body. Similarly, its persistence conditions are independent of whether or not it is any person's body. A human body may be identified as a human body independently of whether it is Smith's or any other person's body. Moreover, since organisms do not lose their membership in their species at death, a human body remains a human body whether alive or dead. In an ordinary, nonviolent death, one and the same human body persists through the change: It is first alive, and then it is dead.

Although a human body starts out as entirely organic, it can acquire non-organic parts. An artificial leg that I think of as my own, and that I can move merely by intending to move it, becomes a part of my (still human) body. Exactly how much replacement of parts a human body may undergo and still remain a *human* body is somewhat vague, but as long as it continues to be sustained by DNA-based organic processes, it should be considered a human body, a member of the species *Homo sapiens*.

Recall the general definition of 'constitution' in Chapter 2. Let *being an F* be x's primary-kind property, and let *being a G* be y's primary-kind property, where *being an F* $\neq$ *being a G*, and let D be G-favorable circumstances. Let F$\star$ be the property of *having the property of being an F as one's primary-kind property*, and let G$\star$ be the property of *having the property of being a G as one's primary-kind property*.[4] Then:

Definition of 'Constitution'
(C) x constitutes y at $t =_{df}$
   (a) x and y are spatially coincident at t; and
   (b) x is in D at t; and
   (c) It is necessary that: $\forall z[(F\star zt \ \& \ z$ is in D at $t) \rightarrow \exists u(G\star ut \ \& \ u$ is spatially coincident with z at $t)]$; and
   (d) It is possible that: (x exists at $t \ \& \ \sim\exists w[G\star wt \ \& \ w$ is spatially coincident with x at $t]$).
   (e) If y is immaterial, then x is also immaterial.

---

4 Again, the reason to distinguish F$\star$ and G$\star$ from F and G is that some x may have the property of *being an F* derivatively, in which case x is an F but *being an F* is not x's primary-kind property. Introduction of F$\star$ restricts the definition to cases to Fs that have the property of *being an F* as their primary-kind property.

Now let Body be a particular human body (i.e., a human organism); let Smith be a particular person. Body's primary-kind property is the property of being a human body; Smith's primary-kind property is the property of being a person. The person-favorable circumstances are the intrinsic and environmental conditions conducive to development and maintenance of a first-person perspective, where the intrinsic conditions include structural properties required to support a first-person perspective. Now apply the definition of 'constitution':

Body constitutes Smith at $t =_{df}$

(a) Body and Smith are spatially coincident at t; and
(b) Body is in intrinsic and environmental conditions at t conducive to development and maintenance of a first-person perspective; and
(c) It is necessary that: for anything that has the property of being a human body as its primary-kind property at t and that is in intrinsic and environmental conditions at t conducive to development and maintenance of a first-person perspective, there is some spatially coincident thing that has the property of being a person as its primary-kind property at t; and
(d) It is possible that: Body exists at t and there is no spatially coincident thing that has the property of being a person as its primary-kind property at t; and
(e) Neither Smith nor Body is immaterial.

Let me make two comments. The first concerns the intrinsic and environmental conditions conducive to development and maintenance of a first-person perspective at t, as cited in (b) and (c). The relevant intrinsic conditions are that the organism, particularly the brain, is developed to the extent that a normal baby's brain is developed at birth. The relevant environmental conditions are those in which the infant naturally develops various senses of 'self,' as described by developmental psychologists.[5] The first-person perspective, on my account, fits easily into the framework of developmental psychology. The second comment concerns (d): It is possible that: Body exists at t and there is no spatially coincident thing that has the property of being a person as its primary-kind property at t. Body could exist at t but be dead; in that case, Body would not be in the relevant intrinsic conditions conducive to development and maintenance of a first-person perspective and so would not constitute a person.

5 For example, see Stern, *The Interpersonal World of the Infant*, and Kagan, *Unstable Ideas*.

As we saw in Chapter 2, the idea of constitution brings with it the idea of having properties derivatively. A person has some of her properties — for example, she has blue eyes, say — in virtue of the fact that she is constituted by a human organism. Those are properties that the person has derivatively. To have a property derivatively is to have constitution relations to something that has it independently of *its* constitution relations. Recall that the idea of having a property derivatively may be spelled out in two definitions: Let H range over properties that are neither alethic properties, nor identity/constitution/existence properties, nor properties such that they are rooted outside times at which they are had, nor hybrid properties.

(I) x has H at t independently of x's constitution relations to y at $t =_{df}$
  (a) x has H at t; and
  (b) Either (1) (i) x constitutes y at t, and
                (ii) x's having H at t (in the given background) does not entail that x constitutes anything at t.
      or (2) (i) y constitutes x at t, and
                (ii) x's having H at t (in the given background) does not entail that x is constituted by something that could have had H at t without constituting anything at t.

(D) x has H at t derivatively $=_{df}$ There is some y such that:
  (a) it is not the case that: x has H at t independently of x's constitution relations to y at t; &
  (b) y has H at t independently of y's constitution relations to x at t.

You and I are persons nonderivatively; we have first-person perspectives nonderivatively. I have the property of having a first-person perspective independently of my constitution relations to my body. This is so because application of the definition of 'constitution' to persons and bodies ensures that (I)(b)(2)(ii) is satisfied: My having a first-person perspective does not entail that I am constituted by something that could have had a first-person perspective without constituting anything. (By (C)(c), an organism's having a first-person perspective necessitates its constituting a person.) On the other hand, you and I are animals derivatively. The organisms that constitute us are animals independently of their constitution relations to us, and it is not the case that you or I is an animal independently of our constitution relations to the animals that in fact constitute us. Conversely, as is equally clear from the definitions, the organisms that constitute us are organisms nonderivatively, and those organisms have first-person perspectives derivatively. Before it comes to constitute a person, an organism has all of its "highest" properties non-derivatively. As soon as an organism comes to have a capacity for a first-person perspective, however, it comes to constitute a person. An organism never has a first-person perspective nonderivatively. Anything that has a first-person perspective nonderivatively, whether it is constituted by an organism or not, is nonderivatively a person.

With the idea of having properties derivatively, I need not deny that the animal that constitutes me is a person; indeed, I insist on it. That animal is a person derivatively: It is a person in virtue of constituting something that is a person. We account for Brown's body's being a person by showing that it is a person derivatively. To see this, consider: Brown has the property of being a person independently of his constitution relations to his body since Brown's being a person does not entail that Brown is constituted by something that could have been a person without constituting anything. Assuming that Brown's body is a person, we see by (I) that it is not a person independently of its constitution relations to Brown, since Brown's body's being a person does entail that Brown's body constitutes something. Now check the relevant instance of (D): (a) Brown's body does not have the property of being a person independently of Brown's body's constitution relations to Brown; (b) Brown is a person independently of his constitution relations to his body. Similarly, we account for the fact that Brown is an animal by seeing that the definitions are satisfied for Brown's being an animal derivatively.

I can even agree that Brown's body, the animal, has a first-person perspective. My point is that when an animal has a first-person perspective or the capacity for one, a new entity comes into being: a person. The person is not a duplicate of the animal; rather, the person is constituted (in the sense defined) by the animal. There are not two animals; there are not two persons. There is one person constituted by an animal. There is one first-person perspective that the person has non-derivatively and the animal has derivatively (according to the preceding definitions). The animal borrows the person's first-person perspective. The animal does not duplicate me; it constitutes me. And it is clear from the definition of 'constitution' that constitution is not duplication.[6]

---

6 I shall develop this point further in Chapters 7 and 8.

The idea of having properties derivatively explains how, say, I can have the property of being overweight. It is not just that my body is overweight; I am.[7] Being overweight is a property that I – the person, constituted by this particular body – have. True, being overweight is a property that I have because my body has it, but my body constitutes *me*. So, I have the property of being overweight derivatively. By contrast, other properties of mine are had by me in virtue of my legal status, or of thinking what I think, or of being a member of a particular community, or of any number of other circumstances that are independent of my having the particular body that I have; I am the primary bearer of these properties. But some of my properties (like being overweight) are had by me in virtue of my having the particular body that I have. And the properties that depend on my having a particular body are no less properties of me than are the others.[8]

Up to now, I have been explaining what a human person is largely in terms of an example, Smith. But what about Smith's body? Is Smith's body a human person too? We need to see how, if at all, the property of being a human person applies to Smith's body, as well as to Smith. I want to conclude this section with a technical account of the bearer(s) of the property *being a human person*. (Feel free to skip to the end of this section if you are satisfied with an intuitive understanding.)

Begin by asking: Does Smith or Smith's body have the property of being a *human person* derivatively? Not according to (D). *Being a person* is a primary-kind property, and *being a human organism* is a primary-kind property. Hence, the property of being a human person is a hybrid property, as defined in Chapter 2. But (D) is not defined for hybrid properties. So, neither you nor your body has this (or any other) hybrid property derivatively, according to (D). The reason that (D) must exclude hybrid properties is this: Suppose that Smith were a human person at t nonderivatively and Smith's body were a human person at t derivatively. Then, by (D), Smith's being a human person at t would be independent of Smith's constitution relations at t. But clearly, Smith's being a human person at t is not independent of Smith's being constituted by a human body at t. The same reasoning would apply, mutatis mutandis, to the supposition that Smith's body was a human person at t

7   This is just an example; it is not intended to be autobiographical.
8   In Chapter 7, I respond to an argument that assumes that if I am not identical to my body, then it can't be true both that my body weighs n kg and that I weighs n kg – unless the bathroom scales read $2n$ kg.

nonderivatively and Smith was a human person at *t* derivatively. Hence, (D) cannot accommodate hybrid properties.

Further examination of hybrid properties, however, will lead to a modification of the definition of 'having a property derivatively' that will accommodate hybrid properties like *being a human person*. By definition, a hybrid property – for example, *being a granite monument, being a cloth flag, being a human person* – is decomposable into two or more properties, which entail or are entailed by distinct primary-kind properties. For any hybrid property, one of the properties into which it is decomposable is basic (e.g., *being a monument, being a flag, being a person*). The basic property is (almost always) the one referred to by a noun – 'monument,' 'flag,' 'person.' If we focus on hybrid properties decomposable into two properties, one property is the basic property of the hybrid, and the other property is a delimiter that specifies a subclass of things that have the basic property – a kind of monument, a kind of flag, a kind of person. (Compare genus and species.) Now the primary bearer of a hybrid property is the thing that has the basic property into which the hybrid is decomposable nonderivatively.

Let us apply this general account of hybrid properties to the property of being a human person. To be a human person at *t* is to be a kind of *person*: It is to be a person who is constituted by a human animal at *t*. The basic property of the hybrid property *being a human person at t* is the primary-kind property *being a person*. So, the primary bearer of the property of being a human person at *t* is something that is a person nonderivatively and a human animal at *t* derivatively: Smith rather than Smith's body. This seems intuitively right. When we think of a human person, we think in the first instance of a person who is human.

Although we have seen that hybrid properties are never had derivatively, according to (D), we need an analogue of having a property derivatively for hybrid properties. This is so, because, on the Constitution View, Smith's body is nonderivatively a human animal and, according to (D), derivatively a person at *t*. So, it would be very odd to deny that Smith's body at *t* is *in any sense* a human person at *t*. Let us say that *x* is a secondary bearer of a hybrid property at *t* if and only if *x* is constitutionally related to a primary bearer of that hybrid property at *t*. So, whereas Smith is the primary bearer of the property of being a human person at *t*, Smith's body is a secondary bearer of that property at *t*. Being a secondary bearer of a hybrid property is analogous to having the property derivatively à la (D). This suggests a modification of (D) to accommodate hybrid properties. The modification requires only that we add a clause for hybrid properties. Let H range over properties that are neither alethic properties, nor identity/constitution/existence properties, nor properties that are rooted outside times at which they are had. Then

(D') x has H at t derivatively = $_{df}$ Either
    (1) H is not is a hybrid property, and there is some y such that:
        (a) it is not the case that: x has H independently of x's constitution relations to y at t, and
        (b) y has H at t independently of y's constitution-relations to x at t; or
    (2) H is a hybrid property, and there is some y such that:
        (a) y is the primary bearer of H at t, and
        (b) x and y are constitutionally related at t

Note that (D'), like (D), is perfectly general, with no special consideration of the case of human persons. (1) just repeats the original (D) and thus presupposes the definition (I) of 'x's having a property independently of constitution relations to y'; (2) extends (D) to cover hybrid properties. As we have seen, Smith is the primary bearer of the hybrid property *being a human person*; but, according to (2), Smith does not have that hybrid property derivatively. Therefore, Smith has it nonderivatively. Now with this enlarged definition (D') of 'x's having a property derivatively,' we can say that Smith is nonderivatively a human person and that Smith's body is derivatively a human person. The account of human persons given here is an account of things that have the hybrid property *being a human person* nonderivatively.

MENTAL PROPERTIES

A discussion of the properties of persons and bodies would be incomplete without considering mental properties. The idea of having properties derivatively also applies to mental properties. For example, many of the pains that I have are such that dogs and other mammals could have pains of the same types. If my pain is of a type that a dog could have, then it is one that I have derivatively: If a dog could have it, then a human organism that did not constitute anything could have it. In that case, my body has the pain (of that type) nonderivatively. Since my being in (that kind of) pain is not independent of my constitution relations to my body, I have that kind of pain derivatively. (I)(b)(2)(ii) is not satisfied, for 'S has a pain (of a kind that a dog could have) independently of S's constitution relations to her body at t' since S's being in pain at t does entail that x is constituted by something that could have been in pain at t without constituting anything at t. Thus, I am committed to a nonCartesian construal of pain. Dogs feel pain, and if I have the same kind of pain that a dog could have, then my pain could be had by an organism with no first-person perspective; in that case, my body (a human animal) could have had that pain without constituting a person, and I have the pain derivatively. This does not imply that the organism that constitutes me has one pain and I have another. Rather, it implies that the person's having the pain does depend on its being constituted by an animal.

On the other hand, the property of hoping that I will not be in pain on my birthday is one that I have nonderivatively. For I have that property independently of my constitution relations to my body since my having it does not entail that I am constituted by something that could have had it without constituting anything. Indeed, since I am constituted by my body, and since only something with a first-person perspective could have that hope, my body could not have that property without constituting a person, according to the Constitution View. Therefore, some of my mental states (e.g., being in pain of certain kinds) I have derivatively; other of my mental states (e.g., hoping that I will not be in pain on my birthday) I have nonderivatively.

Someone may object as follows: "On the Constitution View, you have a brain, and the animal that constitutes you has the same brain. If your having the thought 'I hope that I will not be in pain on my birthday' on a particular occasion is simply a matter of your brain's being in a certain state, then the brain of the animal that constitutes you must be in that same state (since it is the same brain), and hence that animal, too, is having that thought. In that case, if you are distinct from the constituting animal, there must be two simultaneous thoughts. But that's implausible." Of course, I agree that duplication of mental states is implausible. But no such duplication follows from the Constitution View. I have the thought nonderivatively; the animal that constitutes me has it derivatively – solely in virtue of constituting something that has the thought nonderivatively. The definitions make it perfectly clear what it means to say that there is a single thought that I have nonderivatively and that the animal that constitutes me has derivatively.[9]

9   I shall develop this point further in Chapter 8.

Moreover, it is never the case that my thinking "I hope that I will not be in pain on my birthday" is *simply* a matter of my brain's being in a certain state. Even if (contrary to what I have argued elsewhere) particular mental states are always "realized in" particular brain states, being in a particular brain state (a state in the taxonomy of a neurological theory) never suffices by itself to be the realization of such a thought. For in order for a particular brain state to be the realization of a particular thought, certain requirements other than simply being in that brain state must be satisfied. For example, in order for an instance of a brain state B (a state in the taxonomy of a neurological theory) to be a realization of my thought that I hope I will not be in pain on my birthday, I must have the concepts of *pain* and *birthday* in addition to having a first-person perspective. And nothing about B by itself could possibly ensure that I have those concepts.[10] So, a person's brain's being in a particular brain state (where brain states are individuated by neurological theory) never by itself guarantees that the person is having the thought "I hope that I will not be in pain on my birthday."

Suppose that the objector persists: "All the thoughts that express your first-person perspective are also realized in your brain, the brain that you share with the animal that constitutes you. Therefore, the animal that constitutes you also has (albeit derivatively) all those first-person-perspective thoughts. In that case, it is simply arbitrary to deny that that animal is a person too. So, either you have to give up the idea that thoughts are realized in brain states, or you have to give up the idea that you are constituted by an animal with which you are not identical."[11]

This is a false dilemma. For any of my mental states that require a first-person perspective, I have them nonderivatively and the animal that constitutes me has them derivatively. For any of my mental states that do not require a first-person perspective, I have them derivatively and the animal that constitutes me has them nonderivatively. But this does not amount to duplication because to have a property derivatively is nothing other than to be constitutionally related to something that has

10 I derive this point from Kripke's discussion of Wittgenstein with respect to having the concept of addition. See Saul A. Kripke, *Wittgenstein on Rules and Private Language* (Cambridge, MA: Harvard University Press, 1982).

11 This is Eric T. Olson's line of argument in *The Human Animal: Personal Identity Without Psychology* (New York: Oxford University Press, 1997): 98–102. For a critique of Olson's whole approach, see my "What Am I?" *Philosophy and Phenomenological Research* 141 (1999): 151–9.

it nonderivatively (as we shall see in greater detail in Chapter 7). The situation is clear, I think, with respect to mental states. But there is one more wrinkle that I want to work out.

Although I have argued at length against the view that instances of mental states are "realized in" or "constituted by" instances of particular brain states, such realization is not ruled out by the Constitution View of persons. Suppose (contrary to what I really believe) that my thinking at t "I hope that I will not be in pain on my birthday" is realized by an instance of neurological property N. Then the animal that constitutes me nonderivatively has N at t, and I derivatively have N. The property of being in neural state N is always one that I have derivatively (if I have it at all), even if my being in neural state N at t realizes my nonderivative thought "I hope that I will not be in pain on my birthday." This is so because an organism that did not constitute a person presumably could be in neural state N (induced by, say, electronic stimulation). But if the organism (or even a brain in a vat) did not constitute a person, then its being in neural state N would not realize the thought "I hope that I will not be in pain on my birthday." Since the organism that does in fact constitute me could be in neural state N without constituting anything, being in neural state N is one state that my body has nonderivatively.

In general: Any mental property of mine whose exemplification requires a first-person perspective is one that I have nonderivatively, if I have it at all. Any mental property of mine that dogs or chimpanzees (organisms that do not constitute persons) could have is one that I have derivatively. Some mental states of which I am conscious (those that require a first-person perspective) I have nonderivatively; other states of which I am no less conscious (those, like feeling hunger, do not require a first-person perspective) I have derivatively. For any neural property that I have, either I have it derivatively or it is a hybrid property that can be had only by a person constituted by an organism.

This account of mental properties indicates the sense in which the person has control over the animal that constitutes him. The thoughts that a person has nonderivatively can be judgments about the mental properties that a person has derivatively. For example, a person may derivatively have the property of being aware of food in the vicinity, and may nonderivatively have the property of wanting not to be enticed into eating by his awareness of there being food in the vicinity. (An animal that constitutes nothing can be aware that there is food in the vicinity, but only a being with a first-person perspective could have the property of wanting not to be enticed into eating by his awareness of there being food in the vicinity.) An animal may be motivated by the awareness of food in the vicinity to go over there and eat something, but the first-person perspective opens up a new source of motivation. From his first-person perspective, a person can think about his awareness of food in the vicinity and decide whether or not to resist letting that thought motivate him to go over there and eat.

THESES ABOUT HUMAN PERSONS

Let me try to make clearer what I take a human person to be by setting out some theses about human persons, to the necessity of which the Constitution View is committed. As we have seen, on the Constitution View,

(T1) For any object x and time t, x is (nonderivatively) a person if and only if x (nonderivatively) has a first-person perspective or the capacity for one in the sense specified.

Also, as we have seen, something is a human person nonderivatively at t if and only if it is a person constituted by a human animal at t.

(T2) For any object x and time t, x is (nonderivatively) a human person at t if and only if: (1) x is (nonderivatively) a person, and (2) there is some y such that y is (nonderivatively) a human organism (i.e., a member of the species *Homo sapiens*) and y constitutes x at t.

Next, on the Constitution View, persons are essentially psychological/moral entities; human bodies are essentially biological entities. The modality here is *de re*: If x is a person, then x could not exist without having psychological/moral properties. I have argued elsewhere that a statue could not exist without being a statue.[12] Similarly for persons and bodies: Smith's body could exist without constituting a person, but Smith could no more exist without being a person than *Discobolus* could exist without being a statue. When a person comes into being, a new thing – and not just a new exemplification of a property by a previously existing thing – comes into existence. The addition of a person increases

---

12 Lynne Rudder Baker "Why Constitution Is Not Identity," *Journal of Philosophy* 94 (1997): 599–621.

the stock of things that exist, and the subtraction of a person diminishes the stock of things that exist. Nothing can cease to be a person without ceasing to exist. This claim falls out of the Constitution View: Things have their primary-kind properties essentially, and a person's primary-kind property is the property of being a person. So, on the Constitution View, a person is essentially a person.

(T3) For any object x and time t, if x is (nonderivatively) a person, then it is necessary that: if x exists at t, x is a person at t.

Being a human animal is also a primary-kind property. So, if something is a human animal (nonderivatively), then it could not cease to be a human animal without ceasing to exist.

(T4) For any object x and time t, if x is (nonderivatively) a human animal, then it is necessary that: if x exists at t, then x is a human animal at t.

Although a person is essentially a person, a human person is not essentially a human person. What makes human persons *human* is that they are constituted by biologically human bodies, where a biologically human body is an animal, an organism. Although a human organism could not become a nonbiological being and still continue to exist, a human person (originally constituted by a human organism) could come to be constituted by a nonbiological body and still continue to exist. For it may be possible for a human person to undergo gradual replacement of her human body by bionic parts in a way that did not extinguish her first-person perspective; if so, then she would continue to exist, but she would cease to have a human body. And she would continue to exist (and to be a person) as long as her first-person perspective remained intact, whether she continued to be constituted by a human body or not. If she came to be constituted by a nonorganic body, then she would no longer be a *human* person. So, a human person is not essentially a human person.

(T5) For any object x and time t, if x is (nonderivatively) a human person at t, then it is possible that: there is a time t' such that $t' \neq t$ and x exists at t' and x is not a human person at t'.

On the other hand, if x is a human person at the beginning of x's existence, then x is essentially embodied – even if what constitutes her at some later time is not a human animal. To say that she could exist without having an organic body is not to say that she could exist without having any body at all. We have seen that the human organism that constitutes a person at t is itself a human person at t (derivatively); however, the human organism was not a human person (even derivatively) at the beginning of its existence. A human person that is a human person at the beginning of his existence (e.g., Smith as opposed to Smith's body) may continue to exist without being a *human* person, but he could not continue to exist without having a body at all. Although it is possible that he could exist without being constituted by a human body, it is not possible that he could exist without being constituted by some body or other.

(T6) For any object x and time t, if x is (nonderivatively) a human person at the beginning of her existence, then it is necessary that: if x exists at t, there is some y such that y is a body and y constitutes x at t.

What distinguishes two human persons that exist at the same time is that they are constituted by different bodies. This solves one of two very different problems that might be called a 'problem of individuation.' One problem is to say in virtue of what there are two coexisting things of the same kind; the other problem is to say in virtue of what there is a single individual of a given kind over a period of time.[13] I propose to solve the former problem with respect to human persons by saying that there are two coexisting human persons only if there are two coexisting human animals.[14] A human person's body at a given time distinguishes

13 According to Peter Geach, Aquinas distinguished between these two issues. As Geach comments about Aquinas: "Difference of matter is what makes the difference between two coexisting individuals of the same kind, e.g., two pennies." And, as Geach continues, "But identity over a period does not depend on identity of matter." With respect to human persons, I agree on both counts: individuation at a time depends on matter (or, as I prefer, on the body); identity over time does not depend on identity, or even on continuity, of matter. G. E. M. Anscombe and P. T. Geach, *Three Philosophers* (Ithaca, NY: Cornell University Press, 1961): xi.

14 Conjoined twins are two persons who can share organs and limbs. So, 'two animals' does not entail 'two separate animals' or even 'two separable animals.' Rather, there are two animals if there are two centers of control of biological functions. Suppose that conjoined

her from all other persons at that time. (I shall consider the latter problem – the problem of personal identity over time – in Chapter 5.)

On the one hand, a single body cannot constitute two persons at the same time. A single personality may be radically disordered, as in *The Three Faces of Eve* or *Dr. Jekyll and Mr. Hyde*. Or a commissurotomy patient may be manipulated in an experimental situation into trying to put on his pants with one hand and trying to take them off with the other at the same time. But this is evidence not of two first-person perspectives, but rather of one that has been disrupted. Indeed, most of the time a commissurotomy patient behaves normally. If it were possible for a single body to constitute two persons at once, there would be two first-person perspectives on a single body, and there would be monumental incoherence, not just the experimentally induced incoherence of the commissurotomy patient.

If there were any time at which you could share your body with another person, then both of you would have a first-person relation to your body at that time. Part of what it means to say that you have a first-person relation to a body is that that body expresses your intentional states: We can see the coach's frustration in the way he walks down the sideline; we can see the sprinter's effort in the grimace on his face and the strain of his muscles. The athlete's body itself reveals that the athlete is making an enormous physical effort. If S_1 and S_2 are two human persons, then it must be physically possible that S_1 is making an enormous physical effort at a certain time and S_2 is totally relaxed at that time. But if S_1 and S_2 shared a body at time, t, then it would not be physically possible for S_1 to be making an enormous physical effort at t and for S_2 to be totally relaxed at that time. For it is not physically possible for a single body to express both enormous physical effort and total relaxation at the same time. Therefore, there is no time at which S_1 and S_2 share a single body. So, a person's body at a time distinguishes her from all other persons at that time.

On the other hand, a person cannot be constituted by two bodies at the same time. Suppose that Smith were constituted by two bodies, Body A and Body B, at the same time. Then it would be physically possible that Body A operated a car that ran over Body B, and that Body B died while Body A was uninjured, in which case it would be physi-

---

twins are surgically separated, and that of one of the resulting persons is given artificial organs and prosthetic limbs In such a case, it seems natural to me to say that that person is constituted by a different body from before the operation.

cally possible that Smith was both dead and alive. Since it is impossible for one person to be both dead and alive, a person cannot be constituted by two bodies at one time. For each human person at a time, there is one human body at that time; and for each person-constituting human body at a time, there is one human person at that time. So, if body y constitutes a human person x at t, then there is no other human person that y constitutes at t and there is no other body that constitutes x at t.

(T7) For any objects x and y, and time t, if x is (nonderivatively) a human person at t and y constitutes x at t, then:

  (i) $\sim\exists z(z \neq x \ \& \ z$ is (nonderivatively) a human person at $t \ \& \ y$ constitutes z at t); and

  (ii) $\sim\exists w(w \neq y \ \& \ w$ is (nonderivately) a body $\& \ w$ constitutes x at t).

Although I cannot have two bodies at once, my human body may go out of existence and be replaced by, say, a bionic body; since it is possible that I continue to exist with a bionic body, I am not identical to my body. This is so because as we saw in chapter 2, identity is necessary, as Kripke and others contend. That is, if $a = b$ is true, then it is necessarily true: There is no possible world in which a exists and b fails to exist. But it is possible for me to exist and for this body (that constitutes me now) to fail to exist; and, conversely, it is possible for this body to exist (as a corpse, say) and for me to fail to exist.[15] So, as we already know from the definition (C), I am not identical to this body.

(T8) For any objects, x and y, and time t, if x is a human person at t and y is a human animal and y constitutes x at t, then $x \neq y$.[16]

    A person has causal powers that a body would not have if it did not constitute a person. For example, consider the properties of using a passport, enjoying a close friendship, taking a vacation with the children, voting in local elections, and being responsible for a prisoner. These

---

15 The nonidentity of persons and organisms does not imply nonidentity of organisms and bodies of organisms. Something is a tiger just in case it is a body of a certain sort (identifiable as a member of the species *Felis tigris*); and something is a human being just in case it is a body of a certain sort (identifiable as a member of the species *Homo sapiens*). Again, *person* is not a biological concept.

16 Note that in (T8) we do not need the qualification 'nonderivatively' because the clause 'and y constitutes x at t' in the antecedent rules out both x's being a human person derivatively and y's being a human organism derivatively.

properties are clearly causal: One can do things in virtue of have these properties that one could not otherwise have done. And using a passport, enjoying a close friendship, taking a vacation, with the children, voting in local elections, and being responsible for a prisoner are, in the first instance, properties of persons — not properties of bodies. A body that did not constitute a person could have none of these properties. (This is not to deny that other of a person's causal properties — e.g., being able to reach the top shelf — derive from the body that constitutes her.) So,

(T9) For any objects x and y, and time t, if x is (nonderivatively) a human person at t and y constitutes x at t, then x has causal properties at t that y would not have had at t if y had not constituted anything at t.

Both persons and statues are particulars constituted by material objects, but each is the thing that it is (a person, a statue) in virtue of its intentionally specified properties (first-person intentional states, relation to an artworld). Smith is no more a composite of two kinds of entities than was Myron's *Discobolus*. Nevertheless, the analogy between persons and statues can go only so far. The constitution relation between persons and bodies has an "inner" aspect — what I earlier called a 'first-person relation' between persons and their bodies. The first-person relation between a person and her body is "from the inside" what constitution is "from the outside" or from a third-person point of view. Human persons have first-person relations to the bodies that constitute them:

(T10) For any objects, x and y, and time t, if x is (nonderivatively) a human person at t and y constitutes x at t, then it is necessary that: y is (nonderivatively) a body and x has a first-person relation to y at t.

This completes exposition of the conditions under which something is a human person at a given time, according to the Constitution View. Although (T1) − (T10) comprise a theory of what it is to be a human person at a time (nonderivatively), there remain many questions for the Constitution View to answer about the relation between persons and bodies.

MY BODY/MYSELF

Before embarking on further consideration of the relation between persons and bodies on the Constitution View, however, I want to discuss

110

the term 'body' and to defend my use of it. Peter van Inwagen has argued that when philosophers use the term 'human body,' typically they are talking or writing nonsense.[17] Among his samples of "nonsense" are these: 'A person is [is not] identical with his body,' 'A person might have [could not have] different bodies at different stages of his career,' and 'I might [could not] have had a different body from the one I have.' Since I am committed to denying the first and affirming the other two, I want to show that such sentences can be used to say something philosophical.

Van Inwagen asks for a definition of 'body' and proposes a test of adequacy for any such definition: The definition must be nontendentious, that is, it "should not render any of the sentences containing the word 'body' that any of these philosophers uses to state his theory a trivial, verbal falsehood."[18] (For example, to define 'body' as 'what is animated by a soul' would be tendentious.) And we must not define 'body' in such a way that any of the philosophers who believe that the sentence 'There are bodies' expresses a truth would be expected to respond to the definition by saying, "If *that's* what the word means, then there are no 'bodies.' " Although van Inwagen asks for a definition that has as its definiendum 'body,' and although his title implies that his concern is with 'human body,' he immediately shifts to efforts to define '*x*'s body' or 'my body.' He justifies this shift as follows:

For if there is such a concept as the concept of a human body, then simple inspection of philosophers' use of body shows that it is part and parcel of understanding this concept to understand what it is for a given body to be the body *of* a given human being.[19]

Even if we agree with van Inwagen that we ultimately must give an account of '*x*'s body,' we should not try to define '*x*'s body' right off the bat.[20] We will never get anywhere if, for example, we follow Eric

---

17   Peter van Inwagen, "Philosophers and the Words 'Human Body'," in *Time and Cause*, Peter van Inwagen, ed. (Dordrecht, the Netherlands: D. Reidel Publishing Company, 1980): 283–99.

18   Van Inwagen, "Philosophers and the Words 'Human Body'," p. 286.

19   Van Inwagen, "Philosophers and the Words 'Human Body'," p. 287. Philosophers use the term 'human being' in a variety of ways. Given my later definitions, "the body *of* a given human being" is just a human body (nonderivatively), an organism – something identical to an organism. Whatever other philosophers have said, I do not distinguish between an organism and its body.

20   If I were challenged to define '*x*'s body' right off the bat, I'd offer this: '*x*'s body' $=_{df}$ 'that material thing that would occupy the place where *x* is now and would weigh *n*

Olson's suggestion that perhaps "something is a human body only by virtue of being someone's body – by being related in a certain way to some person. . . ."[21] As I see things, and as I use the term 'body,' this is backward. For it precludes there being human bodies independently of there being persons. And that is indeed a heavy philosophical commitment that is certainly not shared by philosophers (such as Descartes) who use the term 'body.' So, to suppose that 'human body' is like 'uncle' in that "to be an uncle is to be *someone's* uncle" fails van Inwagen's test of adequacy. Any definition based on that supposition would be highly tendentious. Let me propose some definitions that I take to be untendentious:

> 'body' = spatially extended, solid entity, all of whose parts are contiguous
> 'human body' = organism; member of the species *Homo sapiens* (living or dead)
> 'x's body' = body some of whose parts x can normally move without moving anything else, simply by intending for them to move

I take an organism to be a kind of body, a body that is or has been self-directing: A living organism is a currently self-directing body, and a dead organism is a formerly self-directing body. I do not distinguish an organism from its body.[22] So, a human body – an organism, a biological entity – is one kind of body. Human bodies are defined biologically and can be identified without consideration of any relations that they may bear to persons. Archeologists identify things as human bodies all the time. Although almost all human bodies at some time constitute persons, that fact is irrelevant to the identification of something as a human body.

On these definitions, and on the Constitution View, "I am a body," when asserted by me, is true – as are "I am a human body," "I am an animal," and "I am less than six feet tall." All of these sentences employ the 'is' of constitution. I have the property of, for example, being an animal or being less than six feet tall in virtue of being constituted by something that has these properties. As I have said, I borrow these

---

pounds if x had a stroke and died right now.' Cf. Michael Tye, "In Defense of the Words 'Human Body,'" *Philosophical Studies* 38 (1980): 177–82.

21 Olson, *The Human Animal*, p. 144.

22 Olson says of "philosophical commonplaces" advanced by Wiggins that each "seems to entail that 'my body' is the name of an object that is different both from me and from the human animal associated with me" (*The Human Animal*, p. 150). This is not my view. Although I do take my body to be nonidentical to me, I take my body (the body that is mine now) to be identical to a particular human organism.

properties from the thing that constitutes me and hence have them derivatively.

I make only three claims for my definitions. First, they are tolerably clear. Second, they satisfy van Inwagen's test of adequacy. Third, they define terms needed for the statement of the Constitution View; 'body' is not replaceable by some less philosophical term like 'animal.'

First, the clarity of the definitions is open to inspection. Second, these definitions are, I submit, untendentious. Neither a materialist nor a Cartesian dualist need demur: Each could use these definitions to state his own theory. Even a Berkeleyan idealist could accept these definitions and refine them further: "If 'spatially extended entities' are understood as existing unperceived, then there are no bodies; but if we construe 'spatially extended entities' in terms of perceptions, then, of course, there are bodies." On these definitions, a living human body is (identical to) the organism that van Inwagen would identify as me. (I'm unsure that van Inwagen would endorse this way of putting his view.)

Third, these definitions define terms that the Constitution View needs. The Constitutionalist has an answer to Olson's rhetorical question: "We have me, the person; and we have the animal (whether or not they are the same). That much everyone can agree on. Why suppose that there is something called 'my body' as well?"[23] I need the term 'body' or 'my body' in addition to 'person' and 'animal' for this reason: Although the body that is mine now is a human organism, the Constitution View allows that an inorganic body could replace the animal that constitutes me now and I could persist through the change. After the replacement, 'my body' would denote the nonhuman body. 'My body now' denotes an animal; 'my body then' denotes something inorganic. ('My body', used attributively, is semantically like 'my lottery number'; it can denote different things at different times when uttered by me.) Since, on the Constitution View, a person can be constituted by a human body at one time and by an inorganic body at another time, the Constitution View needs the more general term 'body' in addition to the terms 'person' and 'animal.'

Finally, I turn to questions that arise about persons and bodies. First is a question concerning the referent of 'I.' Does 'I' refer to a person or a body, or is 'I' ambiguous? The Constitution View has a clear answer: When used comprehendingly and literally by a person, 'I' is not ambiguous. In its standard, literal use, 'I' always refers to the person using or

---

23 Olson, *The Human Animal*, p. 150.

113

thinking it. And having a first-person perspective, I am never wrong about who I mean to refer to when I comprehendingly use 'I.' My use of 'I' refers to me, the person constituted (at this time) by this body. If I say, "I am a fast runner," I am attributing to myself the property of being a fast runner. But the property of being a fast runner is a property that I have in virtue of my body: To say that I am a fast runner is to say that I am constituted by a body that can run fast. We have seen this point before: Some of my properties I have in virtue of being constituted by this body: I have those properties derivatively. If I say, "I wish that I* took up less space," then I refer to myself, the person. Granted, taking up so much space is a property that I (the person) have in virtue of being constituted by a certain body. I (the person) borrow the property from my body, but I (the person) have it nonetheless. However, to have a property derivatively is still to have it.

In sum, there are two points about the referent of 'I': (i) 'I' is a personal pronoun, and as the term 'personal pronoun' suggests, 'I' in its literal and standard use always refers to the person using it. (This would be so, I believe, even if the Constitution View were false.) (ii) Nevertheless, 'I' is often used to attribute bodily properties to oneself. I have the property of being left-handed, of still having my appendix, and of weighing n kg, all derivatively – in virtue of my constitution relations to my body. Hence, the bearer of such physical and biological properties is, nonderivatively, my body. When I attribute to myself properties that my body has nonderivatively, I am thinking of *myself-as-my-body*. On the other hand, for other of my properties, my body has them derivatively. For example, I have the property of being employed or the property of having answered a question nonderivatively. My having these properties is independent of my being constituted by the body that I have. If one said, stiltedly, "My body has the property of being employed," one would say something that would be true in virtue of the fact that one's body constitutes someone who is employed nonderivatively. When I attribute to my body properties that I have nonderivatively, I am thinking of *my-body-as-myself*.

So, it is not as if there were two separate things – my body and myself. There is a single constituted thing – me – some of whose properties depend on my being constituted by the body that I have and other of whose properties do not depend on my constitution relations to my body. Sometimes I think of myself-as-my-body (as when I say that I am a fast runner), and sometimes I think of my-body-as-myself (as when I say that my body is entitled to be located in a particular seat).[24]

There are other matters about the relation between persons and bodies on which the Constitution View weighs in. If, as the Constitution View contends, a person is essentially a psychological entity, and if a human body is essentially a biological entity that may lack psychological properties, then my body and I could have begun to exist at different times. And, indeed, I think that that is the case. My body (the human organism that constitutes me now) began to exist a couple of weeks after conception – after there was no further possibility of the fertilized egg's dividing into identical twins. But that body had no psychological properties; it lacked the relevant neural structures. Hence, that body did not constitute me. I had not yet come into being. On *any* psychological account of a person, a fetus that lacks psychological properties is not a person. On the other hand, a fetus that lacks psychological properties *is* a human organism. A natural conclusion – one that I draw – is that an early-term fetus is a stage of an organism that may or may not come to constitute a human person.

I can speak of 'my body before I existed' in the same way that I can speak of 'my husband before I met him.' So, I can say of a certain fetus that it was my body in the sense that the body that now constitutes me was at one time a fetus; but if it had miscarried or been aborted, it would not have been my body. (I can say of a certain boy that he is my husband, but if he had not married me, he would not have been my husband.) In order for a body to be *my* body, there must be *me* for it to constitute. In the absence of a person – something with capacity for a first-person perspective – the organism that is in fact y's body would not be y's body. However, this does not mean that I must deny that I was ever a fetus. As we have seen, just as there is an 'is' of predication and an 'is' of identity, there is an 'is' of constitution. So, on the Constitution View, it is true to say "I was a fetus."[25] To say "I was a fetus" is to say

---

24 Incidentally, this distinction between primary and secondary bearers of properties is a partial elucidation of Wittgenstein's distinction between the use of 'I' as subject and the use of 'I' as object. In all cases of the use of 'I' as subject, the person is the primary bearer of the property ascribed. The elucidation is only partial because a person could also be the primary bearer of properties whose self-attribution would not be by means of use of 'I' as subject (e.g., I am employed). Wittgenstein, of course, would not put it this way.

25 Similarly, it is true to say "I am an animal." To say "I am an animal" is to say "There is some x such that x is an animal and x constitutes me."

115

"There is some x, and times t and now, such that x was a fetus at t and x constitutes me now." By contrast, to say "My body was a fetus" is to say "There is some x and times t and now, such that x was a fetus at t and x is identical to my body." There is a human organism that at one stage in its career was a fetus, and at another stage in its career was an adult human being, and that organism now constitutes me.[26]

Not only does the human body begin (as an embryo) before it constitutes a person, but also a human body may continue to exist after it has ceased to constitute a person. Irretrievable loss of first-person perspective would be extinction of the person even if the body's metabolic functions continued. Moreover, a human body can cease to function without ceasing to exist. A human body that has stopped functioning is a dead human being, a corpse. To say that a person will become a corpse is to say that the person's body will cease to constitute the person. Similarly, to say that a fetus will become a person is to say that the organism that is now a fetus will come to constitute a person.

Indeed, we can imagine a case (like Karen Ann Quinlan's) in which the human body would continue to exist *as a living human animal* (not just as a corpse) despite loss of first-person perspective if it retained certain of its bodily functions. Suppose that an adult who suffered severe brain damage in an accident survived for a time in a deep coma without being hooked up to life-support machines, but that the brain damage was so severe that there was no physical way for her brain to support first-person reference again. In that case, the human animal (and, of course, the body) would continue to exist, but that body would no longer constitute a person. The view put forth here about the essential role of the first-person perspective accords with (what I take to be) widespread intuitions about human persons and human animals.

CONCLUSION

Human persons are animals but not *just* animals. This is so even if the property in virtue of which entities are persons – having a capacity for a first-person perspective – is a product of natural selection. Animals are essentially biological; they are essentially regulated by DNA. Persons are essentially psychological/moral; they essentially have the capacity for first-person perspectives. This is so whether the first-person perspectives are regulated by DNA or by silicon chips or by something else. Focusing

26   See Chapter 8 for further discussion of this and related points.

on things that are nonderivatively persons and things that are nonderivatively animals, the Constitution View holds this: Persons, human or not, are of a different kind from animals. Yet, because human persons are constituted by animals, they can have biological, as well as psychological/moral, natures. The Constitution View of persons and bodies shows in detail how all this can be true.

5

Personal Identity over Time

There are two central questions about what it is to be a person. One is synchronic: In virtue of what is something a person at a given time? The other is diachronic: In virtue of what is there a single person at two different times? To put the diachronic question another way: Assuming that a person S is considered at time *t* and a person S' is considered at time *t'*, in virtue of what is person S identical to person S'?[1] So far, I have sheared off the question of what it is for *x* to be a person from the related, and much discussed, question of what it is for *x* and *y* to be the same person considered at two times. My answer to the synchronic question was that to be a person is to have a first-person perspective, where I gave an account of what a first-person perspective is; and to be a human person (nonderivatively) is to be a person constituted by a human organism.[2]

Turn now to the diachronic question, the question of personal identity over time: In virtue of what is a person P_1, at t_1, the same person as person P_2, at t_2?[3] All the candidate answers that I know to the question about identity of persons over time (including my own answer) are

---

1 Olson suggests that this question improperly assumes that anything with which something that is a person at one time is identical is also a person. Since I have already answered the syncrhonic question, and since it is a tenet of the Constitution View that anything that is nonderivatively a person is essentially a person, a proponent of the Constitution View begs no questions by this standard question about personal identity over time. Eric T. Olson, *The Human Animal: Personal Identity Without Psychology* (Oxford: Oxford University Press, 1997): Ch. 2.

2 From now on, read 'is an F' as 'is an F nonderivatively' unless otherwise noted.

3 For stylistic reasons, I am saying 'person P_1 at t_1' and 'person P_2 at t_2' instead of 'person P_1, *considered* at t_1,' and 'person P_2, *considered* at t_2.' I do not mean to suggest anything about "person stages" or temporal parts.

either clearly false or not very illuminating. I want now to canvas various answers, and show where they fall down, and then offer my own answer – in the not-very-illuminating category. (Alternatively, I am happy to say that personal identity over time is not analyzable in terms of anything else; it is primitive.[4]) The difficulty – which I believe is insurmountable – is to give informative sufficient conditions for sameness of person over time without presupposing sameness of person. That is, I believe that a reductive account of personal identity is bound to fail. But, unlike others (e.g., Harold Noonan), I also believe that a nonreductive approach can be materialistic.[5]

OTHER VIEWS OF PERSONAL IDENTITY OVER TIME

I shall call the various proposals in answer to the question of personal identity over time 'criteria,' where a criterion need not be something by which we can *recognize* someone as the same person as someone considered at a different time, but must be the condition in virtue of which someone *is* (identical to) the same person as someone at another time. That is, I'm using 'criterion' in a metaphysical, not an epistemological, sense. First consider a bodily criterion of personal identity.

1. Sameness of Person Consists in Sameness of Body

Since the cells in the body die and are replaced continuously, sameness of body does not preclude change of the cells that make up the body. It requires only bodily continuity of the sort exhibited by organisms. It is possible that *a* is the same body as *b* even though *a* and *b* do not even have one single cell in common.

However, bodily continuity seems neither sufficient nor necessary for personal identity. To see that bodily continuity is not sufficient, consider

---

4 Others who have held that there can be no informative criteria of diachronic personal identity include George I. Mavrodes, "The Life Everlasting and the Bodily Criterion of Identity," *Noûs* (1977): 27–39; Baruch Brody, *Identity and Essence* (Princeton, NJ: Princeton University Press, 1980): 49–59; P. T. Mackenzie, "Personal Identity and the Imagination," *Philosophy* 58 (1983): 161–74; E. J. Lowe, *Kinds of Being* (Oxford: Basil Blackwell, 1989): 121–37; David S. Oderberg, *The Metaphysics of Identity Over Time* (New York: St. Martin's Press, 1993); and Trenton Merricks, "Fission and Personal Identity Over Time," *Philosophical Studies* 88 (1997): 163–86. I owe these references to Dean Zimmerman, "Immanent Causation," in *Philosophical Perspectives 11, Mind, Causation and Action*, James E. Tomberlin, ed. (Malden, MA: Blackwell Publishers, 1997): 468, n. 41.
5 Harold Noonan, *Personal Identity* (London: Routledge, 1989).

this: If I leave a corpse when I die, then my body remains, though I am no longer here. If sameness of person consisted in sameness of body, then my corpse would just be me – existing in an undesirable state. But this seems implausible: My dead body would not be (nor would it constitute) me.[6] I may have wishes about my corpse (that it be disposed of in such-and-such way), but I certainly do not care about it in the way that I care about myself. That is because it would not be me. I (this person) would no longer be around.

Judith Jarvis Thomson has said that a person who dies in bed becomes a dead person, just as a cat that dies in bed becomes a dead cat.[7] Her evidence is the linguistic propriety of saying things like "There's a dead person in the house." I think both that the linguistic evidence is mixed (we don't speak consistently about the dead) and that the linguistic evidence, such as it is, betrays the unclarity of our ideas about life and death. We can felicitously say, "There are dead poets" without meaning that there is some x such that x is dead and x writes poetry. Likewise, we can felicitously say, "There's a dead person in the house" without meaning that there is some x such that x is dead and x is in the house and x is a person. On my view, Thomson's analogy between dead people and dead cats is misplaced. Yes, there are dead cats, just as there are dead human beings. What we call 'a dead person' is a dead organism, an organism that no longer functions, and hence that no longer constitutes a person.

2. Sameness of Person Consists of Sameness of Living Organism (Animalism)

A variation on the sameness-of-body criterion would avoid a commitment to saying that my corpse is I. According to the variation, sameness of person consists in sameness of living organism.[8] On this Animalist variation of the sameness-of-body criterion, my corpse, no longer a

---

6 Not everyone agrees. For a discussion by someone who disagrees, see Fred Feldman, *Confrontations with the Reaper: A Philosophical Study of the Nature and Value of Death* (Oxford: Oxford University Press, 1992): Ch. 6.

7 Judith Jarvis Thomson, "People and Their Bodies," in *Reading Parfit*, Jonathan Dancy, ed. (Oxford: Basil Blackwell, 1997): 202.

8 I take this to be what Eric Olson calls the 'Biological Approach,' which he is at pains to distinguish from the Bodily Criterion. Since I (unlike Wiggins, say) take a living human organism to be a special kind of body, not to be constituted by a body, from my point of view, the Biological Approach (or Animalism) is just a version of the Bodily Criterion.

living organism, would not be I.[9] But sameness of living organism seems no more necessary or sufficient for sameness of person than does sameness of body.

Sameness of living human organism is not sufficient for sameness of person. Unless one supposes that a living human organism is ipso facto a person, something could be a living organism, a member of the species *Homo sapiens*, and not be a person at all. The concern here is with personal identity, and there is no personal identity without a person. Suppose that a human organism that goes into a persistent vegetative state caused by the death of cerebral neurons has no hope of recovery. Although it is still a living organism, it is incapable of suffering or of any awareness whatever, and never will be.[10] It is a being that does not, and never will be able to, care about itself or about anything else. If such a (diminished) being is a person, then to be a person simply *is* to be a living human organism. In that case, it is difficult to see why being a person should have any special moral status; for considered as purely biological beings, human organisms have no greater claim to respect than any other kinds of organisms. To hold that to be a person simply is to be a living human organism is to stipulate a meaning of 'person' that has no connection with the historical or contemporary use of the term. Since it seems untenable to hold that a human organism in an irreversible vegetative state is a person at all, sameness of living human organism is not sufficient for sameness of person.[11]

An Animalist variation on the criterion of sameness of living human organism is to hold that sameness of person consists in sameness of living human organism *with a properly functioning brain*. This latter criterion may well be sufficient for sameness of person over time if it turns out that being a living human organism with a properly functioning brain is a sufficient condition for having person-making properties, whatever they

9 The view that we are essentially animals is endorsed by P. F. Snowden in "Persons, Animals, and Ourselves" in *The Person and the Human Mind*, Christopher Gill, ed. (Oxford: Clarendon Press, 1990): 83–107; in Olson, *The Human Animal*; and Peter van Inwagen, *Material Beings* (Ithaca, NY: Cornell University Press, 1990).

10 Ronald E. Cranford, "The Persistent Vegetative State: The Medical Reality (Getting the Facts Straight)," *Hastings Center Report* 18 (1) (1988): 27–32 (cited by Olson, *The Human Animal*, p. 169, n. 2).

11 There is some disagreement about the conditions under which a human organism is no longer living. I am assuming here, along with Eric Olson, that an organism is living as long as its brain can regulate biological functions like metabolism. My point would only be strengthened by lower requirements for brain death (i.e., by a more stringent criterion of living).

are (on my view, a first-person perspective). Nevertheless, sameness of living human organism with a properly functioning brain cannot be a necessary condition of personal identity over time since people routinely survive neural malfunction, even neural malfunction (e.g., strokes) that permanently damages the brain. Suppose that an Animalist drops 'properly functioning' and takes sameness of person to consist in sameness of living organism with a whole brain intact. This would be no better. Whether sufficient or not,[12] sameness of living organism with a whole brain intact is clearly not a necessary condition for sameness of person. It is not necessary since a person may survive removal of part of the brain (see the next subsection). In any case, I believe that the criterion of sameness of human organism with whole brain intact would fail to be necessary for sameness of person for reasons to be given.

Sameness of living human animal is not necessary for sameness of person. In the first place, any version of the idea that sameness of person consists in sameness of living organism seems excessively chauvinistic, for this criterion makes no provision for the possibility of persons that are not constituted by living organisms. Taking some feature such as being (constituted by) a living organism to be necessary for personal identity would rule out the very possibility of there being persons who are not organisms. A criterion of sameness of person over time should reveal what human persons have in common with divine Persons or artificial persons. Our view of human person should allow *person* to be a genus, of which *human person* is a species. So, sameness of living organism is not necessary for personal identity.

Moreover, sameness of living organism seems to me (and to many others) quite implausible as the criterion for sameness of person. If sameness of person consists in sameness of living organism, then it is logically impossible for anyone to have a different body from the body that she in fact has. An organic body is essentially organic. That is, an organic body cannot itself become inorganic. Its parts may be replaced by inorganic parts, but it (the body that was organic) could not persist through near-total replacement of organic parts by inorganic parts. So, if sameness of living organism

12 I do not think that sameness of living organism with a whole brain intact is sufficient for sameness of person. But my argument for insufficiency would rely on my own positive view of a person as having a first-person perspective. A living organism with an intact whole brain may have a brain so disrupted that it cannot support a first-person perspective; inability to support a first-person perspective may not be enough for brain death on the various construals of "brain death." In that case, on my view, the continued existence of the living organism would not be sufficient for the continued existence of the person.

were necessary for sameness of person, then a person would be unable to persist through near-total replacement of organic parts by inorganic parts. It certainly seems metaphysically possible (and perhaps even physically possible) for Jones to have a series of operations that successively replaced enough of Jones's organs with inorganic parts so that Jones's body was no longer the organic body that she started with. But it would not follow that, after the operations, Jones herself no longer existed.

Indeed, if sameness of living organism were necessary for sameness of person, the many thought experiments about bodily transfer would be not merely empirically impossible but metaphysically impossible. Thought experiments from those of John Locke to those of the TV show *Star Trek* suggest that personal identity is independent of bodily continuity. In Locke's thought experiment, a Prince comes to inhabit a Cobbler's body, and everyone quickly recognizes the prince in the Cobbler's body. For those unconvinced by Locke, there is Kafka's vivid story in which Gregor Samsa wakes up to find himself in the body of a gigantic cockroach. (Who has read "The Metamorphosis" and not felt the horror of it?) And it is now routine in science fiction movies to have creatures that take on different shapes (shape shifters) and wholly different bodies. If sameness of person consisted in sameness of living organism, then all of these stories would be not only fictional, but incoherent; what they portray would be not only false, but necessarily false. In that case, why do the stories and thought experiments seem so plausible – so plausible as to tempt some to dualism? Anyone who takes hundreds of years of thought experiments as attempts to depict what is metaphysically impossible should show how so many have gone so badly wrong.

When Kripke said that it was impossible for heat to be anything other than molecular motion, he showed why we seem to have a strong intuition to the contrary. The intuition that we really have (and that is correct) is this: Something other than molecular motion (i.e., something other than heat) could have caused heat sensations in us. Kripke showed how we might have confused a correct intuition about heat with the necessarily false proposition that heat could have been something other than molecular motion. In this way, he diagnosed the error in the thought experiments purporting to show how it is possible that heat is not identical to molecular motion. In general, if a critic claims that a thought experiment, acceptable to many, is incoherent, then the critic owes what Kripke provided: an account of the incoherence, together with an account of our error, of how we could have made the mistake that we did. As far as I know, no such account is forthcoming from those who take personal identity to consist in bodily identity. So, I see no reason to suppose that sameness of living organism is logically necessary for personal identity.

Underlying the failure of an Animalist criterion to be necessary or sufficient for personal identity over time is a deeper reason to reject any Animalist criterion. An adequate account of personal identity over time should have something to do with what is required to be a person at all. And the pretheoretical concept of a person is the concept of something with psychological states, something that can be a rational and moral agent. It is these person-making features that should determine what counts as personal identity over time. But an Animalist criterion of personal identity over time simply leaves out these person-making features. On the Animalist view, "psychology is completely irrelevant to personal identity."[13] Since an Animalist view of personal identity over time has no truck with the properties that pretheoretically distinguish persons from nonpersons, it is difficult to see how it is even a contender as an account of *personal* identity over time.

A further motivation for rejecting sameness of living human organism as necessary for personal identity is the importance of the brain considered in the context of further thought experiments. For example, suppose that future scientists removed Brown's brain and connected it to the nerves in Robinson's body. Call the resulting person (Brown's brain in Robinson's body) 'Brownson.' Who is Brownson? Many say Brown: Where Brown's brain goes, there goes Brown.[14] This leads to a third attempt to understand personal identity in terms of a material object; sameness of brain may be thought to preserve personal identity.[15]

3. Sameness of Person Consists in Sameness of Brain

Sameness of brain also is insufficient for personal identity.[16] Indeed, sameness of brain as a criterion elicits the same response as sameness of

13 Eric T. Olson, "Was I Ever a Fetus?" *Philosophy and Phenomenological Research* 57 (1997): 97.

14 Sydney Shoemaker, *Self-Knowledge and Self-Identity* (Ithaca, NY: Cornell University Press, 1963).

15 Note that people who take sameness of brain to be the criterion of personal identity use the term 'body' in a way that distinguishes body and brain – as we just saw in the Brownson case. As should be apparent, I do not mean to exclude the brain when I use the term 'body.'

16 Versions of the view that sameness of person consists in sameness of brain may be found in Thomas Nagel, *The View from Nowhere* (New York: Oxford University Press, 1986); Peter Unger, *Identity, Consciousness and Value* (New York: Oxford University Press, 1990);

body: If my brain (the material object) is not destroyed at my death, then, on the sameness-of-brain criterion, *I* also survive my death. But surely the merely intact state of my nonfunctioning brain would not suffice for me to survive cessation of my bodily functions.

Nor is sameness of brain necessary for personal identity. As is well known, there are two hemispheres in the human brain. When people have strokes, sometimes one of the hemispheres is rendered totally inoperative. And if one of the hemispheres is incapacitated at an early enough age, the other hemisphere takes over its functions. There is no disagreement in such a case about saying that the person persists with only one hemisphere functioning. It requires only a slight nudge of the imagination to suppose that the nonfunctioning hemisphere could be removed and the person could still survive. But the surviving person, minus a hemisphere, would not have the same brain as before. Thus, sameness of brain is not required for sameness of person.

In the story just told, the person persisted but so did *part* of his brain. So, technically, all the story shows is that sameness of *whole* brain is not necessary for sameness of person. If one wanted to hold on to the sameness-of-brain criterion, one could relax the requirement for same-ness-of-brain to sameness-of-part-of-brain. But then the question would arise: How much? And what part? The answer would no doubt be in terms of function: however much of whatever part it takes to sustain memories and other psychological states. In that case, the criterion of personal identity could be stated directly in terms of psychological continuity. Thus we have a new proposal:

4. Sameness of Person Consists in Psychological Continuity

Some kind of psychological continuity is perhaps the most prevalent criterion of personal identity today.[17] Sydney Shoemaker has a provocative thought experiment that purports to show that psychological continuity does not require sameness or even continuity of any kind of matter (or

J. L. Mackie, *Problems from Locke* (Oxford: Oxford University Press, 1976): Ch. 6, esp. p. 200.

17 Versions of the view that sameness of person consists in psychological continuity may be found in David Lewis, "Survival and Identity," *Philosophical Papers*, Volume I (New York: Oxford University Press, 1983): 55–77; John Perry, "Can the Self Divide?" *Journal of Philosophy* 69 (1972): 463–88; Derek Parfit, *Reasons and Persons* (New York: Oxford University Press, 1984); Sydney Shoemaker, "Person Identity: A Materialist's Account," in *Personal Identity* by Sydney Shoemaker and Richard Swinburne (Oxford: Basil Black-well, 1984): 67–132.

even continuity of any kind of immaterial stuff). Suppose that with advances in medical technology, scientists invent a brain-state transfer device that records the brain patterns from one brain and imposes them on a second brain by restructuring the second brain so that it is in exactly the same state as the first brain was at the beginning of the procedure. Suppose also that, at the same time, the device removes the patterns from the first brain. Suppose that the first and second brains are in similar but obviously different bodies. There is no transfer of any bodily organ or part of a bodily organ from the first-brain person to the second-brain person. In the words of Shoemaker, "All that is transferred, it is natural to say, is 'information.' "[18] There is a direct causal connection between the first-brain person's states and the successor states of the second-brain person. At the end of the procedure, the second-brain person has psychological states continuous with those of the first-brain person. For example, if Smith was the first-brain person, the second-brain person now has Smith's apparent memories, intellectual abilities, quirks, character traits, and so on. Moreover, the second-brain person now claims to be Smith, knows Smith's mother's maiden name and Smith's social security number, and so on.

In the literature, this kind of thought experiment is commonplace among materialists.[19] Shoemaker uses it to claim that the brain-state-transfer device is person-preserving. Others make the weaker claim that the second-brain person is only a psychological duplicate of the first-brain person, who does not survive. But nobody doubts that the second-brain person is psychologically continuous with the first-brain person and that this psychological continuity is achieved "without the identity of any body, even though nothing non-physical is involved."[20] Although I am doubtful that such a procedure is empirically possible, I do not want to take issue with the point that it purports to establish – namely, that on a materialist view, psychological continuity does not require continuity of body or of matter of any sort. It is thus possible that there is psychological continuity throughout an interval during which there is no spatiotemporal continuity of body.[21]

18 Shoemaker, "Personal Identity: A Materialist's Account," p. 110.
19 See, e.g., Bernard Williams, "The Self and the Future," in *Problems of the Self* (Cambridge: Cambridge University Press, 1973): 47; Robert Nozick, *Philosophical Explanations* (Cambridge, MA: Harvard University Press, 1981): p. 39; Shoemaker, "Personal Identity: A Materialist's Account," pp. 108ff.
20 Shoemaker, "Personal Identity: A Materialist's Account," p. 111.
21 Peter van Inwagen, "Materialism and the Psychological-Continuity Account of Personal Identity" in *Philosophical Perspectives, 11, Mind, Causation, and World, 1997*, James E.

The criterion of psychological continuity, which to many of us is initially the most attractive, is now widely recognized to be subject to a troublesome objection – the duplication problem.[22] Suppose that Shoemaker's brain-state transfer device transfers Smith's intentional states from the brain in Smith's body – call it 'body 1' – to a brain in a different body – call it 'body 2.' Now *whatever* the relation between Smith's body-1 intentional states and the intentional states of the person with body 2, it is metaphysically possible that that relation also hold between Smith's body-1 intentional states and the intentional states of a person with body 3. That is, the brain-state transfer device could transfer Smith's body-1 intentional states both to the person with body 2 and to the person with body 3. No matter how stringently we conceive the nature of psychological continuity, if Smith's body-1 intentional states are psychologically continuous with the intentional states of the person with body 2, then they could equally well be psychologically continuous with the intentional states of the person with body 3. That is, there could be "branching." In that case, Smith would have exactly the same relation of psychological continuity with two distinct persons – the person with body 2 and the person with body 3.

So, if psychological continuity (no matter how it is spelled out) sufficed for personal identity, Smith – *per impossibile* – would be identical both to the person with body 2 and to the person with body 3. Of course, it is impossible for Smith to be identical to both since they are not identical to each other.[23] So, taking psychological continuity to be sufficient for personal identity (without further qualification) leads to contradiction. In short, the problem for the psychological continuity criterion is this: It is metaphysically possible for there to be two distinct persons whose intentional states bear the same relations of causal continuity to Smith's body-1 states; but it is metaphysically impossible for two distinct persons both to be Smith.

Tomberlin, ed. (Malden, MA: Blackwell Publishers, 1997): 305–20, argues against psychological-continuity views of personal identity like Shoemaker's that purport to be materialistic. Shoemaker has some replies in "Self and Substance," also in *Philosophical Perspectives 11*, pp. 283–304. I cannot take up that debate here.

22 According to John Perry (*A Dialogue on Personal Identity and Immortality* [Indianapolis: Hackett Publishing Company, 1978]: 50), duplication arguments apparently originated with an eighteenth-century freethinker, Antony Collins, who used a duplication argument to raise difficulties for the doctrine of immortality.

23 This is on the widely held assumption that there cannot be one person with two bodies at the same time. I explicitly hold this view when I take bodies to individuate persons at a time.

This problem – the duplication problem – is a well-known problem for any account of personal identity that implies this: Person x is the same person as y if and only if x is connected to y in some way R, where R leaves open the possibility that x is also connected to some z ($z \neq y$) in that way R. There are three kinds of response to this problem: (a) One can restrict personal identity to cases in which duplicates are de facto absent. (b) One can replace personal identity with a weaker relation and argue that the weaker relation is all that we really care about anyway. (c) One can come up with a nonempirical criterion of personal identity that precludes satisfaction by qualitative duplicates. Shoemaker takes the first line: He restricts personal identity to cases in which duplicates are de facto absent by adding to the requirement of psychological continuity a requirement of "no branching." So, his view is that x is the same person as y if and only if (i) there is appropriate continuity between x's psychological states and y's psychological states and (ii) there is no z distinct from y such that z's psychological states are connected to x's psychological states in the same way that y's psychological states are.

On Shoemaker's view, if Smith's psychological states are transferred from body 1 (Smith's original body) to body 2, then Smith endures as the body-2 person – unless Smith's body-1 psychological states remain intact or Smith's psychological states are also transferred to body 3. In the case of a second "offshoot," Smith himself does not survive. The mere existence of two persons psychologically continuous with Smith would extinguish Smith. Smith survives if there is one offshoot and Smith's body-1 psychological states are destroyed, but not if there are two persons psychologically continuous with Smith. Now this new requirement solves the duplication problem by ruling out duplicates, but it does so by stipulation. I know of no principled argument that Smith's survival should depend on whether or not there is another person just like Smith. There seems to be no logical reason why mere duplication of Smith's psychological states should destroy Smith. So, the no-branching solution to the duplication problem seems unsatisfactory.

Other materialists (e.g., Parfit, Lewis) try to soften the no-branching solution to the duplication problem by claiming that identity does not really matter to us anyway. Such materialists claim that satisfaction of Smith's desire to survive does not require that the person who survives be identical to Smith. On this view, Smith would be satisfied if he himself did not survive, but someone with psychological states continuous with his survived. For example, in a branching case in which Smith had two psychologically continuous descendants A and B – related in the same way to Smith – neither A nor B would be identical to Smith. But, say these materialists, no matter: What Smith (and, by extension, the rest of us) would care about with respect to survival is psychological continuity, not identity.

There is good reason to think that this weaker relation than identity is not what we are interested in in ordinary cases of survival.[24] Suppose that A is subjected twice to the brain-state transfer device (or to "fission") and that B and C are the offshoots. Since A cannot be identical to both B and C, A does not survive. But, according to the view that what concerns us is survival in a sense that does not entail identity, it matters little that B and C are not identical to A but are only psychologically continuous with A. However, I submit, if that were so, then our ordinary practices of agency and morality would be incoherent. Suppose that A had been on the verge of apologizing to her former fiancé for breaking off their engagement. Should B and C, who now both have A's memories, both apologize to the former fiancé for the broken engagement? The former fiancé would be startled to have apologies from two people; after all, he was engaged to only one. Or suppose that A had promised D to buy her lunch. Are B and C both obligated to fulfill that promise? How could one be obligated to fulfill A's promise but not the other? Does A's promise now entitle D to two lunches? Or, to consider another kind of case, suppose that A was a politician who vowed to become the first woman Democratic presidential candidate. B and C, each of whom reports remembering A's vow, are both infuriated by the unexpected (and unfair?) competition. Suppose that B becomes the first woman Democratic presidential candidate. B says, elatedly, "Since I am the first woman Democratic presidential candidate, I've totally fulfilled the intention that I remember before the operation." A says dejectedly, "Since I am not the first woman Democratic presidential candidate, the intention that I remember before the operation is totally unfulfillable." How can a single intention both be totally fulfilled and totally unfulfillable? Our practices of apologizing, promise keeping, and intending become incoherent if we suppose that our interest in identity really is interest only in psychological continuity.

Moreover, speaking for myself, psychological continuity without identity is not what concerns me in matters of survival. I want to know:

---

24 For a challenge to the view that in general the question of survival can be freed from presuppositions about identity, see Gareth B. Matthews, "Surviving As," *Analysis* 37 (1977): 53–8.

Will I be around? Not: Will someone just like me be around? Suppose that I discovered that someone else had qualitatively the same memories, the same character, personality traits, habits, and so on that I have. Should I care? Should I have the same concern for her as I have for myself? Should I have the same concern for her as I have for my closest friend or my husband? Even if I've never met her? In fact, regardless of how many psychological replicas of me there are, I would not have the same concern for any of my psychological replicas as I have for myself. I would not even care about those replicas as much as I care for my family and friends. We are interested in identity because we are interested in particular individuals (*de re*), and not just in whoever fits a particular description (*de dicto*). I am interested in the survival of me, not just in the survival of someone who has my memories, interests, habits, and so on. We do in fact have an interest in identity, for which our interest in psychological continuity is no match.

We have considered two attempts to avoid the duplication problem – by introducing a no-branching requirement and by claiming that our interest in survival does not require identity anyway. Both ploys seem to me desperate and ad hoc. The implausibility of these responses to the duplication problem has been for some philosophers an inducement to dualism.[25] For if dualism is correct, there seems to be a ready criterion of personal identity.

5. Sameness of Person Consists in Sameness of Soul

Since souls are conceived of as indivisible and immaterial substances, the duplication problem does not arise for a dualist. Even with a brain-state transfer device, there is no possibility that two offshoots could both have the original person's soul. But another question of personal identity arises for the dualist. The question of personal identity over time arises in the first place because a person undergoes various changes, and we want to know which kinds of changes the person would survive and which kinds of changes the person would not survive.[26] But that question would also arise for indivisible, immaterial souls.

---

25 For example, Richard Swinburne, "Personal Identity: The Dualist Theory," in Shoemaker and Swinburne, *Personal Identity*, pp. 1–66.

26 On the Constitution View, for a person to survive at all is to survive as a person. Since being a person is essential to its (nonderivative) bearer, there is no question of a person's surviving and not being a person. I think that dualists share this view.

To see that the question of identity over time arises for souls as much as for persons, consider: Either an immaterial soul is subject to change or it is not. If it is not subject to change, then a soul could undergo no moral or psychological development. In that case, the point of postulating a soul – which is to be a seat of moral and psychological properties – would be undermined. For a soul that could not become more corrupt or more refined or coarser is not a likely candidate as the bearer of moral and psychological properties.

So, suppose that an immaterial soul can change over time. If a soul can undergo change (perhaps profound change – think of Augustine before and after his conversion) between time t and time t', then the question arises: In virtue of what is a soul s at t (before moral or psychological transformation) the same soul as a soul s' at t' (after transformation)? I have never heard a dualist give criteria for sameness of soul over time. The only answer that I can think of is that there was a single person who persisted through the change and whose soul at t was s and whose soul at t' was s'. But on this answer, the idea of sameness of soul depends on the idea of sameness of person, in which case appeal to sameness of soul to account for sameness of person is viciously circular. So, the immaterialist's account of personal identity just reraises the question that it is supposed to answer. Hence, although it is largely out of favor these days, dualism would not offer an illuminating solution to the problem of personal identity even if one supposed that people had immaterial souls.

I believe that I have canvassed the main types of positions on personal identity – at least on our ordinary conception of three-dimensional objects enduring through time; I shall not consider the conception of four-dimensional temporal parts that do not endure. All of the attempts surveyed seem to me to fail, and the reason is not difficult to find. There is no account of personal identity over time that is (a) informative, (b) noncircular, and (c) plausible. This is hardly surprising since we do not have accounts of identity over time for other kinds of things. (The problem of the ship of Theseus has been around for millennia.) We can use sameness of body, sameness of living organism, sameness of brain, and psychological continuity as *evidence* of personal identity, but none of these proposed criteria show what personal identity consists in. Again, this is no surprise: Why would anyone assume (as almost everyone does) that personal identity consists in any *other, nonpersonal facts* anyway? But if personal identity does not consist in other, nonpersonal facts, then the truth about personal identity is bound to be circular (as is the truth about intentionality, among other things). Personal identity over time is, in an important sense, unanalyzable. With this disappointing feature in mind, let us see what illumination the Constitution View can shed on personal identity.

THE CONSTITUTION VIEW OF PERSONAL IDENTITY OVER TIME

As I have just mentioned, I doubt that there are any noncircular, informative, plausible criteria of personal identity to be stated. In the first place, a person is defined in terms of a first-person perspective. So, person P_1 at t_1 is the same person as person P_2 at t_2 if and only if P_1 and P_2 have the same first-person perspective. [27] I firmly believe this to be true. The difficulty is that I cannot give noncircular conditions under which a first-person perspective considered at one time is the same first-person perspective as a first-person perspective considered at another time. So, sameness of first-person perspective is almost, but (as I hope to show) not quite, unsatisfactory as a criterion of personal identity over time.

In the first place, since I gave a synchronic account of what a first-person perspective is in Chapter 3, recourse to sameness of first-person perspective over time connects the diachronic aspect with the synchronic aspect of an account of persons. In the second place, even though 'sameness of first-person perspective over time' is almost empty, it does avoid the difficulties found in other materialist accounts; in particular, it courts neither indeterminacy about the identity of a person nor the "closest-continuer" theory, according to which whether a certain person is you depends on the nonexistence of someone else. In the third place, although I cannot give informative conditions for sameness of *person* over time, I can give a sufficient condition for sameness of *human* person over time. I will elaborate on the latter two points, which I shall label '(A)' and '(B).'

(A) The idea of sameness of first-person perspective avoids the difficulties found in other materialist accounts of personal identity over time; in particular, it courts neither indeterminacy about the identity of a person nor the closest-continuer theory that threaten other accounts.

27 Early-term fetuses have no psychological properties at all and, according to the Constitution View, are not persons. Therefore, questions of personal identity do not arise for early-term fetuses.

Before showing how the Constitution View escapes indeterminacy and closest-continuer accounts, let me quickly say why sameness of first-person perspective is superior to the other proposed materialistic criteria of personal identity – sameness of body, sameness of living organism, sameness of brain. Sameness of first-person perspective allows that one could survive a complete change of body, including brain. It is nonchauvinistic. It allows that there could be nonhuman persons and reveals what human persons would have in common with such nonhuman persons (if there are any). Hence, sameness of first-person perspective is not subject to the criticisms of sameness of body or, mutatis mutandis, of sameness of living organism or of sameness of brain as a criterion for personal identity.

Sameness of first-person perspective also escapes the difficulty of the criterion of psychological continuity. For a first-person perspective is not susceptible to the duplication problem. The argument here is similar to the one we just considered in the case of fissioning. If a person, Smith, has two offshoots, A and B, then, as we have seen, A and B are both psychologically continuous with Smith. But both cannot be Smith. So, psychological continuity is not by itself sufficient for personal identity over time. But the Constitution View does not hold that psychological continuity is sufficient for personal identity over time. For a single first-person perspective cannot be shared by two people at the same time. A and B could not both have Smith's first-person perspective – although both would have memories qualitatively indistinguishable from Smith's memories, and so on. We may not be able to determine which one, if either, is Smith. But my point here is only that the Constitution View does not have the unhappy consequence that two offshoots could have the same first-person perspective. It is logically possible that a body just like mine constitutes someone else who has a first-person perspective that is qualitatively indistinguishable from mine, but that first-person perspective would not be mine. Nor would that person be me. Hence, if the criterion of personal identity is sameness of first-person perspective, the duplication problem cannot arise. So, the Constitution View comes out better than the psychological continuity view in that the Constitution View can avoid the desperate expedients of making my survival depend on the mere nonexistence of somebody else or of denying that what we care about in survival is . . . well, ourselves.

Now I want to develop what I have already suggested – namely, that the Constitution View avoids both indeterminacy about personal identity and the closest-continuer view. I shall defend two conclusions: first,

133

that there is a fact of the matter (perhaps unknowable, but a fact nonetheless) about whether a given person in the future is you or not; and second, that whether you are x does not depend on the nonexistence of someone else.

(I) No indeterminacy: On the Constitution View, there is a fact of the matter as to whether some future person is I. Consider a person – an eighty-year-old person S – at some time in the future. *Pace* Parfit, there is a determinate (although perhaps unknowable) answer to the question: Is person S I or not?[28] I am person S with body b if and only the first-person perspective that I now have ever includes a first-person relation to body b. Now it is possible that no one knows whether or not that eighty-year-old person S is I. I may know all the nonpersonal facts of the case: I may know what happens to my body, what happens to my brain and still not know now whether the resulting body or brain will be mine; I may know how my apparent memories will change and not know whether the person with those apparent memories is I. But there is still a fact of the matter as to whether or not the eighty-year-old person S is I – and the answer is determined by whether or not my first-person perspective includes a first-person relation to S's body. Moreover, if I have a first-person relation to a particular body at a certain time, then I know it at that time – even if I could not have foreseen in advance that I would have a first-person relation to that body. It may be that the identity (or nonidentity) of person(s) S considered at t and S' considered at t' is unknowable, but realism about persons allows that there may be unknowable facts of the matter.

It is a paramount virtue of the Constitution View that it is a materialistic view that does not imply indeterminacy. Even proponents of alternative views who are willing to live with indeterminacy acknowledge that the thought that there must be a determinate answer to the

---

28 Parfit uses spectrum cases as arguments for the claim that personal identity is indeterminate. He points out that the spectrum cases would have no force against the view that persons are Cartesian egos. "If we had reasons to believe this [Cartesian-ego] view, it would provide an answer to my argument." I agree. But notice that the same should be said for the Constitution View: If we had reasons to believe the Constitution View, that view too would provide an answer to his argument. My project is to give reasons for the Constitution View, which, if sustained, would defeat Parfit's Reductionist View. Parfit, *Reasons and Persons*, p. 237. (Parfit claims that one can hold that personal identity is determinate only if one holds that persons are "separately existing entities" like Cartesian egos. As far as I can see, Parfit supports this claim mainly with rhetorical questions; in any case, I think that the Constitution View is a counterexample to the claim.)

question of whether, say, the survivor of a certain operation will be S is very strong. Why does the inclination to hold that such questions must have determinate answers have such a grip on us?[29] I think that the answer concerns what it is to be a person. To be a person, according to the Constitution View, is to have a first-person perspective. Either I will experience waking up after the operation or I will not. From my own first-person point of view, there can be no indeterminacy. It would be incoherent to suppose that there will be an experience of waking up after the operation had by someone who is partly me and partly someone else. There can be no such entity who is partly me and partly someone else.

(II) No closest-continuer view of personal identity: On a closest-continuer view, whether or not I am person S depends on whether or not there is some other person who is a closer continuer to S than I am.[30] Materialist views seem pushed toward closest-continuer views by considerations like this:[31] If personal identity consisted in sameness of brain states, then in a case of fissioning that was only partly successful – so that half of A's brain was transplanted into B's head and the other half was thrown away – B would be A because B is A's closest continuer. However, if the fissioning were successful, so that B and C were equally "continuous" with A, then A would not have a closest continuer. Or, in the case of Shoemaker's brain-state transfer, if A's brain states were transferred only to B's brain, then B would be A; but if A's brain states were transferred to both B's and C's brain, there would be no closest continuer and neither would be A.

However, the Constitution View is committed to no such line. In the case of successful fissioning or brain-state transfer to two offshoots, the Constitution View does not say whether one of the resulting persons is the original; but (i) it has the resources to avoid saying (as it must

29   For example, see Judith Jarvis Thomson, "Persons and Their Bodies," pp. 225–6.
30   See Nozick, *Philosophical Explanations*, pp. 29–47. Any closest-continuer view will violate the "only x and y principle." See Harold Noonan, "The Only x and y Principle," *Analysis* 45 (1985): 79–83.
31   In the context of arguing that van Inwagen's materialism leads to a closest-continuer account of personal identity, Dean Zimmerman pronounces himself "convinced that any materialism concerning human beings that eschews temporal parts [as both van Inwagen and I do] can be driven in similar fashion toward a closest continuer account of human persistence conditions." Dean W. Zimmerman, "The Compatibility of Materialism and Survival: The 'Falling Elevator' Model," in *Faith and Philosophy*, forthcoming. For Peter van Inwagen's view, see *Material Beings*.

avoid saying!) that both are identical to the original, and (ii) it does say what must be the case for one of the resulting persons to be the original. (i) First-person perspectives for human persons are individuated at a time by bodies that constitute the person at that time; so, no matter how qualitatively similar B's and C's first-person perspectives are to A's, the fact that B and C are constituted by different bodies, according to the Constitution View, ensures that they are distinct persons and hence are not both A. (ii) What would make it the case that B (but not C) is A is for B to have A's first-person perspective. Whether B (or C) has the same first-person perspective as A is not a matter of continuity; so, the Constitution View does not imply that B is A unless there is a competitor, C, who is equally continuous with A.[32] Let me try to make this clearer by looking at the situation from a first-person point of view.

The following seem to me to be incontrovertible facts, easily discernible from a first-person perspective: Every morning when I wake up, I know that I am still existing – without consulting my mirror, my memory, or anything else. I can tell. Perhaps I even have a dramatic experience that I might express by exclaiming, "I'm alive! I'm alive!" I do not have to (indeed, cannot) identify myself as the one who is having that experience, and I cannot believe, "Well, it's partly me and partly somebody else who is having this experience." The subject of the experience of realizing that she★ is still alive is either I, or it is not I. If it is not I, then I cannot be aware (without being told) that such an experience is being had. And if it is I, then I know without being told that I am the subject of that experience. If I have such an experience after fissioning, then I survive, constituted by whatever body I find myself related to via a first-person relation.

What is peculiar about the first-person perspective is that, from the first-person perspective, I do not identify (or misidentify) myself at all. I do not pick out myself on the basis of appearance or memory or any bodily continuity or any other criterion. Others may be indistinguishable from me both physically and psychologically; even if no one else could figure out which one was I, I would have no trouble. Nor would any of the others have any difficulty knowing which one she★ was. From a first-person perspective, there is always an asymmetry between oneself★ and everyone else. I may be totally mistaken about my past; I may have

---

32 So, the Constitution View accepts Harold Noonan's "Only x and y principle," according to which "no facts about any other individual can be relevant to whether x is y." See Noonan, Personal Identity, p. 17.

complete amnesia; but I am never in doubt about my own existence. And this is so even if the others and I are physically and psychologically indistinguishable.

So, it is not on the basis of any criterion that I know which of a number of people present is I. This fact wards off both the closest-continuer account of personal identity and indeterminacy about personal identity. To see that the Constitution View accommodates this fact and is not pressed into a closest-continuer account or into indeterminacy, consider an argument to show the following: On the Constitution View, after successful fissioning or multiple application of the brain-state transfer device to my brain, there is a fact of the matter whether I still exist, and that fact does not depend on the nonexistence of duplicates of me. Suppose that after the operation (either fissioning or total brain-state transfer) there are two people, B and C, with an equal claim to being me. If either B or C had my first-person perspective, then I would know it. For B's (or C's) experience of thinking "I'm alive" would be *my* experience of thinking "I'm alive." (I would be B if B's experience were my experience, and I'd be C if C's experience were my experience.) Even if someone else physically and psychologically indistinguishable from me were thinking "I'm alive" at the same time, I would still be thinking "I'm alive." And if *I* were thinking, "I'm alive," (whether or not someone else was having a qualitatively similar thought), then there would be a fact of the matter that I was alive at that time. Therefore, if one of the resulting people, B or C, were I, there would be a fact of the matter which one I was.

Alternatively, if after the previously described experiment neither B nor C had my first-person perspective, then I would no longer exist. Neither B's nor C's experience of thinking, "I'm alive" would be my experience. Since, as I have just said, there would be a fact of the matter when B's (or C's) experience of thinking, "I'm alive" was my experience, there would equally be a fact of the matter when B's (or C's) experience of thinking, "I'm alive" was not my experience. Therefore, if neither B nor C had my first-person perspective, then there would be a fact of the matter that I was neither B nor C.

I do not know whether I would survive the operation. But my point is that whether I survive or not does not depend on the (non)existence of a psychological or physical duplicate of me. So, with its reliance on the first-person perspective, the Constitution View avoids the closest-continuer theory of personal identity. Likewise, indeterminacy seems reasonable only if we disregard the first-person perspective. There is no indeterminacy about whether the subject of a given experience is I. From a first-person perspective, there is never any doubt about whether some present experience is mine; nor do I ever mistake someone else's present experience for my own. And the Constitution View agrees with intuition that the idea of a subject of present experience that is partly I and partly not I is unintelligible.

In sum, according to the Constitution View, personal identity over time is unanalyzable in any more basic terms than sameness of first-person perspective. Although the Constitution View has no noncircular (i.e., reductive) account of personal identity over time, it does better than its rivals, and it allows for robust realism about persons and determinacy about questions of personal identity. This is one of many reasons to prefer the Constitution View to its competitors.

(B) Although I cannot give informative conditions for sameness of person over time, I can give a sufficient condition for sameness of *human* person over time. In order to see what this amounts to, I need to distinguish between two questions that are often not distinguished.

(i) Under what conditions is a person x at t identical to a person y at t'?
(ii) Under what conditions is x at t identical to y at t', where x is a person at t?

Question (i) is the question that we have been considering under the rubric 'personal identity.' Question (ii) is the question about persistence conditions for beings that are persons at some time. On the Constitution View, if x is a person at any time during x's existence, x is a person at all times of x's existence, so, the Constitution View gives the same answer to (i) and to (ii).[33] However, on the Constitution View, it is possible that x is a human person during a part of x's existence and x is a bionic person (i.e., not a human person) during other parts. So, although I give the same answer to (i) and (ii) in terms of sameness of first-person perspective, I give different answers to questions about *human* persons analogous to (i) and (ii). The question that I can answer for human persons is this:

(i') Under what conditions is a human person x at t identical to a human person y at t'?

The question about human persons analogous to (ii) is this:

33. But other views may not. For example, an Animalist could give a psychological condition (in terms of continuity and connectedness, say) to (i) and a biological condition (in terms of metabolism, etc.) to (ii).

(ii') Under what conditions is x at t identical to y at t', where x is a *human person* at t?

Question (ii'), like question (ii), is a question about persistence conditions. Since *person* (not *human person*) is a primary kind, if x is a person (whether human person, bionic person, or some other kind of person), x has the persistence conditions of a person. So, the Constitution View gives the same answer to (ii') that it gives to (ii). But it can give a more informative answer to (i'). It can do so by taking advantage of the fact that, necessarily, human persons have human bodies. In detail:

Recall that for human persons, bodies individuate at a time. So, for any time t, if x and y are human persons at t, then $x = y$ if and only if, necessarily, any body that constitutes x at y constitutes y at t, and conversely. So,

(H) For all objects, x and y and time t, if x is a human person at t and y is a human person at t, then $x = y$ if and only if for all human bodies z, necessarily: z constitutes x at t if and only if z constitutes y at t.

We can use this fact about bodies and constitution to specify conditions for x and y to be the same human person considered at different times. The human person x at t is identical to the human person y at t' if and only if, necessarily, any body that constitutes x at t constitutes y at t and conversely, and any body that constitutes y at t' constitutes x at t', and conversely. Sameness of human person considered at two times consists in necessary sameness of constituting bodies at each of the times.

(T) For all objects, x and y and times t and t', if x is a human person at t and y is a human person at t', then $x = y$ if and only if for all human bodies, z, w, necessarily: (z constitutes x at t if and only if z constitutes y at t) and (w constitutes x at t' if and only if w constitutes y at t').

(T) allows for a bodily criterion of sameness of human person over time, and it also accommodates the intuitions about the possibility of bodily transfer. For (T) can easily be applied to the thought experiment in which Prince, constituted by body b at t, came to be constituted at t' by the body, b', that used to constitute Cobbler at t. Calling the person who has body b' at t' 'Joe,' in the current scenario Prince = Joe. Also, necessarily (b constitutes Prince at t if and only if b constitutes Joe at t) and (b' constitutes Prince at t' if and only if b' constitutes Joe at t'). So, if Prince comes to be constituted by the body that used to constitute Cobbler, both sides of the biconditional of (T) are true.

Consider a case in which there is no body switching but rather branching. Suppose that Prince undergoes a brain-state transfer in which Bob acquires all Prince's memories, abilities, dispositions, desires, preferences, and so on, but Prince's psychological states remain intact. Bob is psychologically continuous with Prince, but Prince's brain states remain unchanged. The result of the branching case is that, after the brain-state transfer, we have two people, Prince and Bob. Check (T). Since the second conjunct of the right side of the biconditional in (T) is obviously false, it follows from (T), as it should, that Prince ≠ Bob. Hence, if Prince and Bob are not the same person, then (T) returns the correct verdict.

Before drawing the conclusion that I want about (T) from these two cases, let me deflect a reply to the Prince/Bob example: "This just commits you to a closest-continuer view of personal identity. For if, as in the story, Prince undergoes a brain-state transfer that leaves him psychologically unchanged, then Bob is not Prince. But if Prince had been destroyed in the process, then Bob would have been Prince." Let me emphasize again that this is not my view: I am not committed to any claim about the conditions (if any) under which a brain-state transfer is person-preserving. I am only saying that in the case described (in which Bob is clearly not Prince), (T) renders the right answer.

The only moral that I want to draw from (T) is that (T) is correct, not that it is epistemologically useful. To show that (T) is incorrect, we would need a thought experiment in which x was a human person at t and y was a human person at t', and one side of the biconditional was true and the other false. I cannot think of any such thought experiment. So, I am inclined to think that (T) is correct. But even if (T) is correct, it does not enable us to determine whether or not Prince exists at a certain time and, if so, what body constitutes Prince at that time. However, our quest was only for a metaphysically sufficient condition for personal identity over time, and I do think that (T) provides just that for human persons. So, I tentatively conclude that, although the Constitution View cannot provide noncircular sufficient conditions for sameness of *person* over time, it can provide noncircular sufficient conditions for sameness of *human* person over time.

These conclusions allow for realism about persons without reduction to nonpersonal elements and without dualism. Traditionally, the view that personal identity over time is unanalyzable has been associated with the view that a person is a simple substance – an immaterial soul.[34] The

34. See Descartes, *Meditations* II; Joseph Butler, "Of Personal Identity," in *Personal Identity*, John Perry, ed. (Berkeley: University of California Press, 1975): 99–105; Thomas Reid,

Constitution View shows that unanalyzability of personal identity need not lead to the view that a person is a simple (or immaterial) substance. For a constitutionalist can take it to be necessary that a human person is constituted by a body (and hence not a simple) and yet deny that personal identity can be analyzed in terms of nonpersonal facts.

IS BODILY TRANSFER IMPOSSIBLE?

I find the traditional thought experiments about bodily transfer – for example, the Prince and the Cobbler – utterly convincing when considered from a first-person point of view. Suppose that I wake up and look in the mirror and see a strange new body. What makes that person me, no matter what body constitutes her (or him!), is that she has my first-person perspective. I am certain that I am this person (with the unfamiliar body), no matter how many other people also look in the mirror and find similar unfamiliar bodies. Now suppose that these other people with unfamiliar bodies that look just like my unfamiliar body are also psychologically continuous with me: They have the same apparent memories, the same apparently intimate knowledge of my past and so on. Each of the others also thinks that she is L. B.

As we have seen, one of us is right about being L. B. (I am, actually) and the others are wrong – even though no one (including each of us who thinks that she is L. B.) can be certain which one really is L. B. You may convince me to believe that I'm wrong to think that I'm L. B., but you could not convince me that I am wrong to believe that I'm me or that I exist. Even though 'L. B.' and 'I' uttered by me both rigidly designate the same individual, I could have amnesia and fail to believe that this person (designating myself, L. B.) is L. B. without failing to believe that this person (designating myself again) is I.

If numerous people woke up all thinking that they were L. B., perhaps no one could discover which one really was L. B.; but I would know with certainty which one was I, and each of the others would know with certainty which one was she. There is only one of those people (namely, me) who would think that she was I, and she would be right. Even though each of many other people could believe that she was L. B., it is not the case that any of the others could believe that she

---

"Of Identity," in Perry, op. cit.: 107–12; Roderick Chisholm, "On the Simplicity of the Soul," in *Philosophical Perspectives 5: Philosophy of Religion, 1991*, James E. Tomberlin, ed. (Atascadero, CA: Ridgeview Publishing Company, 1991): 167–81.

was I. Since each of the others' first-person perspectives includes a relation to a body, and each of us is constituted by a different body, none of the others could have my first-person perspective. So, it seems to me quite conceivable that I – with my first-person perspective – could wake up in a different body. Furthermore, no matter how many others were physically and psychologically indistinguishable from me, none of the others could have my first-person perspective. I would always know which one was I, even if (on the one hand) others thought that they were L. B. or (on the other hand) I did not think that I was L. B.

In light of the intuitive plausibility of the thought experiments, I would need a powerful argument that the bodily transfer is metaphysically impossible (not just that I can't figure out how such a thing could happen) before I would give up the intuitions that support the thought experiments. Now I want to consider whether a recent argument offered by Peter van Inwagen is such a powerful argument that it should dislodge all the thought experiments.

Van Inwagen has mounted a forceful attack on the following combination of philosophical views: "materialism, realism about human persons and their endurance through time, and a belief in the possibility of bodily transfer."[35] If his argument succeeds, it shows that bodily transfer, in the context of the other assumptions, is metaphysically impossible. Van Inwagen directs his attack at proponents of the view that personal identity over time consists in psychological continuity, a view that is not mine. However, since I am committed to materialism, realism about human persons and their endurance through time, and a belief in the possibility that human persons could come to have different bodies from the ones that they now have, I may well be a potential target of the attack.

Specifically, given the assumptions of materialism and realism about persons who endure through time, van Inwagen offers a reductio of the following conjunction: (i) a person is identical to a human organism, and (ii) a person can undergo bodily transfer in virtue of a flow of information from one human organism to another (as in Shoemaker's brain-state transfer device). Since I deny (i), we can see right off the bat that van Inwagen's reductio as it stands does not straightforwardly apply to the Constitution View. That is, a constitutionalist would avoid van

---

35. Van Inwagen, "Materialism and the Psychological-Continuity Account of Personal Identity," p. 305.

Inwagen's contradiction not by denying (ii) – as van Inwagen would have us do – but by denying (i). So, the question for us becomes this: If we reformulate van Inwagen's reductio in terms of the Constitution View, can we still derive a contradiction?

To answer this question, let us first consider the argument as van Inwagen presents it. Suppose that there are two organisms, one at place p_1 and the other at place p_2. Suppose that at t_1, the organism at p_1 is (identical to) you. The information from the brain of the organism at p_1 is transferred to the brain of the organism at p_2. According to the view that van Inwagen opposes, the transfer of information is person-preserving; so, at t_2, after the information transfer, the organism at p_2 is (identical to) you. To see that this thought experiment is incoherent, note that the organism at p_2 was at p_2 all along, but you were not at p_2 all along. You were at p_1 at t_1 and at p_2 at t_2. So, if you are identical to an organism, at t_2 the organism at p_2, who is you after the information transfer, can truly say, "At t_1 I was here, and it is not the case that at t_1 I was here." In detail:

(1) You = this human organism at p_2 at t_2.
(2) At t_1, this human organism was at p_2. (the organisms are stationary)
(3) It is not the case that at t_1, you were at p_2. (you were the p_1 organism at t_1)
(4) At t_1, you were at p_2. (by substitution of identicals in (2))

Since (3) and (4) are directly contradictory, van Inwagen takes this to be a reductio of bodily transfer. He notes that Shoemaker, who also holds that persons are constituted by bodies, would deny (1); but van Inwagen thinks that Shoemaker's adversion to constitution does not get to the heart of the problem that he has raised. For van Inwagen says that his point does not depend on supposing that human persons are strictly identical to human organisms.

Nevertheless, if one is a materialist and if one believes that persons really exist, then one must concede that every person is strictly identical with *some* material thing. Someone who holds views like Shoemaker's is therefore committed to the proposition that there could be two simultaneously existing material things such that one of them could become strictly identical with the other simply in virtue of a flow of information between them.[36]

Here van Inwagen challenges the materialist who believes in bodily transfer to specify some material thing to which a human person is

---

36. Van Inwagen, "Materialism and the Psychological-Continuity Account of Personal Identity," p. 312.

identical. Any such material thing, he suggests, will be subject to an analogue of the preceding reductio.

I would like to show that a proponent of the Constitution View escapes the reductio (even if a proponent of a psychological-continuity view of personal identity like Shoemaker's does not). Of course, a human person is strictly identical to some material thing: himself or herself. It would be nonsensical to require that there be *something else* to which a human person is strictly identical; and it would beg the question against the Constitution View to disallow that *human person* is a material-object category.

For according to the Constitution View, *human person* has as great a claim to be a material-object category as *marble statue* does. Van Inwagen points out that one of the advantages of the psychological-continuity view of personal identity, against which his reductio is specifically aimed, is that it is supposed to be ontologically neutral about persons. The Constitution View, as I have developed it, is decidedly not ontologically neutral about persons: It takes *human person* to be a material-object category. So, the Constitutionalist is *not* "committed to the proposition that there could be two simultaneously existing material things such that one of them could become strictly identical with the other simply in virtue of a flow of information between them [or in virtue of anything else]." Indeed, if x and y are two simultaneously existing material things, then it is metaphysically impossible that "one of them could become strictly identical with the other" by any means whatever.

Adapting the bodily transfer case to the Constitution View, we have two organisms, one at p_1 and the other at p_2, and one person who is constituted at t_1 by the organisms at p_1 and who is constituted at t_2 by the organism at p_2. I simply see no logical problem. Consider a variation of van Inwagen's reductio:

(1') You = this person at p_2 at t_2.
(2') At t_1, this person was at p_2.
(3) It is not the case that at t_1, you were at p_2.
(4) At t_1, you were at p_2. (by substitution of identicals in (2))

Obviously, this argument does not touch the Constitution View. For (2') is clearly false on the Constitution View. At t_1, the organism that constitutes you (the person) at t_2 was at p_2, but at t_1 *you* were at p_1 (where the organism that constituted you at t_1 was). Therefore, we can derive neither (4) nor a contradiction between (3) and (4).[37] So, I do not believe that van Inwagen's argument shows the impossibility of bodily transfer if the Constitution View is correct.

My response to van Inwagen's reductio has done nothing to show how bodily transfer can be effected. All that I have tried to show is that a certain argument does not demonstrate that bodily transfer, in the context of the other assumptions, is metaphysically impossible. So, there is no logical bar to holding that the conditions for personal identity allow that in the future I could be constituted by another body. The Constitution View is committed only to the metaphysical possibility of bodily transfer. To see this, consider the following:

If x constitutes y at t, nothing about constitution per se either precludes or guarantees that y could be constituted by something other than x in the future at t'. Whether or not y could come to be constituted by something different from x depends on the primary kind of things that y is. For example, the persistence conditions of statues differ from those of rivers. If Piece constitutes Michelangelo's *David* at t, I doubt that *David* could exist at t' without being constituted by Piece. But if a certain aggregate of molecules constituted a river at t, that very river could exist at t' without being constituted by that aggregate of molecules. With respect to identity conditions, I believe that persons are more like rivers than like statues. I believe that a human person, constituted by a human organism at t, could come to be constituted by a bionic body at t'. In that case, the person would still exist, although no longer constituted by a human organism. (I'm not claiming that this kind of bodily transfer is effected solely in virtue of transfer of information.) So, I am committed to holding that it is metaphysically possible that there be a person constituted at t by body b and constituted at t' by body b', where $b \neq b'$. And, although van Inwagen is not concerned with this particular claim, it is important to see that what the Constitution View is committed to does not fall to his reductio. In short, I do not believe that van Inwagen's reductio precludes the metaphysical possibility of bodily transfer.

---

37. Van Inwagen says that the only things in the literature that he knows of that offers an escape from his reductio resort either to relative identity or to four-dimensionalism. The Constitution View, I believe, offers another way to escape the reductio.

Descartes was right about this much: I know with certainty that I exist, even if I am ignorant of almost everything else about myself. It seems to be a brute fact that a particular experience now is mine and that a particular experience yesterday was mine, whether I remember it or not. My first-person perspective shows itself in my ability to conceive of an experience as mine. Oddly, the significance of the first-person perspective has been neglected in standard accounts of personal identity. Even discussions of the memory criterion are typically conducted in terms of conditions statable without recourse to the first person – such as the condition that if x remembers doing A, then x must be identical to the doer of A. But it is the first-person perspective that makes questions of personal identity even more intractable than other questions of identity, for example, the identity of ships or cats.

The matter of personal identity over time is a vexing question. I have canvassed the proposed answers known to me and found them all wanting. I conclude that there will not be an answer in wholly nonpersonal terms. Nevertheless, the Constitution View, I have argued, affords a picture of personal identity over time in terms of sameness of first-person perspective. Although this picture is theoretically unsatisfying, there are at least three things to be said for it: First, this picture avoids the difficulties faced by other views of personal identity – for example, species chauvinism and the duplication problem. Second, the picture of personal identity offered by the Constitution View accords well with our ordinary self-understanding: that there is a fact of the matter whether a certain future person is I, and that that fact does not depend on the nonexistence of yet some other person. Third, the picture of personal identity in terms of sameness of first-person perspective unites the diachronic question to the synchronic question. It ties what it is to be a person enduring through time with what it is to be a person in the first place. For these reasons, I believe that the picture of personal identity offered by the Constitution View is superior to its rivals.

6

The Importance of Being a Person

According to the Constitution View, what is ontologically most important about human persons is that they are *persons*. According to the Animalist View, by contrast, what is ontologically most important about human persons is that they are *animals*. In this chapter, I want to show the difference that being a person makes.

It is the first-person perspective, in virtue of which we are persons, that gives rise to what matters to and about us. First, we matter to ourselves in a way that, logically, animals that lack first-person perspectives cannot matter to themselves. Nonhuman animals can attempt to survive and reproduce, but only beings with first-person perspectives can have conceptions of their own futures. Only persons can have fears and hopes about the future, and only persons can attempt to shape their futures according to their own ideas of the kinds of beings that they want to be. In short, animals that do not constitute persons cannot be important to themselves in the same way that persons are important to themselves. This is so because the first-person perspective allows us to think about, and conceive of, ourselves in a unique way.

So the significance, to persons, of being persons is simply incalculable. And it is difficult to see how to dismiss this apparent significance as merely parochial. I suspect that such dismissal requires a degree of self-deception. We may gaze at the sky and think how vast is the universe and how inconsequential are humans, but that does not (and should not!) stop us from worrying about how we are going to take care of our aging parents. In any case, there is an importance of being persons that in a sense transcends our own interests. Persons are important in the scheme of things as bearers of normativity.

With the emergence of persons comes new normativity in at least

147

two ways. First, beings with first-person perspectives are moral agents who are subject to moral judgment. A person who torments babies is reprehensible; a cat that torments mice is not. The lion that rips apart and eats a gazelle has nothing to account for (indeed, from a biological point of view, the eating of the gazelle was a positive good – for the lion). We may construe elephants' behavior as mourning their dead or chimpanzees' behavior as taking care of their sick brethren, but if on occasion they displayed different behavior, it would make no sense to blame them. (We may praise or blame dogs that we are trying to train, but our words do not carry the moral weight that they do for persons capable of reflecting on what they have done.)

Second, beings with first-person perspectives are rational agents who engage in normative activities. To be a fully rational agent, one must not only have goals and pursue them, one must also be able to evaluate one's goals. Higher nonhuman animals like cats and dogs and chimpanzees appear to reason about means to ends and thus to exhibit instrumental rationality, but nonpersons cannot subject the ends that they find themselves with to critical scrutiny. They cannot ask "Is this a goal that I really should not have?" A person who fails ever to consider whether his goals are the ones he ought to have is irrational; a cat that fails ever to consider whether his goals are the ones he ought to have is not. Indeed, it is metaphysically impossible for a cat, lacking a first-person perspective, to consider whether his goals are the ones he ought to have. The difference that being a person makes cannot be overestimated.

The ideas of moral agency and rational agency are complex and profound. Each is worthy of a book (or even a lifetime of study) on its own. So, full discussion of these ideas is out of the question here. However, I want to show that whatever the final truth is about moral agency and rational agency, the first-person perspective will be found to be at the heart of what they are.

MORAL AGENCY

Being a person is intimately linked to being a moral agent. Necessarily, all moral agents are persons, and all persons are, or in the normal course of things will be, moral agents. To show how moral agency presupposes personhood, I want to raise considerations that bring out the centrality of the first-person perspective, the defining characteristic of persons, for moral agency and moral life.

To begin, let us distinguish between being a moral agent and being morally responsible for a particular occurrence. A moral agent is a being who can be called to answer for what she does. To be a moral agent is to be accountable and to be subject to moral judgments of praise and blame. To be morally responsible for a particular deed, one must not only be a moral agent, one must also satisfy further conditions. The further conditions typically include conditions like these: One must have contributed to bringing about the occurrence, that is, one must have some causal responsibility for the occurrence, and one must have known what one was doing under an appropriate description. To take a commonplace example, if somebody set off a car bomb inadvertently by flipping a light switch that (unknown to him) was hooked to a bomb, the person – although a moral agent – was not morally responsible for the explosion. Or the schizophrenic who thought that he was hitting a pillow when in fact he was beating his child may not have been morally responsible for the child's injuries (although clearly he was causally responsible). Nevertheless, the schizophrenic remains a moral agent if he can appreciate the fact that he has done things in the past even if he is not morally responsible for some particular deed.

The sine qua non for moral agency in general is the ability to appreciate the fact that one does things and has done things in the past. Only those who can appreciate the fact that they themselves have done things can be held accountable and can be subject to moral judgments of praise and blame. To say that one must be able to appreciate the fact that one does things and has done things in the past is not to impose any requirement about memory. There is no memory requirement because such appreciation does not imply that one remembers any particular thing that she has done. What is required is that a being be able to think of herself in the first person as the doer of deeds. And a person with total amnesia can think of herself in the first person as the doer of deeds. She may well realize that she has done things in the past, even if she cannot remember what things she has done. What is required for moral agency is the recognition that one has done things.

In order to be able to appreciate the fact that one has done things in the past, one must have been able to "do things." What is the relevant sense of 'doing things'?

(DS) S does something in the relevant sense if and only if there is some occurrence o and some attitude of S's such that o would not have occurred if S had not had that attitude.

'Doing something' in the relevant sense is conceptually tied to having attitudes like beliefs, desires, and intentions. If it turned out (per impossibile, in my opinion) that no one ever had a belief, as eliminative materialists have held, or that beliefs and other attitudes are not genuinely explanatory, then it would also turn out that no one has ever done anything in the relevant sense.[1] (DS) is very broad and very weak in ways that I shall now illustrate.

(1) (DS) applies both to things done that require some bodily motion and to things done that require no visible bodily motion. Much of what one does involves some motion of one's body – for example, the soldier's arm moves when he salutes an officer. There is an occurrence (a salute) and an attitude that the soldier has (e.g., a belief that he has come into the presence of an officer) such that the salute would not have occurred if the soldier had not had that attitude. But some of what one does involves no such motion of one's body – for example, the actor silently rehearses his lines in a play while riding a bus. The actor as well as the soldier is doing something in the sense of (DS). There is an occurrence (a rehearsal of the lines) and an attitude that the actor has (e.g., his desire to perform well) such that the rehearsal of the lines would not have occurred if he had not had that attitude. (Even though silent and lacking visible manifestation, the rehearsal is an occurrence since it has effects: As a result of rehearsing his lines, the actor performs without prompting.)

(2) (DS) applies to both 'basic actions' (e.g., the soldier's raising his arm) and 'nonbasic actions' (e.g., the soldier's saluting). The raising of the arm would not have occurred if the soldier had not wanted to salute; the salute would not have occurred if the soldier had not believed that he had come into the presence of an officer. So, according to (DS), the soldier both raises his arm and salutes.

(3) (DS) applies in cases of wayward causal chains. To use an example from Donald Davidson, a climber may want to get rid of his business partner and believe that if he loosens his grip on the rope, he will get rid of his partner. The climber is so distracted by his belief and desire that he loosens his grip without choosing to.[2] In this case, the belief and

---

1   I discuss these matters in *Saving Belief: A Critique of Physicalism* (Princeton, NJ: Princeton University Press, 1987) and in *Explaining Attitudes: A Practical Approach to the Mind* (Cambridge: Cambridge University Press, 1995).

2   See Donald Davidson, "Freedom to Act," *Essays on Actions and Events* (Oxford: Clarendon Press, 1980): 79.

desire caused the loosening of the grip, but not in the standard way that explains intentional action. Nevertheless, according to (DS), the climber in this scenario did something: There was an occurrence (the loosening of his grip) such that if the climber had not had the relevant belief and desire, the loosening of his grip would not have occurred.

This shows that one can do something in the sense of (DS) even if one does not do it intentionally. However, we need not worry that (DS) would allow that there could be some S such that *everything* that S did was done unintentionally. This is not a worry because of the nature of attitudes. If nothing that S did were intentional, then S would not fulfill conditions for having attitudes in the first place.[3] Hence, there would be no attitudes that satisfied (DS).

(4) (DS) applies in cases in which a single occurrence guarantees that more than one person did something. For example, a professor puts *Naming and Necessity* on the syllabus that she hands out the first day of class because she wants her students to read *Naming and Necessity* at the end of the semester. Midway into the semester, a student who wants a good grade opens *Naming and Necessity* for the first time and begins to read it. In this case, there is an occurrence (the opening of *Naming and Necessity*) and there is an attitude of the professor's (wanting her students to read *Naming and Necessity*) without which the opening of *Naming and Necessity* would not have occurred. Also, there is an attitude of the student's (wanting a good grade) without which the opening of *Naming and Necessity* would not have occurred. So, by (DS), both the professor and the student did something.

(5) Conversely, (DS) applies in cases in which a single attitude plays the same role with respect to two occurrences (as I individuate occurrences): a raising of an arm on a certain occasion and a vote for the school budget. Suppose that I raised my arm in order to vote for the school budget at *t*. If I had not wanted the school budget to pass, neither the arm raising nor the vote for the school budget would have occurred at *t*. Alternatively, if I had wanted the school budget to pass, but I had believed wrongly that the chair had asked for "no" votes at *t*, neither the arm raising nor the vote for the school budget would have occurred at *t*. In either case, by (DS), raising my arm was doing something and voting for the school budget was doing something.

---

3 See *Explaining Attitudes*.

These examples illustrate how broad and how weak a requirement (DS) imposes. Only a being who does things in the sense of (DS) is a moral agent. But more is required to be a moral agent. As I have mentioned, a moral agent is a being who can appreciate the fact that she does things in the sense of (DS). Now let me explain what I mean by 'appreciates' when someone appreciates the fact that she can do things. First and most obviously, if someone can appreciate the fact that she can do things, then she is in a position to claim (or disclaim) causal responsibility for various occurrences that satisfy (DS). She is in a position to say, "I realize that I did that," and she is equally in a position to deny that she did it. (Of course, even if she accepts that she did whatever it was, she may go on to say, "That was the right thing to do in the circumstances," or "I was wrong to do that," or something else.)

Second, if someone can appreciate the fact that she does things in the sense of (DS), then she can realize that she would do things differently if she had different attitudes. And if she can realize that she would do things differently if she had different attitudes, then she can try to change her attitudes. She may profess inability to change her attitudes–"I was just brought up that way" – but this profession would not blunt my point. Someone who says "I was just brought up that way" simply declines to try to change. The ability to try to change does not guarantee that anyone will (or should) try to change. Moreover, I am not claiming that one will be successful in changing one's attitudes if one appreciates that one does things in the sense of (DS). The claim is only that such a being has the ability to try to change – whether or not it is a good idea to try to change and whether or not she would be successful if she did try to change. The ability to try to change one's attitudes is built into the notion of 'appreciates' in 'appreciates the fact that she does things in the sense of (DS).'

This point is entirely outside the controversy between those who take freedom to be compatible with determinism ('compatibilists') and those who take freedom to be incompatible with determinism ('incompatibilists'). If S does something in the sense of (DS), then there is some occurrence o and some attitude of S's such that if S had not had that attitude, then o would not have occurred. If S can appreciate the fact that she does things in the sense of (DS), then she can appreciate the fact that certain things would not have happened if she had had different attitudes. And if she can appreciate that fact, then she is in a position to try to change her attitudes. A compatibilist is just as likely to try to change her attitudes as an incompatibilist. The compatibilist tries to set up causal conditions that will bring it about that she has different attitudes. Of course, if compatibilism is true, whoever tries to set up causal conditions that will bring it about that she has different attitudes is caused to do so. But that fact is irrelevant to the current point. The current point is that the compatibilist and the incompatibilist can agree that one can try to change one's attitudes, and that appreciation of the fact that one does things in the sense of (DS) implies that one has the ability to try to change one's attitudes.

Now we have two conditions for moral agency: (i) doing things in the sense of (DS) and (ii) appreciating of the fact that one does things in that sense. A compatibilist could accept these two conditions as necessary and sufficient for moral agency; an incompatibilist could accept them as necessary, but not sufficient, for moral agency. The reason that the incompatibilist would deny that (i) and (ii) are sufficient for being a moral agent is this: It is possible both that S satisfies (i) and (ii) and that S is caused to have all the attitudes that she has (including any attitudes that lead her to try to change other of her attitudes). And if S is caused to have all the attitudes that she has, then the causal sources of her attitudes are ultimately "outside" S and hence beyond her control. And if S's attitudes cause her to do what she does, and her attitudes themselves have causal sources beyond S's control, then there is a sense (an incompatibilist sense) in which S could not do otherwise than she does. An incompatibilist holds that if S could not do otherwise than she does (in this incompatibilist sense), then she is not morally responsible for anything that she does. And if she is not morally responsible for anything that she does, she is not a moral agent. Hence, an incompatibilist would deny that (i) and (ii) give a sufficient condition for moral agency.

Although I cannot begin to resolve, or even to do justice to, the debate between compatibilists and incompatibilists, I think that there is a prima facie reason to come down on the side of compatibilists, and hence to accept (i) and (ii) as sufficient as well as necessary for moral agency. The reason is this: For all we know, some kind of determinism – psychological, physical, or theological – is true.[4] Suppose that some version of determinism is true, and suppose that we came to know that determinism is true. Would the idea of moral agents go the way of the idea of witches? I do not think so. (If we came to know that determin-

---

4 At the beginning of this section, I said that all persons are, or in the normal course of things will be, moral agents. Note that an incompatibilist is in no position to affirm this, since according to incompatibilism, if determinism is true, *no* person is a moral agent.

ism was true, then if we abandoned the idea of moral agency, we would be caused to do so; and if we retained the idea, we would be caused to do that as well; but that point is irrelevant here.) Whether I am right about the survival of the idea of moral agency in the face of knowledge of the truth of determinism or not, incompatibilists could still accept (i) and (ii) as necessary for moral agency and add a clause to get a sufficient condition for moral agency. For example, an incompatibilist could hold:

(MA-I) S is a moral agent if and only if (i) S does things in the sense of (DS), (ii) S appreciates the fact that she does things in that sense, and (iii) S has incompatibilist freedom.

I suspect that anything having incompatibilist freedom will satisfy (i) and (ii) automatically; in that case, (MA-I) may be reformulated for elegance. But I want to leave (i) and (ii) explicit because I think that any adequate account of moral agency will entail that a moral agent satisfies (i) and (ii). Now a compatibilist could hold that (i) and (ii) are by themselves sufficient, as well as necessary, for moral agency. So, the compatibilist version is just this:

(MA-C) S is a moral agent if and only if (i) S does things in the sense of (DS) and (ii) S appreciates the fact that she does things in that sense.

For ease of reference, I shall take what (MA-I) and (MA-C) have in common to be a necessary condition for moral agency on any adequate account:

(MA) S is a moral agent only if (i) S does things in the sense of (DS) and (ii) S appreciates the fact that she does things in that sense.

Now it remains to be shown that only persons satisfy (MA) and hence that only persons are moral agents. I think that it is clear that a dog, lacking a first-person perspective, can do things in the sense of (DS). A dog that digs in a certain place by moving its paws in a certain way is doing something in the sense of (DS). The moving of the paws in that way would not have occurred if the dog had not wanted to dig there; and the digging there would not have occurred if the dog had not believed that a bone was buried there. So, a dog does things in the relevant sense and thus satisfies the first condition for moral agency. But the dog is not a moral agent; it is not accountable for what it does. To be a moral agent, one must also be able to appreciate the fact that one has done things in the past. Since the dog cannot appreciate the fact that he has done things in the past, the dog fails to satisfy condition (ii) of (MA). So, (MA) returns the correct verdict on dogs.

Someone may object that a dog really can appreciate the fact that he has done something. For example, suppose that Rover defecates on the rug; on discovery, Rover's owner shows Rover the results of his misbehavior in order to make the dog appreciate what he has done and then punishes the dog. After repeated episodes of this kind, the dog learns not to defecate on the rug. Shouldn't we say that part of the learning was that the dog came to appreciate what he had done? No, because there's a simpler explanation: Rover came to associate feces on the rug with punishment. To see that all that is going on with Rover is mere association, consider: If Rover came and saw feces left on the rug by Fido, Rover would cower or run away or manifest other punishment-avoiding behavior when his owner returned. No appreciation of the fact that it was he – he himself – who had done something is required to explain anything about Rover.

The reason that the dog does not appreciate the fact that he has done something in the past, of course, is that the dog lacks a first-person perspective. For the relevant sense of 'appreciation of the fact that one has done something' is that the doer can understand herself (in the first person) as the author of the deed; she must be in a position to acknowledge in the first person, "Yes, I did that." This acknowledgment requires a first-person perspective. Moreover, appreciation of the fact that one has done something brings with it the ability to try to change one's attitudes; however, Rover is in no position to try to change his attitudes. So, Rover, who lacks a first-person perspective, lacks the ability to appreciate the fact that it was he who had done something. It is for this reason that absence of a first-person perspective is what prevents Rover from being a moral agent.

So, dogs fail to satisfy (MA), which gives necessary conditions for moral agency. Dogs and other nonhuman animals do things in the sense of (DS) and hence satisfy clause (i) of (MA): They perform actions explainable in terms of beliefs and desires. But, because they lack first-person conceptions of themselves as themselves, dogs and other nonhuman animals do not have the ability to appreciate the fact that they have done things; and hence they do not satisfy clause (ii) of (MA). And, as we saw in Chapter 3, to have a first-person conception of oneself as oneself just is to have a first-person perspective. Therefore, having a first-person perspective is a necessary condition for being a moral agent. Since, on the Constitution View, having the capacity for a first-person perspective is both necessary and sufficient for being a person, it follows that only persons are moral agents.

Is having a first-person perspective also sufficient for satisfying (MA)? Having a first-person perspective is sufficient for satisfying (MA) if and only if having a first-person perspective is sufficient for the ability to do things and to appreciate the fact that one has done things.

First, consider whether or not having a first-person perspective is sufficient for the ability to do things. (Since dogs, lacking first-person perspectives, do things, we already know that having a first-person perspective is not necessary for the ability to do things.) As we saw in Chapter 3, a being with a first-person perspective ipso facto has many attitudes. Is it possible to have many attitudes and yet not be able to do things? No. As I argued in *Explaining Attitudes*, the attitudes are conceptually connected to what one would do, say, or think in various circumstances. If S did not do anything in the sense of (DS) – that is, if there were no occurrence *o* and attitude of S's such that *o* would not have occurred if S's attitude had been different – then S would not have any attitudes. Similarly, if there were no belief explanations, there would be no beliefs. There is no logical room for attitudes that do no explanatory work. In short, a being with a first-person perspective has many attitudes, and a being with many attitudes can do things. So, having a first-person perspective is sufficient for being able to do things.

Second, assuming that a having a first-person perspective is sufficient for being able to do things, is it also sufficient for being able to appreciate the fact that one has done things? Yes. Consider a dog, which can do things but cannot appreciate the fact that he has done things. If that dog were to develop a first-person perspective (and hence come to constitute a canine person), then ipso facto that canine person would be able to appreciate the fact that he has done things. Such appreciation is just what a first-person perspective confers. Since having a first-person perspective is sufficient for the ability to do things and is sufficient for the ability to appreciate the fact that one has done things, having a first-person perspective is sufficient for satisfying (MA).

In sum, having a first-person perspective is sufficient for (i) of (MA), and having a first-person perspective is necessary and sufficient for (ii). (Having a first-person perspective is not necessary for (i) since dogs can satisfy (i) without having a first-person perspective.) Therefore, on the compatibilist model (MA-C) of moral agency, having a first-person perspective is both necessary and sufficient for being a moral agent. And on the incompatibilist model (MA-I) for moral agency, or on any other model with a claim to adequacy, having a first-person perspective is necessary for being a moral agent. Since our being moral agents is one of the most important things about us, the importance of being a person resides partly in the fact that all moral agents are persons.

Let me conclude this discussion of moral agency with a comment about moral life. In general, a first-person perspective makes possible a moral life, a life that has moral (or immoral) significance. Much of one's moral life – reflections on the kind of individual that one wants to be, struggles with temptation, attempts to discern and purify one's motives, deliberations about what is the right thing to do – would be metaphysically impossible without a first-person perspective. For example, to deliberate about what is the right thing to do, I must think of various alternatives that are open to me to do. There is no deliberation if I cannot envisage myself as myself doing one thing or another. But, of course, to have the ability to envisage myself as myself at all is to have a first-person perspective.

Or, again, in order to struggle with temptation, I must not only want to do a certain thing – call it 'A' (have an extramarital affair? cheat on my income tax?) – but I must also realize that I want to do A and that I ought not to do A. Merely to desire to do A cannot get temptation off the ground. To be tempted to do A, one must not only desire to do A, one must also believe that one should not desire to do A. Temptation requires a clash. In order for doing A to be a temptation, I must be able to entertain the thought that I want to do A and know that I should not do A. Of course, the ability to have *this* thought requires a first-person perspective.

Even the most quotidian aspects of moral life require a first-person perspective. Ordinary moral sentiments like guilt and regret depend on having a first-person perspective. If I could not appreciate the fact that I had done something, I could not regret having done it. Even if one feels guilt inappropriately – about something that one did not do, for example – the capacity to feel guilt requires that one be able to conceive of oneself as oneself. If one did not have a first-person conception of who one was and of the kind of person that one wanted to be, there would be no logical space for guilt. (Even if you feel guilty for something that your ancestors did, you must be able to think of them as *your* own ancestors in order for their deeds to induce feelings of guilt in you.) The very possibility of our having these morally significant properties at all depends on our being persons.

A rational agent deliberates about what to do, attempts to evaluate and rank preferences and desires and goals or ends, attempts to evaluate her beliefs, taking into account all available evidence and trying to resolve conflicts among them, and so on. I want to show that having a first-person perspective is necessary and sufficient for engaging in these essentially normative activities.

A first-person perspective is necessary for being a rational agent. The ability to engage in means–end reasoning is not enough to make a being a rational agent. A dog may engage in means–end reasoning. When the dog sees his owner roll up a newspaper, he may infer that the owner is about to hit him and run away. (Means–end reasoning: I want to avoid punishment; if I run away, I'll avoid punishment; so, RUN.) But a dog does not, cannot, rank his preferences and desires; he simply acts on them. He lacks the resources to evaluate his desires and hence is not a rational agent. What is required in order to be able to evaluate one's desires is a first-person perspective. In order to evaluate your desires, you have to realize that you have certain desires, and you have to be able to conceive of yourself as being one motivated by one kind of desire as opposed to another. You evaluate your desires according to your conception of the kind of person that you want to be. But to have a conception of your being one kind of person and not another requires a first-person perspective. So, having a first-person perspective is necessary for being a rational agent.

A first-person perspective is also sufficient for being a rational agent. As we have seen, anything that has a first-person perspective has many attitudes – including beliefs, desires, preferences, and so on – and has a first-person conception of herself. A being with a first-person perspective not only has desires but also can identify her own desires as her own, and hence can have desires about which first-order desires to satisfy.[5] A being who can have desires about which first-order desires to satisfy is in a position to evaluate and order her desires and preferences. But why should she try to evaluate and order them? Because, by its very nature, a desire is something that one has an inclination to satisfy; otherwise, it would not be a desire. And desires often conflict; they cannot all be satisfied. If one tries to satisfy conflicting desires, the result is likely to be

---

5 See Harry Frankfurt, "Freedom of the Will and the Concept of a Person," *Journal of Philosophy* 68 (1971): 5–20.

chaos that satisfies none of them. So, if one has the ability to evaluate and order desires, one will attempt to do so. And a first-person perspective entails the ability to evaluate and order desires. Therefore, a being with a first-person perspective will try to evaluate and order desires. Hence, a first-person perspective is both necessary and sufficient for being a rational agent.

SOME COGNITIVE AND PRACTICAL CAPACITIES

In the spirit of Wittgenstein's project of assembling reminders, let me quickly canvass a number of things not yet mentioned that are pretheoretically our important features and then show how they are made possible by the first-person perspective. I'll divide these into two groups: things that we can *conceive of* only because we have first-person perspectives and things that we can *do* only because we have first-person perspectives.

In the first group are cognitive abilities that we have only because we have first-person perspectives: (1) It is often said that we are the only beings who know that we are going to die. We can know this only because we have first-person perspectives. Perhaps a being without a first-person perspective could know that all human persons (or animals) eventually die; but only a being with a first-person perspective could know that she – she, herself – was going to die eventually, and know this despite the fact that she is at the peak of health and in no immediate danger. (There is a felt difference between assenting to the proposition that all persons are mortal and being struck by the thought that some day I am going to die. The latter, but not the former, depends on a first-person perspective.) (2) We can envisage many alternative possibilities for our own futures. To imagine oneself in this or that situation requires conceiving of oneself as oneself, in the first person, not as someone who fits a description or is picked out by a third-person demonstrative. But again, to be able to conceive of oneself in this way is to have a first-person perspective. (3) Only beings with first-person perspectives could make sense of the ancient dictum "Know thyself," much less attempt to follow it. To see this, try to imagine teaching a chimpanzee or any other being without a first-person perspective to "Know thyself."

In the second group are practical abilities that we have only because we have first-person perspectives: (1) We can have life projects and plans; we can choose our ideals and assess our desires and try to change them to conform better to our ideals. One can try to rid oneself of a desire only if one can conceive of one's desire as one's own, and to conceive of one's desire as one's own is to have a first-person perspective. Simply to be able to take a hard look at one's life and decide that one is on the wrong (or right) track requires a first-person perspective. (2) We do not simply act in accordance with laws of nature. We also follow rules and even make up rules for ourselves.[6] I could not set for myself a rule – even as silly a rule as "Don't step on the cracks" – if I could not decide that I will not step on the cracks or try not to. But to decide that I will not step on the cracks requires, yes, a first-person perspective. A dog or a chimpanzee could have habits, but he could not set himself to follow one rule rather than another or none at all. (3) We can decide what matters to us (within limits). Things no doubt matter to dogs, but dogs do not decide to care about one thing rather than another. To choose to value, say, mercy over justice (or vice versa) is to align oneself in a certain way. A being can decide to align herself in one way rather than another only if she has a first-person perspective. Unlike a person, a dog has no first-person conception of himself, which would enable him to set himself to be one kind of individual rather than another. (4) We can ask, "What am I? Who am I? What kind of life ought I to lead?" Such questions could not even be understood, much less seriously asked, by a being without a first-person perspective.

The cognitive abilities are put to use in exercising the practical abilities. For example, decisions about what really matters to one and about one's life projects are obviously informed by knowing that one is going to die sooner or later and being able to envisage various alternative futures for oneself. And the conceptual capacity to understand (and follow) the dictum "Know thyself" is surely advantageous to one deciding to pursue one kind of life rather than another.

One of the most striking features of our lives is what we might call 'interiority.' By 'interiority,' I mean those aspects of ourselves that we can report but that are not directly observable by others. (I am using 'directly observable' here in an ordinary, nontechnical sense.) For example, an actor may mentally rehearse his lines in a play while riding on a bus; or a very young child may have imaginary playmates with whom he entertains himself for hours; or a mentally ill person may have delusions of grandeur. The mental rehearsal, the imaginary characters, and

---

6 I am not suggesting that our setting rules for ourselves violates any laws of nature.

the delusions may be entirely invisible to outsiders, but the fact that they can be reported makes them part of the interior lives of the the actor, the young child, or the mentally ill person. Our ability to answer the question "What are you thinking about?" manifests our interiority. To anyone who professes not to know what I am talking about when I speak of interiority or of our inner lives, I would mention that one's inner life is made up of things that one is apt to report to a confessor or a psychiatrist. Any individual who has ever imagined himself or herself in some nonpresent circumstances has an inner life. The possibility of an inner life in the relevant sense depends not just on conscious experience (that dogs, for example, have), but also on a first-person perspective. To imagine oneself receiving an award or being arrested for speeding is to exercise a first-person perspective.

All of these cognitive and practical capacities are "structural" in a certain way. They do not dictate the content of our values, our rules, or our ideals. They do not determine what kinds of inner lives we have. They do not guide us in answering questions like "What am I?" Rather, these capacities are required for us even to formulate such questions; to reflect on our own values, rules, and ideals; and to consider whether or not they are the ones that we ought to have. Asking such questions and embracing ideals are absolutely characteristic of persons, and of no other kind of thing.

UNITY OF CONSCIOUSNESS

What I called 'weak first-person phenomena' in Chapter 3 suffices for a weak kind of unity of consciousness. The dog, which enjoys weak first-person phenomena, sees the stick land in the bushes and orients himself to run to the bushes and retrieve the stick. To accomplish this, the dog has to perceive the stick, the bushes, the spatial relation between the stick and the bushes, and his spatial relation to the bushes. (The dog's perception of where the bushes are in relation to himself is knowledge of the relation between "here" and "there"; this perception does not require anything deserving to be called self-knowledge.[7]) Furthermore,

---

7 In "Unity of Consciousness and Consciousness of Unity" (*The First-Person Perspective and Other Essays* (Cambridge: Cambridge University Press, 1996): 176–97), Sydney Shoemaker also notes that for sense perception to guide action, it must "include information about the relation of the thing perceived to the perceiver." He goes on to suggest that this amounts

this complex visual perception must be tied to the dog's desire to retrieve the stick. If the belief and desire were not thus connected, with the dog as subject of both the belief and the desire, then the belief and desire could not combine to move the dog to run to the bushes.[8] The dog is the subject of both.

What I mean by 'the dog as subject' here does not require what I am calling a first-person perspective. The dog's being a subject only implies that the dog is the origin of a perspective, and all of the dog's beliefs and desires have the dog's spatial (and temporal) location as origin. If the dog could speak, he would indicate himself as the origin of his perspective by saying "I": for example, "I see the stick over there in the bushes and I want to retrieve it." But lacking a first-person perspective, he would have no grasp of "I." "I" in the mouth of a speaking dog would just be a default, indicating the origin of a particular perspective. All of the dog's perceptions, beliefs, and desires are automatically from the dog's own first-person point of view.

But merely having a first-person point of view (as a dog has) does not suffice for a first-person perspective. There is a stronger kind of unity of consciousness than what we attribute to the dog. What a first-person perspective adds to the dog's first-person point of view as origin of a perspective is awareness that it *has* a perspective; and with this awareness comes a conception of himself as the origin. So, although the dog has a first-person point of view, the person *knows* that she has a first-person point of view. She conceives of herself as the origin of a perspective and in so doing adds consciousness of unity to the unity of consciousness (that a dog has). Call the unity of consciousness underwritten by a first-person perspective 'strong unity of consciousness.'

I am not claiming that strong unity of consciousness is a necessary condition for something to be a single person. The reason that strong unity of consciousness is not necessary for something to be a single person is that bizarre thought experiments – like Parfit's "divided consciousness" – suggest that a single person may have two streams of consciousness that are causally and phenomenologically insulated from each other.[9] Although I seriously doubt that such divided consciousness

---

to a kind of self-knowledge. Call it 'self-knowledge' if you like, but it is what I called in Chapter 3 a 'weak first-person phenomenon,' well short of a first-person perspective in my sense – although not in Shoemaker's sense. See his "The First-Person Perspective" in *The First-Person Perspective and Other Essays*, pp. 157–75.

8   Gareth Matthews urged this point on me.

9   Derek Parfit, *Reasons and Persons* (Oxford: Clarendon Press, 1984): 246.

is possible, if it were possible, I would count the subject of both streams of consciousness as one person. Isolating what goes on in one hemisphere of the brain from what goes on in the other could not call forth a second first-person perspective, nor could such isolation replace a first-person perspective with two "successor" first-person perspectives. Divided consciousness (if it is even possible) would disrupt the unity of consciousness, while the first-person perspective and hence the person persisted. Hence, if we countenance the possibility of divided consciousness, we should not take unity of consciousness to be a necessary condition for there to be a single person.

Nevertheless, strong unity of consciousness is characteristic of persons, and there is no way to understand strong unity of consciousness independently of a first-person perspective. As one with a first-person perspective, I have a conception of myself as myself. Not only do I have mental states (as a dog has), but I can also think of myself as the subject of mental states. And those mental states of which I think of myself as the subject are in fact *my* mental states. Strong unity of consciousness consists in my thinking of certain states as my mental states, where the metaphorical glue that holds those mental states together is my first-person perspective. So, a first-person perspective accounts for the strong unity of consciousness that characterizes our inner lives.

CONCLUSION

Since all and only persons have a capacity for a first-person perspective, the question of the importance of being a person comes down to the importance of having a first-person perspective. The first-person perspective, or the abilities that it brings in its wake, may well be a product or a by-product of evolution by natural selection. My claim is this: However the first-person perspective came about, it is unique and unlike anything else in nature, and it makes possible much of what matters to us. It even makes possible our conceiving of things *as* mattering to us. The first-person perspective − without which there would be no inner lives, no moral agency, no rational agency − is so unlike anything else in nature that it sets apart the beings that have it from all other beings. The appearance of a first-person perspective makes an ontological difference in the universe.

Much of what is distinctive about us and much of what we care most deeply about − our ideals, values, life plans; our status as rational and moral agents − depends on our being persons. If, as on the Constitution

View, we are most fundamentally persons, then our uniquely characteristic abilities, which require a first-person perspective, stem directly from
our being the kind of entities that we are. If, on the other hand, we are
most fundamentally animals, then our uniquely characteristic abilities do
not stem from our being the kind of entities that we are. This is so,
because on the Animalist View, what we are most fundamentally –
human organisms – can exist and persist without first-person perspectives. Having a first-person perspective, on the Animalist View, is irrelevant to the kind of being that we most fundamentally are. By contrast,
on the Constitution View, our unique characteristics and what we care
deeply about depend squarely on what we fundamentally are: persons.

In sum: Our moral agency, our rational agency, the cognitive and
practical abilities that require a first-person perspective, and the ability
to have an inner life are all unique to persons. And these things, I
submit, are among the most significant things about us. It is a signal
virtue of the Constitution View that it directly connects what is most
important to us and about us to what we most fundamentally are.

Part Three

The Constitution View Defended

7

The Coherence of the Idea of Material Constitution

The approach to the material world in terms of constitution without identity has been subjected to a barrage of criticism. Some objections have been leveled at the very idea of constitution-without-identity; others have challenged the specific application of the idea of constitution-without-identity to the problem of persons and their bodies. In this chapter, I want to defend the idea of constitution-without-identity. In the next chapter, I want to defend the Constitution View of human persons and their bodies.

Some of the objections just refuse to take the general idea of constitution-without-identity seriously. For example, David Lewis speaks for many when he remarks, "It reeks of double-counting to say that here we have a dishpan, and we also have a dishpan-shaped bit of plastic that is just where the dishpan is. . . ."[1] But this is just a bit of polemics. There is no double-counting; we count by sortals, and 'piece of plastic' is a different sortal from 'dishpan.' The "reek of double-counting" comes from Lewis's tendentious use of 'dishpan-shaped' to describe the piece of plastic. The less tendentious way to express what constitution-without-identity implies is to say: Here we have a dishpan constituted by an S-shaped piece of plastic, where 'S-shaped' is a more neutral expression denoting the actual shape of the piece of plastic. To see that Lewis's remark gets its bite from being amusing, consider a less amusing (and by now tired) example of a piece of sculpture constituted by a hunk of gold. In this case, it is perfectly natural to distinguish between the sculpture and the hunk of gold. It makes perfectly good sense to ask: Which do you want to preserve? The gold hunk has a meltdown value

---

1   David Lewis, *On the Plurality of Worlds* (Oxford: Basil Blackwell, 1986): 252.

167

of $1,000. Unlike the gold hunk, the sculpture would not survive being melted down; it would just cease to exist. If you inherit the ugly old sculpture from a distant relative, whether you melt it down or not may depend on whether you could sell the sculpture for more than $1,000. So, not only do we have theoretical reasons (which I have rehearsed at length) for denying the identity of the sculpture and the hunk of gold, or of the dishpan and the piece of plastic, but we may also have practical reasons as well. Constitution–without–identity is a serious position that will not just fall to ridicule.

Before turning to the serious criticism of constitution–without–identity, let me set out again the bare bones of the idea. In Chapter 2, I explicitly defined 'constitution.' This is the general idea that I want to defend and that I shall refer to as 'constitution–without–identity.' Let *being an F* be *x*'s primary-kind property, and let *being a G* be *y*'s primary-kind property, where *being an F ≠ being a G*, and let D be G-favorable circumstances. Let F$\star$ be the property of *having the property of being an F as one's primary-kind property*, and let G$\star$ be the property of *having the property of being a G as one's primary-kind property*.[2] Then:

(C) *x* constitutes *y* at $t =_{df}$
   (a) *x* and *y* are spatially coincident at *t*; and
   (b) *x* is in D at *t*; and
   (c) It is necessary that : $\forall z[(F\star zt \ \& \ z$ is in D at $t) \rightarrow \exists u(G\star ut \ \& \ u$ is spatially coincident with *z* at *t*)]; and
   (d) It is possible that: (x exists at $t \ \& \ \sim\exists w[G\star wt \ \& \ w$ is spatially coincident with *x* at *t*]); and
   (e) If *y* is immaterial, then *x* is also immaterial.

Several of the objections to the coherence of the idea of constitution–without–identity may be turned aside by the distinction between having properties nonderivatively and having them derivatively. Recall that in Chapter 2, I defined the idea of 'having properties derivatively' by means of two definitions, (I) and (D).[3] Where H is a property that is neither

---

2   The reason to distinguish F$\star$ and G$\star$ from F and G is that some *x* may have the property of *being an F* derivatively, in which case *x* is an F but *being an F* is not *x*'s primary-kind property. Introduction of F$\star$ restricts the definition to cases to Fs that have the property of *being an F* as their primary-kind property.

3   In Chapter 4, I modified (D) to (D′) by adding a clause to accommodate hybrid properties. Since I know of no additional objections that this modification raises, I shall stick to the original (D) for purposes here.

alethic, nor constitution/identity/existence, nor rooted in times outside those at which it is had:

(I) x has H at t independently of x's constitution relations to y at $t =_{df}$
    (a) x has H at t; and
    (b) Either (1) (i) x constitutes y at t, and
                (ii) x's having H at t (in the given background) does not entail that x constitutes anything at t.
       or (2) (i) y constitutes x at t, and
                (ii) x's having H at t (in the given background) does not entail that x is constituted by something that could have had H at t without constituting anything at t.

And:

(D) x has H at t derivatively $=_{df}$ There is some y such that:
    (a) it is not the case that : x has H at t independently of x's constitution relations to y at t; &
    (b) y has H at t independently of y's constitution relations to x at t.

I shall consider three kinds of objections. The first kind encompasses objections that the notion of constitution-without-identity leads to incoherence. The second kind concerns my approach to constitution as a relation between things of different kinds rather than as a mereological relation between parts and wholes. The third kind concerns the relation between constitution and theses of supervenience.

CONSTITUTION AND INCOHERENCE

The first attack on the coherence of the notion of constitution-without-identity comes from Michael B. Burke: If Piece constitutes *David*, then Piece and *David* "consist of the very same atoms."[4] Given their qualitative identity, Burke asks in exasperation, "[w]hat, then could *make* them different in sort?" Burke sees only two possible answers: (1) they differ in their histories or (2) they differ in their persistence conditions. But each of these answers, he says, is explainable only by reference to their

---

4 Michael B. Burke, "Copper Statues and Pieces of Copper: A Challenge to the Standard Account," *Analysis* 52 (1992): 14.

differing in sort. Hence, neither answer can explain how Piece and *David* are of different sorts.

First, Burke overlooks a third possibility: Piece and *David* differ in sort in virtue of the fact that they differ in their essential properties. Here is the reason that we know that Piece and *David* have essential properties at all: As I argued in Chapter 1 (under the heading "The Road to Essentialism"), anything that can go out of existence altogether has *de re* persistence conditions, and anything that has *de re* persistence conditions has essential properties. So, assuming that it is possible for Piece and *David* to cease to exist, Piece and *David* have essential properties. Here is the reason that Piece and *David* differ in their essential properties even though they are intrinsically just alike: There are relational properties that *David* has essentially but that Piece does not have essentially. It is metaphysically possible for Piece, but not for *David*, to exist in the absence of an artworld or an artist or anybody's intentions, for that matter.

Burke and others who share his worry do not see how things that are exactly the same internally can be of different kinds or have different persistence conditions. But this worry arises only in the context of a particular metaphysical assumption. The assumption is that sameness of primary kind is a matter of intrinsic similarity.[5] Reflection on the *David*/ Piece example shows that this assumption is false, or at least is question-begging. *David* and Piece are intrinsically indistinguishable, but they differ in primary kind. Hence, intrinsic similarity is not sufficient for sameness of primary kind. Conversely, Big Ben and my travel alarm clock have little if any intrinsic similarity, but they are of the same primary kind (clock); hence, intrinsic similarity is not necessary for sameness of primary kind.

Now that we see that, in general, a thing's primary kind need not be determined by some qualitative intrinsic property, we can extend this insight to cases of constituted things whose primary kinds are in fact determined by intrinsic properties. In these cases, two things may have the same qualitative intrinsic properties, and their primary kinds may be determined by their intrinsic properties; yet, they may differ in primary kind. How can this be? What determines their primary kinds are not merely the qualitative intrinsic properties that they share, but rather their having certain of their qualitative intrinsic properties essentially. They

---

5 I say "primary kind" because a thing may be of many different kinds, but its primary kind is what determines its persistence conditions.

differ in having different of their shared qualitative intrinsic properties essentially. F may be a qualitative intrinsic property of both x and y, but it may be that x has F essentially and y has F contingently.

For example, whether or not something is a river is determined in part by the configuration of the molecules that make it up at a given time. Yet, on my view, the river is not identical to the aggregate of H_2O molecules that make it up at that time. For whether or not something is an aggregate of molecules has nothing to do with the configuration of molecules. Since rivers (in virtue of being rivers) have different essential properties from those of aggregates of H_2O molecules (in virtue of being aggregates of H_2O molecules), *river* is a different primary kind from *aggregate of H_2O* molecules. Another way to see the difference in primary kind between rivers and aggregates of molecules is to notice that the identity of an aggregate of molecules is determined solely by the existence of the very molecules in the aggregate, but the identity of a river is not so determined. The same river can be made up of different H_2O molecules at different times: A river can gain and lose H_2O molecules and continue to exist; an aggregate of H_2O molecules cannot.

Return to Burke's question, "Given the qualitative identity of these objects [e.g., a river and an aggregate of H_2O molecules that make up the river at a given time], what explains their alleged difference in sort?" The answer is this: Rivers and aggregates of H_2O molecules have different essential properties and hence are of different kinds. To ask what explains the fact that nothing can be a river without being a stream of water is to ask a senseless question. That's what rivers are. (More on this point is presented in the section "Constitution and Supervenience.") So, in the case of constituted things whose identity is determined by intrinsic properties, the answer to Burke is that the constituted thing differs from the qualitatively similar constituting thing because of this: There is some intrinsic property (e.g., being a stream of water) that the constituted thing has essentially but the constituting thing has accidentally, or vice versa. And this difference in essential properties grounds the difference in primary kind.

So, what justifies us in holding that rivers and aggregates of H_2O molecules are different primary kinds? Burke bars explaining difference in primary kind by difference in persistence conditions (e.g., an aggregate of H_2O molecules would still exist if it were scattered, but a river would cease to exist if the constituting aggregate were scattered) by claiming this: If difference in persistence conditions is used to explain difference in sort (primary kind), then "there will be no apparent way to explain the difference in their persistence conditions."[6] But on my view, *both* difference in persistence conditions *and* difference in primary kind are explained by differences in essential properties. A river and an aggregate of H_2O molecules have different properties essentially: Nothing is a river that fails to be have a bank or at least an edge. Nothing is a river that isn't a continuous stream of water. But aggregates of H_2O have none of these properties essentially: Something can be an aggregate of H_2O molecules and fail to have a bank, or an edge, and fail to be a continuous stream of water. Difference in (nonindividual) essential properties justifies us in holding that rivers and aggregates of H_2O molecules are of different primary kinds.

If being a river is a distinct primary-kind property from being an aggregate of molecules, then it is easy to see that a river is constituted at *t* by a particular aggregate of H_2O molecules to which it is not identical. Check definition (C): (a) The aggregate of H_2O molecules and the river are spatially coincident at *t*; (b) the aggregate of H_2O molecules is in the circumstance of being configured in a river-favorable way; (c) for anything whose primary kind is to be an aggregate of H_2O molecules that is in the circumstance of being configured in a river-favorable way, there is a spatially coincident river; (d) it is possible that the aggregate of H_2O molecules exists and that there is no spatially coincident river (the aggregate of molecules may be scattered throughout the universe); (e) neither the aggregate of H_2O molecules nor the river is immaterial. Therefore, assuming that rivers and aggregates of H_2O molecules are of different primary kinds, it follows from (C) that the relation between the aggregate of H_2O molecules and the river is constitution and not identity.

So, we can all agree that if *x* constitutes *y* at *t*, then *x* and *y* consist of the same atoms at *t*. But the fact that *x* and *y* consist of the same atoms at *t* is no bar to *x*'s and *y*'s being of different primary kinds – whether those primary kinds are defined by relational properties or not.

Consider another objection raised by Burke. On what he calls the 'standard account' of the relation between copper statues and pieces of copper, *David* has the property of being a statue but Piece does not.[7] If this is the standard account, then my construal of constitution, à la (C), is not an example of the standard account. For, as we have just seen, I do not want to deny that Piece has the property of being a statue; rather,

---

6 Burke, "Copper Statues," p. 16.
7 Burke, "Copper Statues," p. 14.

I want to insist that Piece is a statue and to explicate that fact in terms of having a property derivatively.[8] However, if *David* and Piece are both statues, there seems to be a problem. For consider the following argument, which aims to saddle the Constitution View with an unpalatable conclusion:

(P_1) If x is an F & y is an F & $x \neq y$ & x is spatially coincident with y, then there are two spatially coincident Fs.

(P_2) *David* is a statue, and Piece is a statue, and *David* $\neq$ Piece, and *David* and Piece are spatially coincident.

$\therefore (C_1)$ There are two spatially coincident statues.

(C_1) follows from a general principle, (P_1), and an instance of the Constitution View, (P_2), and (C_1) is indeed an unpalatable conclusion. But the proponent of the Constitution View is not committed to (C_1); for the proponent of the constitution view would reject (P_1) as begging the question against constitution. If the antecedent of (P_1) were augmented by the addition of another conjunct (". . . and neither x constitutes y nor y constitutes x"), then it would be acceptable. But in that case, (P_2) would not be an instance of the revised (P_1), and the argument would be invalid. The point of constitution is to open up a *via media* between identity and separateness, and as it stands, (P_1) disregards this *via media*. Given that the notion of constitution is coherent – as, I think, the definition (C) shows that it is – it would hardly be effective to argue against it by ignoring it.

The reason that, where *David* is, there are not two spatially coincident statues is that Piece has the property of being a statue derivatively. That is, Piece is a statue only in virtue of its constitution relations to something that is a statue nonderivatively. *David* and Piece are not separate statues; they are not even separable.[9] (You can't take them apart and get two statues; you can't take them apart at all.) Indeed, I want to say that

---

8   So, I do not have Burke's problem of saying in virtue of what *David* is a statue and not a piece of marble. Indeed, I have a clear answer to Burke's question: "In virtue of what does the object identified under 'statue' *satisfy* 'statue'?" ("Copper Statues," p. 15). Since *David* is a statue nonderivatively and Piece is a statue derivatively, this question has a disjunctive answer. Let F be the complex property of being presented as a three-dimensional figure in an artwork, given a title, and put on display. Now: x is a statue if and only if $\exists y[y$ has F nonderivatively & ($x = y$ or x constitutes y)].

9   Philosophers who discuss constitution in terms of "spatially coincident objects" sound as if they take the idea of constitution-without-identity to imply that there are two independent objects that just happen to occupy the same location at the same time. Constitution, as we have seen, is a much more intimate relation than talk of spatially coincident objects suggests.

Piece is the *same statue* as *David*. John Perry has argued that, where 'F' ranges over sortals, '*x* is the same F as *y*' should be analyzed as '*x* = *y* and F*x*.'[10] But, on my view, Piece is the same statue as *David* in virtue of constituting *David*, not in virtue of being identical to *David*. So, I suggest amending Perry's analysis to take account of constitution:

(S) *x* is the same F as *y* at *t* $=_{df}$ [(*x* = *y* or *x* has constitution relations to *y* at *t*) and F*xt*].

From (S), it follows that although Piece is the same statue as *David*, Piece might not have been the same statue as *David*. (Piece might not have been a statue at all.). In general, if *x* and *y* are constitutionally related and *x* has the property of being an F derivatively, then *x* and *y* are the same F. Anyone who accepts (S) will reject (P$_1$) and declare the argument unsound.[11]

Why should we accept (S)? (S), I believe, accords with the way that we actually count things.[12] Constitution is intended as a third alternative between identity and separate existence. How are we to count using this three-way classification? We may count either by identity ('If *x* and *y* are Fs, then there is one F only if *x* = *y*') or by nonseparateness ('If *x* and *y* are Fs, then there is one F only if *x* and *y* are nonseparate,' where *x* and *y* are nonseparate if and only if either *x* = *y* or *x* is constitutionally related to *y*). Constitution, as I have urged, is like identity in some ways and unlike identity in other ways. Our practices of counting, I believe, align constitution with identity; *x* is the same F as *y* only if: *either x = y or x* has constitution relations to *y*. Those who would adhere to Perry's principle in effect insist on aligning constitution with separate existence: *x* is the same F as *y* only if *x* = *y*. Since I do not think that we count

10 John Perry, "The Same F," *Philosophical Review* 79 (1970): 181–200. Notice that my construal no more invokes relative identity than does Perry's.

11 Note that those who accept the Christian doctrine of the Trinity are in no position to reject (S) out of hand simply because they endorse Perry's analysis. For from an orthodox Trinitarian point of view, Perry's analysis must be incorrect. I'm not saying that (S) will help illuminate the Trinity, only that a Trinitarian has no grounds for insisting on Perry's analysis.

12 Harold Noonan comments, "It is a deeply engrained conviction in many philosophical circles that if *x* is an F and *y* is an F and *x* and *y* are not identical then *x* and *y* cannot legitimately be counted as *one* F." He notes, however, that it "is perfectly possible to count by a relation weaker than, i.e., not entailing, identity." See "Constitution Is Identity," *Mind* 102 (1993): 138. In discussing fission cases of persons, David Lewis justifies counting by a weaker relation than identity in "Survival and Identity" in *The Identities of Persons*, Amelie Oksenberg Rorty, ed. (Berkeley: University of California Press, 1976): 26–8.

by identity (but rather by nonseparateness), I reject (P_1) and, with it, (C_1).[13]

There may seem to be another problem with taking Piece to be a statue.[14] Here is a proposed counterexample to the claim that Piece is a statue (in virtue of having the property of being a statue derivatively). Suppose that Piece existed before *David* – in, say, 1499. *David* came into existence in 1504. Now suppose that Jones pointed to *David* in 1506 and said, "There is a statue over there that existed in 1499." If, as I have urged, we say that Piece is a statue, and that Piece existed in 1499, then what Jones said was true. But, one may object, what Jones said was not true since Piece did not constitute a statue in 1499.

To this charge, let me reply. What Jones said is ambiguous, and on one reading what she said was true – albeit misleading. There is something over there – namely, Piece – that has the property of being a statue and that existed in 1499. Of course, since Piece acquired that property by borrowing it from *David* and since *David* did not exist in 1499, Piece did not have the property of being a statue in 1499. But this situation has a familiar structure.[15] For "There's a statue over there that existed in 1499" is parallel to "There's a husband over there who existed in 1950," when the husband was six years old in 1950. "There's a husband over there who existed in 1950" is true on one reading and false on another. It is true if taken as: $\exists x(x$ is over there & x is a husband & x existed in 1950); but it is false if taken as: $\exists x(x$ is over there & x was a husband in 1950). Exactly the same can be said about "There's a statue over there that existed in 1499." It is true if taken as: $\exists x(x$ is over there & x is a statue & x existed in 1499); but it is false if taken as: $\exists x(x$ is over there & x was a statue in 1499). So, although Jones's sentence "There is a statue over there that existed in 1499" is highly misleading,

---

13 Note that with (S) there is no problem about counting with respect to hybrid properties like *being a human person*. As we saw in Chapter 4, *being a human person* is a hybrid property borne both by Smith at t and by Smith's human body at t. Since Smith's human body constitutes Smith at t, (S) delivers the desired result: Smith's human body is not a different human person from Smith. Where Smith (constituted by Smith's human body at t) is at t, there is just one human person.

14 This was brought to my attention by Anil Gupta.

15 Although the Piece/1499 case is analogous to the husband/1950 case with respect to the truth conditions of the respective sentences, there are important metaphysical differences. For when the piece of marble that had existed in 1499 came to constitute a statue, a new thing came into existence; but when the person who had existed in 1950 became a husband, nothing new came into existence. The person just gained a property. Cf. Chapter 2.

we need not deny that it is true (on one reading). Hence, the proposed counterexample does not impugn the claim that Piece has the property of being a statue (derivatively).

Consider this popular argument against the coherence of constitution-without-identity. It is charged that constitution-without-identity has false consequences. For example, if your body weighs 180 pounds, then you too weigh 180 pounds; and if you are not identical to your body, then, the objection goes, the scale should read 360. But the scale does not read 360. So, constitution-without-identity must be wrong. In the context of Piece and *David*, here is the argument:[16]

(P₃) If *David* ≠ Piece, then if *David* weighs n kg and Piece weighs n kg, then the shipping weight of the statue is 2n kg.

(P₄) *David* weighs n kg and Piece weighs n kg, but the shipping weight is not 2n kg.

∴(C₂) *David* = Piece.

Since Piece constitutes *David*, (P₃) simply ignores constitution (and hence begs the question against the view set out here). To make (P₃) true, we would have to add a clause to its antecedent ". . . and *David* and Piece are not constitutionally related." But with such a clause added to (P₃), the conclusion does not follow. Indeed, since Piece is the same statue as *David*, Piece's weighing n kg and *David's* weighing n kg do not combine to entail that something weighs 2n kg.

The objector may persist: "If Piece weighs n kg, and *David* ≠ Piece and the scales do not read 2n, then *David* does not genuinely have the property of weighing n kg. In that case, strictly speaking, *David* must be weightless. But that seems wrong." Indeed, I agree, it would be wrong; but my position does not commit me to denying that *David* has weight. *David* actually weighs n kg: Put *David* on the scale and see. The point is that *David* weighs n kg wholly in virtue of being constituted by something that weighs n kg. To explicate the fact that *David* weighs n kg is not to deny that *David* weighs n kg. The fact that *David* has its weight derivatively only implies that *David's* weighing n kg is a matter of *David's* being constituted by something that weighs n kg nonderivatively. Since *David* has its weight derivatively, from the facts that *David* weighs n kg

---

16 Dean Zimmerman, "Theories of Masses and Problems of Constitution," *Philosophical Review* 104 (1995): 53–110, discusses this issue. Also, Alvin Plantinga proposed a similar counterexample to constitution-without-identity at the Notre Dame Conference on Philosophy of Mind, November 3–4, 1994.

and Piece weighs n kg, it does not follow that anything should weigh $2n$ kg.

Examples could be multiplied: From the fact that Mondrian's *Broadway Boogie-Woogie* and the constituting canvas share the property of having yellow of a certain saturation at a particular location, it does not follow that at that location there is a color of twice that saturation. *Broadway Boogie-Woogie* borrows its yellow-of-that-saturation at that location from the constituting canvas. (That's why Mondrian could change the properties of the painting by changing the properties of the canvas.) The account of having properties derivatively also shows why derivative quantitative properties (e.g., being of a certain saturation, weighing m kg) cannot be added to their nonderivative sources. The reason that derivative properties are not "additive" is that *there is nothing to add:* x's having F derivatively is nothing other than x's being constitutionally related to something that has F nonderivatively. Look at it this way: If x and y have constitution relations and x is an F, then x is the same F as y.[17] If x is the same F as y, then it is obvious that x's quantitative properties cannot be added to y's. Piece is the same statue as *David* (in virtue of constitution relations), and Tully is the same person as Cicero (in virtue of identity). So, Tully's quantitative properties cannot be added to Cicero's and Piece's quantitative properties cannot be added to *David*'s. It is no more legitimate to add *David*'s weight to Piece's in order to ascertain the "total" weight than it would be to add the number of hairs on Cicero's head to the number of hairs on Tully's head in order to ascertain the "total" number of hairs.

The idea of having properties derivatively walks a fine line. On the one hand, if x has H derivatively, then x really has H – piggyback, so to speak. Assuming that persons are constituted by bodies, if I cut my hand, then *I* really bleed. It would be wrong for someone to say, "You aren't really bleeding; it's just your body that is bleeding." Since I am constituted by my body, when my body bleeds, I bleed. I have the property of bleeding derivatively, but I really bleed. But the fact that I am bleeding is none other than the fact that I am constituted by a body that is bleeding. So, not only does x really have H by having it derivatively, but also – and this is the other hand – if x has H derivatively, then there are not two independent instances of H: for x's having H is entirely a

---

17 This is true for most "ordinary" properties – i.e., properties that are neither alethic, nor constitution/identity/existence, nor rooted outside times at which they are had.

matter of x's having constitution relations to something that has H nonderivatively.

A final worry about the coherence of constitution-without-identity is that constitution-without-identity makes a mystery of the fact that the statue and the piece of marble that constitutes it have in common all of what we might call 'ordinary properties' – first-order properties whose instantiation is independent of what is the case at other possible worlds. It cannot be just an accident, the objection goes, that the piece of marble and the statue have the same size, weight, color, smell, value, and other ordinary properties. The notion of having properties derivatively dissolves this worry. For the notion of having properties derivatively accounts for these otherwise remarkable similarities: The statue has its size, weight, color, and smell derivatively, and the piece of marble has its astronomical value derivatively. So, the notion of having properties derivatively answers the question: If x and y are nonidentical, why do they have so many properties in common?

But now a question arises from the other side: Assuming that x constitutes y, if x and y are so similar, how can they differ at all?[18] The answer is straightforward: *David* and Piece have different essential properties. If there were no artworld, there would be no *David*, but Piece could exist in a world without art.[19] As theories of art make clear, being an artwork at all – and hence being a statue – is a relational property. When Piece is in certain (statue-favorable) circumstances, a new entity (a statue, *David*) comes into existence. Piece has the property of being a statue because – and only because – Piece constitutes something that is a statue. So, despite the fact that *David* and Piece are alike in atomic structure, they differ in kind: The relational properties that *David* has essentially Piece has only accidentally. Hence, the needed asymmetry to make *David* and Piece different in kind is secured.

So, it is no mystery that *David* and Piece share so many of their properties without being identical: Constitution, defined by (C), ensures nonidentity; and the notion of having properties derivatively accounts for the fact *David* and Piece are alike in so many of their properties. In sum, if x and y are constitutionally related, to say that x has a property

18 Burke, "Copper Statues," pp. 12–17. Burke can imagine only two possible answers: (1) they have different histories, and (2) they have different persistence conditions. He argues that neither of these can ground a difference in sort. I discuss Burke's argument in Lynne Rudder Baker, "Why Constitution Is Not Identity," *Journal of Philosophy* 94 (1997): 599–621.

19 I have extended discussions of this point in "Why Constitution Is Not Identity."

H derivatively highlights the difference between x and y, and hence the fact that constitution is not identity; but to say that H is, nevertheless, a genuine property of x highlights the unity of x and y, and hence the similarity of identity and constitution. (This aspect of constitution is a consequence of trying to mark off an intermediate position between identity and separateness.) Constitution is an intimate relation – almost as intimate as identity, but not quite.

After this survey, I conclude that none of these attempts to impugn the coherence of constitution-without-identity ultimately succeeds.

CONSTITUTION AND MEREOLOGY

Philosophers typically treat constitution as a matter of relations between things and their parts. What worries many philosophers is that some things seem more tightly tied to their parts than do others: An ordinary thing (like your car or my house) seems to be able to gain and lose parts and change size, while its "constituting matter" cannot survive similar material change.[20] The question that occupies many philosophers is this: How can "brittle objects" – objects that can neither gain nor lose parts or particles nor can change size – coincide spatially with familiar objects that can gain or lose parts and particles and can change size?[21]

There is a deep metaphysical reason why I do not approach constitution from the standpoint of mereology. A mereological approach to medium-sized objects would identify each object – a statue, a person, whatever – with the sum of its parts. 'Mereological sum' may be defined as follows:[22]

---

20 Mark Johnston uses the term "constituting matter' in "Constitution Is Not Identity," *Mind* 101 (1992): 89–105.

21 The term 'brittle objects' comes from Crawford L. Elder, "Essential Properties and Coinciding Objects," *Philosophy and Phenomenological Research* 58 (1998): 317–33. See also Judith Jarvis Thomson, who casts the issue in terms of differences in how tightly different things are tied to their parts, in "The Statue and the Clay" *Noûs* 32 (1998): 149–73; and Michael Rea, who says that the problem "arises whenever it appears that an object a and an object b constitute one another and yet are essentially related to their parts in different ways," in "The Problem of Material Constitution," *The Philosophical Review* 104 (1995): 527. Others who start with a similar problematic (but propose different solutions) recently include Michael Burke, "Preserving the Principle of One Object to a Place: A Novel Account of the Relations Among Objects, Sorts, Sortals, and Persistence Conditions," *Philosophy and Phenomenological Research* 54 (1994): 591–624; and Zimmerman, "Theories of Masses."

22 Peter van Inwagen, *Material Beings* (Ithaca, NY: Cornell University Press, 1990): 29.

y is a mereological sum of the $xs =_{df}$ the xs are all parts of y, and every part of y overlaps (has a part in common with) at least one of the xs.

David Lewis has pointed out that a sum "is nothing over and above its parts, so to describe it you need only describe the parts."[23] From the point of view of mereology, we would be unable to distinguish between, say, a flag (or any other symbolic or sacred object) and an ordinary piece of cloth: A description of its parts would not distinguish a flag from a scrap of cloth.[24] In any event, a description of the parts of, say, a person is far from a description of the person. So, I see no prima facie motivation to think of persons in terms of mereology.

The importance of mereology, as Jaegwon Kim has noted, "seems to derive largely from the belief that many crucial aspects of a whole including its existence and nature are dependent on those of its parts. That is, mereological relations are significant because mereological determination . . . is, or is thought to be, a pervasive fact."[25] Similarly, Dean Zimmerman simply appeals to "the plausibility of *mereological supervenience*, the thesis that the existence and nature of a whole is determined by the fact that its parts exist and are interrelated in certain ways."[26] Since, as I have argued at length, the nature and existence of many things – statues, flags, human persons – are not determined by the nature and existence of their parts, in general mereological supervenience or mereological determination has no claim to be a basis for metaphysics.

Coupled with rejection of mereological supervenience as a basis for metaphysics is rejection of the claim that if x and y have all and only the

---

23 David Lewis, *Parts of Classes* (Oxford: Basil Blackwell, 1991): 80.

24 Max Cresswell pointed out to me that this would not be so if we countenanced modal parts. He also noted that everything that I say can be modeled in David Lewis's mereological system and that this fact affords the basis for a "relative consistency" proof of my view.

25 Jaegwon Kim, "Concepts of Supervenience," in *Supervenience and Mind: Selected Philosophical Essays* (Cambridge: Cambridge University Press, 1993): 54.

26 Dean W. Zimmerman, "Immanent Causation," in *Philosophical Perspectives 11, Mind, Causation and World*, James E. Tomberlin, ed. (Malden, MA: Blackwell Publishers, 1997): 440. Zimmerman appeals to mereological supervenience in his account of the persistence conditions of masses of K, and my counterexamples are not masses of K. However, the principle of mereological supervenience is stated in full generality; it is not confined to masses of K; he says that "surely such features as shape, color, disposition to move or change shape, and – most importantly for my purposes – general *kind* of object, should supervene in this way" (p. 441). And I see no reason to deny that flags, statues and human persons are general kinds of objects.

same parts, then $x = y$. If we assume that an atom is part of whatever it makes up, then at the level of atoms, *David* and Piece share all the same parts. So, it would follow from this axiom that *David* = Piece. Moreover, it would follow that if the same aggregate of cells composed a human organism and a human person (at the same time), then the organism and person would be identical. Since the burden of my view is that the relation between the organism and the person is constitution, and not identity, I reject standard theories of mereology.[27] Notice that my explicit rejection of standard mereological theories renders it question-begging simply to invoke those theories against my account of constitution.

I have no regrets about departing from mereology in order to understand constitution, for several reasons. First, even if a constituting thing is usually or always more "brittle" than what it constitutes, or even if a constituted thing is usually or always more "mereologically incontinent" than what constitutes it, such a fact seems to me not at the heart of constitution. Constitution is not so much a matter of parts and wholes as it is a matter of relations between kinds of things. Constitution concerns relations among kinds of things, where whether or not x is of kind K may be determined by x's relational properties that do not supervene on the intrinsic properties of x's parts or on the parts' relations to each other. So, I would not consider mereology a promising way to understand constitution anyway.

Second, as we have seen, if x constitutes y, then x and y consist of the same atoms. But is it obvious that they share all the same parts? Pretheoretically, I would have thought that *David* had a nose as a part but that Piece did not. Part of Piece is (i.e., constitutes) *David*'s nose; but Piece itself does not have a nose. Or so I would have thought. And my view explains this intuition: Noses are proper to statues (and to animals); but pieces of marble do not have noses unless they constitute artworks. So, whereas *David* has a nose nonderivatively, Piece has a nose derivatively. Hence, agreement that x and y consist of the same atoms when x constitutes y does not imply that x and y nonderivatively have all the same parts. It is true that, on my view, *David* and Piece share all the same parts if we include those parts that they have derivatively. But the sense in which *David* and Piece share all the same parts depends on

---

27 As does Judith Jarvis Thomson, who uses a nonstandard mereological approach to work out a view of constitution-without-identity. Note that Thomson's constitution relation applies to artifacts, but not to people.

the fact that Piece constitutes *David*. This is another reason not to suppose that the notion of parts is a key to understanding constitution.

Third, mereologists who introduce the term 'part' as an ordinary concept and then use it to denote whatever satisfies the axioms of mereology are susceptible to an ad hominem argument. For a significant distinction with respect to 'part' that is made in ordinary language gets lost in mereological theories. In ordinary language, 'part' is used both as a count noun and as a mass term. A muffler is both a part of the car and part of the car. But, pretheoretically, *x* can be part of *y* without being *a* part of *y*. For example, a particular molecule may be part of the water in this glass without being *a* part of the water in this glass. Or if part of the silver vase is tarnished, it doesn't follow that *a* part of the silver vase is tarnished. The difference in ordinary language between 'part' and 'a part,' I think, is this: '*x* is a part of *y*' entails that *x* has some integrity as an object, but '*x* is part of *y*' does not entail that *x* has any integrity as an object. '*x* is part of *y*' means '*x* is *some* of *y*' – for example, the left side of *y* is part of *y*.[28] A homogeneous sphere of solid gold does not have parts in the count–noun sense, but it does have parts in the mass-term sense. For example, there is the part of the sphere that is invisible from here. But the part that we can't see from here is not *a* part of the sphere. Mereologists may not feel bound by the idiosyncrasies of ordinary language; but since 'part' is typically taken as a primitive term in mereological theories, our understanding of those theories presupposes our ordinary-language understanding of 'part.'

Moreover, I think that mereologists use 'part' to denote two very different kinds of relation. One relation is "vertical," and the other relation is "horizontal." 'Part' is used horizontally if we say that part of the vase is tarnished or that my cat is part of the sum of cats; and it is used vertically if we say that a particular molecule is part of the water in this glass. The relation between the water in this glass and a particular molecule is not the same as the relation between a vase and the fraction of it that is tarnished. Nor is it the same relation as the relation between my cat and the sum of all cats. Since in mereology 'part/whole' is used for both a horizontal and a vertical relation, mereology is unsuitable for understanding constitution: Whereas the part/whole relation is construed ambiguously as both a vertical and a horizontal relation, constitution is construed unambiguously as a vertical relation.

---

28 David Sanford distinguishes between 'part' and 'a part' in "The Problem of the Many, Many Composition Questions, and Naive Mereology," *Noûs* 27 (1993): 219–22.

Finally, as I have already suggested, I believe that mereologists begin with two mistaken assumptions that make it impossible to come to a coherent view of constitution. The two assumptions are that (1) the nature and identity of a thing are determined wholly by the nature and identity of its parts and (2) if x and y consist of the same atoms, then they have all the same parts. In light of these two assumptions, the question "If x and y consist of the same atoms, how *could* they differ in kind?" seems to have no answer. So, any mereological approach based on these two assumptions seems to me a nonstarter for understanding constitution. Moreover, as I have argued repeatedly, the first assumption is false and can be seen to be false by noticing that there are things like statues, whose nature and identity are obviously not determined by the nature and identity of their parts.[29]

Having rejected mereology as an avenue to understanding constitution, let me say a bit more about mereology. According to Lewis, if you are already committed to some things, a commitment to their mereological sum is no further commitment. "Commit yourself to their existence all together or one at a time, it's the same commitment either way."[30] I need not take issue with this aspect of mereology. A sum of the atoms in my body at t is no more than just the atoms in my body at t. I agree! Also, I can agree that the atoms in my body at t have only one mereological sum. I can well assume that mereological summation (unlike constitution) is identity: The "many − one relation of many parts to their [sum] . . . is like identity."[31] However, I would not suppose that my body is identical to that sum of atoms; much less would I suppose that *I* am identical to that sum of atoms. That sum of atoms may constitute my body at a certain time, and that body may constitute me; but constitution, as I have developed it, is not identity.

So, I can agree that the mereological sum of all the parts of a thing is nothing over and above just those parts. Mereological summation is just a way to get one (a sum) out of many (parts). But unlike the mereologist, I would not suppose that the thing itself is identical to the mereological sum of its parts. If x is an object (like a statue) that has relational properties essentially, then although the sum of its parts requires nothing more than a commitment to its parts, the existence of its parts (summed

---

29 As I implied earlier, on my view, if the consequent of the second assumption is interpreted as 'they have all the same parts nonderivatively,' then the second assumption is false.
30 Lewis, *Parts of Classes*, p. 81.
31 Lewis, *Parts of Classes*, p. 82.

or taken severally) does not entail the existence of x. This is the reason that for many kinds of things, the mereological notion of 'the sum of its parts' must be supplemented by another notion, like 'constitution.'

Lewis insists: "Mereology is ontologically innocent."[32] Suppose that it is. Then mereology would not seem to be a basis for metaphysics. For given the atoms in Jack's body, no further commitment is incurred by supposing that the sum of the atoms exists. But given the atoms in Jack's body, a further commitment is incurred by supposing that Jack exists. Therefore, Jack is not identical to the sum of the atoms in his body. Whereas an "ontological ascent" is required to "get from" the atoms in Jack's body to Jack, no such ontological ascent is required to "get from" the atoms in Jack body to their mereological sum. Mereological theories, if ontologically innocent, simply *assume* that there is no further ontological commitment in supposing that Jack exists than there is in supposing that the atoms in Jack's body exist. But this reductive assumption itself is hardly innocent.

In short: A mereological theory either is or is not ontologically innocent. If it is not ontologically innocent, then it is reductive (e.g., it would simply assume that the atoms in Jack's body are identical to Jack). If a theory is reductive in this unargued-for way, it carries a substantive commitment that is unpalatable to those who are not antecedently reductionists. On the other hand, if mereology is ontologically innocent, then it is not a good tool for understanding what there is. I do not see how anything that really is ontologically innocent could be a basis for metaphysics.

Constitution, on my view, is anything but ontologically innocent. For constitution shows how new things of new kinds come into existence. Nothing that is really ontologically innocent can even recognize genuine novelty. Mereology, taken as ontologically innocent, should be confined to ontologically innocent tasks. Mereological summation is one such ontologically innocent task, but understanding persons is not.

So, I make no apology for not taking a mereological approach to constitution. In any case, as I mentioned earlier, the proof of the pudding is in the eating. If my view of constitution is theoretically illuminating and otherwise coherent, then the fact that it takes an atypical approach is no criticism. In any case, a mereological approach to constitution seems plausible only if one overlooks things (like artworks) that

32   Lewis, *Parts of Classes*, p. 81.

have nonintrinsic properties essentially.[33] To understand a thing – like most familiar medium-sized things – whose identity is not determined by the identity of its parts and the parts' relations to each other, we need to look beyond mereology.

CONSTITUTION AND SUPERVENIENCE

A third line of criticism of constitution-without-identity is that it violates plausible principles of supervenience. Constitution is a relation between things; supervenience is a relation between properties or families of properties.[34] The relation of supervenience is a relation of dependence or determination. The generic idea is that if a family of A properties supervenes on a family of B properties, then fixing the B properties thereby fixes the A properties.

Let me be more precise about which thesis of supervenience we are talking about. Although various kinds of supervenience have been defined precisely, two are of interest here: 'strong supervenience' and 'global supervenience.'[35] Define 'strong supervenience' as follows: Let A and B be families of properties.

A strongly supervenes on B if and only if necessarily for each x and each property F in A, if x has F, then there exists a property G in B such that x has G, and necessarily if any y has G, it has F.

Consider the following supervenience thesis:

(SS) All properties of a macrophysical object strongly supervene on its microphysical properties.

33 See my "Why Constitution Is Not Identity." The argument there entails: $\exists x \exists y \forall z [(z$ is a part of $x \leftrightarrow z$ is a part of $y) \& x \neq y]$. Where things (like statues) have relational properties essentially, mereological considerations cannot answer questions about constitution.

34 In philosophy of mind, much confusion has resulted from not distinguishing between the thesis that beliefs are constituted by brain states and the thesis that beliefs supervene on brain states; the term 'is realized by' is sometimes used equivocally for 'is constituted by' and for 'supervenes on.' For thorough discussion of issues of supervenience, see Part I of Jaegwon Kim's *Supervenience and Mind*.

35 Jaegwon Kim, "Supervenience and Supervenient Causation," in *Spindel Conference 1983: Supervenience*, Terence Horgan, ed. (*Southern Journal of Philosophy* 22, supplement [1984]); 49.

If, as has been customary in discussions of strong supervenience, we restrict the properties in B to properties that are intrinsic to the macrophysical object, then (SS) is false.[36] This is so because with the restriction, (SS) would claim that all of a thing's "higher-level" properties would supervene on local microstructure. And, as we have seen, the property of being a statue does not supervene on local microstructure. This counterexample to (SS) has nothing to do with considerations of constitution; the mere fact that the property of being a statue does not supervene on local microstructure shows that (SS) is false – regardless of how issues concerning constitution are resolved. *Statue* is an essentially relational kind. This gives us conclusive reason, independent of constitution-without-identity, to reject (SS). So, it is no criticism of constitution-without-identity to say that it is incompatible with (SS).

But there is another supervenience thesis that is more plausible. Define 'global supervenience' as follows. Let A and B be families of properties:

A globally supervenes on B if and only if any two worlds with the same distribution of B properties have the same distribution of A properties,

where sameness of distribution of properties means "roughly 'sameness of distribution throughout time and space among the objects of that world'."[37] Consider the following supervenience thesis:

(GS) All properties globally supervene on microphysical properties.

Although (GS) appeals to many philosophers, I am not committed to it. Nevertheless, in light of the popularity of (GS), it would be a strength of constitution-without-identity if it were compatible with (GS). Is it?

The question about the compatibility between supervenience and constitution-without-identity, as I construe it, boils down to this: Is (GS) compatible with the claim that there is a property that a statue has

---

36 But strong supervenience can be understood without restricting the properties in B to those intrinsic to their bearers. See, e.g., Jaegwon Kim, "Postscripts on Supervenience" in *Supervenience and Mind*, pp. 161–71.

37 R. Cranston Paull and Theodore Sider, "In Defense of Global Supervenience," *Philosophy and Phenomenological Research* 52 (1992): 833–54.

essentially, but that the piece of clay that constitutes the statue at t does not have essentially? The answer is, "Of course." To say that the statue has a property F essentially but that the piece of clay that constitutes the statue at t does not have F essentially is only to say that there is no possible world in which the statue exists without having F, but that there is a possible world in which the piece of clay exists without having F. But this is obviously compatible with holding that there are no two worlds having the same distribution of particles but differing in, say, whether or not an object has F. What (GS) requires is only this: Given any distribution of particles, it is settled whether or not any object has F and hence whether or not any statue exists. And this is fully compatible with constitution-without-identity. In short, I claim that constitution-without-identity is compatible with (GS), and that (SS) is false, independent of any position on constitution.

Dean Zimmerman has raised a problem about supervenience for constitution-without-identity. One of his basic criticisms is that, given constitution-without-identity, if x constitutes y, then x and y "are supposed to differ in the sorts of physical changes they can undergo *without* differing in their physical construction; explaining these differences by appeal to ungrounded sortal differences is merely to insist that the two do in fact differ in these ways."[38] I think that Zimmerman, along with Burke and others, is overlooking the possibility of kinds, like *statue*, that have relational properties essentially. But once one notices that what makes something a statue are its relational properties, there is no mystery about why x and y can be of different primary kinds without differing in their physical construction. And if they are of different primary kinds, then there is no mystery about why they "differ in the sorts of physical changes they can undergo *without* differing in their physical construction." Moreover, there is no appeal to ungrounded sortal differences: The claim that *David* is a statue is hardly ungrounded; *David* is a statue in virtue of its relation to an artworld. So, I think that at least part of Zimmerman's worry can be deflected by recognizing relational kinds.

Part of his worry, but perhaps not all. For not all primary kinds have relational properties essentially. Some kinds do seem determined by arrangements of particles. Suppose that *river* is a primary kind that

---

38 Zimmerman, "Theories of Masses," p. 90.

187

does not have relational properties essentially.[39] Now adapting Zimmerman's criticism to the river/aggregate of molecules case, we have him saying:

If the difference between being [a river] and being a mere [aggregate of molecules] is *not* grounded in more fundamental intrinsic physical differences, then we still have physical indiscernibles that nonetheless differ in their ability to survive certain physical changes: one can persist in scattered form, while the other cannot; one can survive the destruction of some [molecules], while the other cannot.[40]

This statement is correct; it is a consequence of constitution-without-identity. But where is the criticism? As we have seen, a river has properties essentially that an aggregate of molecules does not have essentially. It is this difference in essential properties, not a difference in actual physical construction, that accounts for the difference in their ability to survive certain changes. But Zimmerman will persist: "What the 'subvenient' physical states are apparently not sufficient to determine is which object is which. . . ."[41] On my view, "which object is which" – which is the river and which is the aggregate of molecules – is determined by which has what essential properties. Perhaps someone would want to press on and ask: What determines which has what essential properties?

On the one hand, there is *nothing* that explains the fact that things of certain kinds have certain properties essentially. It simply makes no sense to ask "What determines that rivers are essentially streams of water?" or "What explains the fact that being transitive is an essential property of the relation 'greater than'?" And if it makes no sense to ask these questions, it makes no sense to demand that a proponent of constitution-without-identity furnish an answer.

On the other hand, if (GS) is true, then fixing the distribution of microphysical properties in a world determines what modal properties are exemplified. For exemplification of modal properties is governed by where the world is vis-à-vis other possible worlds; and where the world is vis-à-vis other possible worlds may be determined by the distribution of microphysical properties in the world. In order to show a conflict

39 Actually, this is not quite right. *Webster's New Universal Unabridged Dictionary*, 2nd ed. (1983), defines "river" like this: "a natural stream of water, larger than a creek, and emptying into an ocean, a lake, or another river."
40 Zimmerman, "Theories of Masses," p. 90.
41 Zimmerman, "Theories of Masses," p. 90.

between constitution-without-identity and (GS), one would need to show that constitution-without-identity implies that there could be two worlds, w_1 and w_2, with the same distribution of microphysical properties, but in w_1, x has F, and in w_2, x does not exist or x does not have F. I do not think that any such case is in the offing.

So, the prospect of global supervenience presents no threat to constitution-without-identity.

CONCLUSION

I have surveyed the various charges that have been brought against the general notion that the relation of material constitution is not one of identity. Some of the charges regard constitution as little more than the idea that two objects happen to occupy the same place at the same time. Constitution-without-identity, as defined by (C), is a much richer notion than one of simple spatial colocation, and I have tried to show that constitution-without-identity can withstand the various charges.

It seems clear to me that any attempt to develop a comprehensive account of material reality is bound to have some aspects that are less than desirable. Everybody has to bite some bullet or another, and I have tried to be candid about the bullets that I am willing to bite. Let me now mention several bullets that I am happy not to have to bite: Constitution-without-identity does not have to tamper with classical, strict identity or with deep-seated intuitions about what exists. It needs no recourse to contingent identity, relative identity, or temporary identity.[42] It need not postulate unusual persistence conditions.[43] It need not deny the existence of familiar medium-sized objects like artifacts or artworks or people.[44] It need not deny that there are three-dimensional objects that endure through time.[45]

In addition to its coherence and the unsavory bullets that its proponent does not have to bite, the idea of constitution-without-identity, as defined by (C), has further virtues. First, it affords a unified account of material reality that postulates no gap between things that have intentional states and things that do not. Second, the idea of constitution-

---

42 Allan Gibbard appeals to contingent identity, Peter Geach to relative identity, and Arthur Prior to temporary identity.

43 Burke, "Preserving the Principle," postulates unusual persistence conditions.

44 Peter Unger denies the existence of any ordinary things; Peter van Inwagen denies the existence of ordinary things except for organisms.

45 David Lewis is a leading proponent of the four-dimensional view.

without-identity is compatible with materialism in the form of global supervenience. Third, it is nonreductive in that it recognizes the genuine reality of familiar medium-sized things – the things that, for good or ill, shape people's lives.

8

The Coherence of the Constitution View of Human Persons

The general idea of constitution-without-identity, as we have just seen, has the resources to meet the charge of incoherence. In this chapter, I want to show that the specific application of the idea of constitution to human persons likewise can meet this charge. The most serious challenge to the Constitution View today comes from those who hold that we are not merely constituted by animals, but that we are identical to animals. It is to such Animalists that I primarily want to respond. I shall begin with a series of objections that have been raised against a 'coincidence' view of person and body, and I shall show that, if these objections were taken to apply to the Constitution View, they would seriously mischaracterize the Constitution View as I have developed it. Next, I shall respond to three problems that are thought to attend the denial that I am identical to an animal: the "how many" problem; problem of linguistic incoherence; and the "fetus problem." Finally, I want to respond to a putative counterexample to the application of the idea of constitution to persons and their bodies.

CONSTITUTION IS NOT MERE "COINCIDENCE"

Eric Olson combats a view according to which I am "associated with" a human animal with which I share the same matter and to which I am not identical. He calls this view "coincidence" and subjects it to a blistering attack. I want to begin with criticisms that Olson aims against "coincidence" to show that if applied to the Constitution View, these criticisms would miss their mark. Of the four criticisms that I shall consider, three are based on mischaracterizations and the fourth rests on a false philosophical assumption. It is simply not the case that the Con-

191

stitution View entails any of the following: (1) each of us is "associated with" or "connected with" or "accompanied by" an animal that is a duplicate of us; (2) we (human persons) are not animals; and (3) animals are not conscious or rational. The fourth misplaced criticism is that (4) if *x* constitutes *y* and the nature and identity of a thing are not determined by its intrinsic properties, then I could easily be mistaken about whether or not I am a person.

(1) Olson repeatedly refers to the view that he is criticizing as one in which there are human animals "associated" with us, or "connected" to us, and that these associated animals are not people.[1] He speaks of "the human animal that accompanies you."[2] It should be abundantly clear that such is not the Constitution View. First, constitution is not mere association or connection, as a glance at the definition of 'constitution' shows. Second, human animals typically are persons. The converse also holds: Human persons are human animals. Of course, proponents of the Constitution View interpret the two preceding sentences as containing the 'is' of constitution. But that can hardly be a criticism of the view that explains exactly how to understand the 'is' of constitution.

In general, Olson speaks as if 'coincidence' were duplication. For example, "You and the animal are now made up of the same atoms, arranged in the same way. This would appear to make you and the animal exactly alike: you are, now at least, perfect duplicates of one another."[3] Olson makes it sound as if, according to the Constitution View, there are two copies of something – rather as 'cat' and 'cat' are two tokens of the same type. He indicates that he thinks of duplicates as copies when he speaks of things' being exact physical duplicates, "whether or not they share their matter."[4]

The elaborate definition of 'constitution' given in Chapter 2 makes it obvious that the "animal" and you are not two separate things, one of which is a duplicate of the other. Your body is not a duplicate of you; it constitutes you. A look at the definition and its defense shows how intimate and complex a relation constitution is. If *x* constitutes y, then *x* and *y* are not two independent things that rather mysteriously come

---

1 Eric T. Olson, *The Human Animal: Personal Identity Without Psychology* (New York: Oxford University Press, 1997): 107.
2 Eric T. Olson, "Was I Ever a Fetus?" *Philosophy and Phenomenological Research* 57 (1997): 101.
3 Olson, *The Human Animal*, p. 98.
4 Olson, *The Human Animal*, p. 102.

to coincide. You and "the animal" are as closely related as *David* and the piece of marble, things of different primary kinds that are a unity in virtue of being constitutionally related.

The reason that Olson takes you and "the animal" to be mere duplicates/copies is that you share actual intrinsic physical properties. But there are not two sets of intrinsic physical properties. As explained in Chapter 2, you have your physical properties derivatively: You are six feet tall and weigh 180 pounds (or whatever) in virtue of being constituted by something that could have been six feet tall and 180 pounds even if it had not constituted anything. So, the sense in which you and your body share the property of being six feet tall is quite different from the sense in which you and your friend share the property of being six feet tall. Since all this is spelled out in detail, a charge that the Constitution View entails that persons are just duplicates or copies of bodies would be unwarranted.

(2) Olson says that the coincidence view entails that "you and I are material objects but not animals" – a thesis that he calls incoherent.[5] But we have seen at length how the idea of having properties derivatively can be used to affirm the fact that you and I most certainly *are* animals. You have the property of being an animal derivatively because you are constituted by something (an animal) that has that property nonderivatively. This follows from a perfectly general account that I defended in Chapter 2, where I set out an explicit definition of '*x*'s having a property derivatively.' A look at the definition will reveal that it straightforwardly implies that human persons – you and I – are animals. True, we are animals only because we are constituted by animals. But that sounds exactly right: If we were constituted by bionic bodies, then we would not be animals. Similarly, if a river that is in fact constituted by an aggregate of H_2O molecules were constituted by an aggregate of molecules of 'heavy water,' then it would not be an aggregate of H_2O molecules. As it is, however, we are animals in exactly the sense that rivers are aggregates of H_2O molecules.

So, Olson is simply mistaken if he thinks that the Constitution View "entails that, although we are material beings, we are not human animals: we are not members of the species *Homo sapiens*."[6] On the Constitution View, of course, we are human animals, just as rivers are

5 Olson, *The Human Animal*, p. 100.
6 Olson, "Was I Ever a Fetus?" p. 101.

aggregates of H_2O molecules; we have our numerous biological properties in virtue of the fact that we are constituted by organisms. What the Constitution View denies is that persons are *identical* to animals. I shall consider the consequences of denying that persons are identical to animals in the next section.

(3) Olson says that proponents of "coincidence" might try to defend their view by arguing that "animals belong to the wrong 'category' to be rational or conscious."[7] But there is no need to deny that animals are rational or conscious. In developing the idea of the first-person perspective in Chapter 3, I simply assumed that nonhuman animals are not only conscious but that, as problem solvers, are instrumentally rational as well. So, the Constitution View does not deny that animals have psychological features.

On the Constitution View, there is not a great divide between beings with mental or psychological properties and beings without them; rather, the great divide is between beings with first-person perspectives and beings without first-person perspectives. Only beings with first-person perspectives have the ability to care about and value their own futures, the ways that they appear to others, whether they are being treated justly and respectfully, and so on. And the ability to care about and value such things, I hazard to guess, is what makes civilization possible. Indeed, I would go on to speculate that all and only planets populated by beings with first-person perspectives would have civilizations – organized social structures that include conventions about various kinds of behavior and sanctions for flouting them. Beings that are merely "rational or conscious," as dogs and chimpanzees are rational and conscious, are incapable of having art, religion, science, government, economic systems, and the other appurtenances of civilization. And if I am right, this difference between chimpanzees and us is grounded in an ontological difference between beings with first-person perspectives and beings without them. On the Constitution View, the person/animal distinction is not in any way a mind/body distinction. Nonhuman animals, as well as human animals that do not constitute persons, may well be psychological beings.

(4) Another of Olson's criticisms is that "coincidence" theorists reject a philosophical claim that I shall label '(Assumption),' and that rejection of (Assumption) has a dire consequence. Here is (Assumption):

7   Olson, *The Human Animal*, p. 101.

194

(Assumption) The nature and identity of a thing are determined by its actual physical intrinsic properties.

Olson thinks that denial of (Assumption) implies that I could easily be mistaken about whether or not I am a person.[8] I shall give his argument later. But first, let me (i) give evidence that Olson does endorse (Assumption) and (ii) remind you why the Constitution View is committed to denying (Assumption). Then I shall (iii) give Olson's argument that denial of (Assumption) leads to the conclusion that I could easily be mistaken about whether or not I am a person and show that denial of (Assumption) has no such consequence.

(i) Throughout, Olson assumes that a person and the animal that constitutes her cannot differ in persistence conditions unless there is some actual intrinsic difference between the person and the animal. He says, "It is a problem about how any two material objects, whether or not they share their matter, can be exact physical duplicates of one another and yet have different persistence conditions."[9] The only reason to think that exact physical duplicates cannot differ in their persistence conditions is to suppose that the nature and identity of a thing are determined by its actual physical intrinsic properties. And to suppose that the nature and identity of a thing are determined by its actual physical intrinsic properties is just to hold (Assumption).

(ii) As we have seen, the Constitution View is committed to denial of (Assumption). For on the Constitution View, persons and the animals that constitute them share all their actual physical intrinsic properties. Yet, the persistence conditions of animals – all animals, human or not – are biological; and the persistence conditions of persons – all persons, human or not – are not biological. So, on the Constitution View, persons and animals do differ in persistence conditions without any actual physical intrinsic difference between them. But if a difference in persistence conditions does not require any actual physical intrinsic difference, then neither does a difference in the nature and identity of things.

Indeed, I have given independent arguments, based on consideration of artworks and artifacts, that (Assumption) is false.[10] As I argued in

8 Olson, *The Human Animal*, p. 105.
9 Olson, *The Human Animal*, p. 102.
10 See Chapters 2 and 7 and also in "Why Constitution Is Not Identity," *Journal of Philosophy* 94 (1997): 599–621.

Chapter 7, once we see that a thing can have relational properties essentially, we are freed from supposing that if x and y differ in primary kind, then there must be an actual physical intrinsic difference between x and y. And being freed from that supposition, we can see how an animal may have certain biological properties essentially, and a person may have those same biological properties contingently. What grounds a difference in primary kind is difference in essential properties, whether intrinsic or relational. As we have seen repeatedly, it is an error to assume that a difference in essential properties is ipso facto a difference in intrinsic properties. And without the assumption that all essential properties are intrinsic properties, the worry about how x and y can have all the same actual intrinsic properties and yet differ in persistence conditions disappears. So, we have good reason to reject (Assumption).

(iii) But Olson thinks that rejection of (Assumption) leads the "co-incidence" theorist to the conclusion that I can easily be mistaken about whether I am a person. Here's the argument: Rejection of (Assumption) implies that a person may have relational properties essentially. And if a person has relational properties essentially, then I could be mistaken about whether I am a person. Olson says: "If I could fail to be a person just by having the wrong relational or modal properties, then I could easily be wrong about whether I am a person, for I cannot discover by introspection what my modal and relational properties are."[11] And this is an untenable consequence.

This criticism simply does not apply to the Constitution View. First, on the Constitution View, there is no way that *I* could fail to be a person at all. If there were no person here, there would be no *me* here: On the Constitution View, persons are persons essentially. Second, and more important, is the reason that I cannot be wrong about whether I am a person. On the Constitution View, if x can entertain the thought "I wonder whether I* am a person" or "I believe that I* am a person," then x is a person.[12] (And this is so even if, as I argued in Chapters 3 and 4, there is a sense in which the property that distinguishes persons from nonpersons – the first-person perspective – is relational.) The first-person perspective is defined in such a way that all and only those with

11   Olson, *The Human Animal*, p. 105.
12   If x can entertain the thought "I wonder whether I* am a person?" nonderivatively, then x is a person nonderivatively; if x can entertain the thought "I wonder whether I* am a person?" derivatively, then x is a person derivatively. I'll consider issues of first-person reference later.

first-person perspectives have the ability to entertain such thoughts. So, I cannot falsely believe that I am a person because I could not even entertain the relevant thoughts if I were not a person.

This point furnishes the materials to reply to other of Olson's criticisms: "If you could be biologically indistinguishable from an organism without being an organism yourself, perhaps something could be psychologically just like a person without really being a person. If there are pseudo-organisms, indistinguishable from real organisms, there might also be pseudo-people, indistinguishable from real people."[13] Assuming that Olson intends this as a serious criticism of the Constitution View, he wrongly imputes to the Constitution View the thesis that I am a pseudo-organism. But of course, the Constitution View does not imply that I am "biologically indistinguishable from an organism without being an organism [myself]." I am not a pseudo-organism; I am constituted by a genuine organism. And we have just seen that on the Constitution View, it is impossible that something could be psychologically just like a person without really being a person.

A similar response awaits Olson's further criticism: "You think that you are a person. That animal thinks so too, and with the same justification; yet it is mistaken. In that case, how do you know *you* aren't making the same mistake?"[14] We have seen that I cannot be mistaken in thinking that I am a person. Does "that animal" mistakenly think that it is a person? No. An animal that did not constitute a person could not possibly have the thought that it was a person. When I think "I am a person," there are not two separate thoughts, entertained by two separate thinkers, one of whom may be right and the other wrong. There is one thought – "I am a person" – entertained nonderivatively by the person constituted by the organism and hence entertained derivatively by the organism.

So, these criticisms that Olson aims at the view that he calls "coincidence" do not apply to the Constitution View as I have set it out.

THE "HOW MANY" PROBLEM AND LINGUISTIC
INCOHERENCE

There are a number of arguments against the Constitution View based the charge that the Constitution View entails that where you are, there

---

13 Olson, "Was I Ever a Fetus?" p. 101.
14 Olson, "Was I Ever a Fetus?" p. 102.

are two persons (or two speakers, or two thinkers). Here is one such argument.[15] Suppose that you are a person, and 'H' is a name for the animal that constitutes you.

(a) Either H is a person or H is not a person.

(b) It is unacceptable to deny that H — a being that can think, is self-conscious, can deliberate, hold moral opinions, and so on — is a person.

∴(c) H is a person.

(d) If H is a person, then anywhere you are, there are two persons — you and H.

(e) It is absurd to say that anywhere you are, there are two persons — you and H.

∴(f) H is not a person.

Since (c) and (f) are contradictory, the objection goes, the original assumption that you are constituted by an animal — H — to which you are not identical is false.

This argument does not touch the Constitution View. On the Constitution View, H is a person; hence (c) is true. But in this case, (d) is false. For it does not follow from the Constitution View that wherever a person is, there are two persons — the original person and the constituting animal. As I showed in detail in Chapter 7, if x constitutes y and x is an F and y is an F, it does not follow that there are two Fs. Since H is a person solely in virtue of constituting me, H is not a different person from me. I have the property of being a person nonderivatively (and essentially), and H has the property of being a person derivatively (and contingently). So, the Constitution View neither denies that H is a person nor implies that wherever you are, there are two persons — you and H. You and H are the same person.

Since I am an animal in virtue of being constituted by something that is nonderivatively an animal, I am an animal derivatively. Since the animal that constitutes me is a person only because it constitutes something that is a person nonderivatively, it is a person derivatively. As we have seen, if I am an animal derivatively, then I am not a *different* animal from the animal that constitutes me; and if the constituting animal is a person derivatively, then she is not a *different* person from me. This is why it is not the case that wherever I am, there are two persons or two animals.

15 This argument is a paraphrase of one given by P. F. Snowden on p. 94 of "Persons, Animals, and Ourselves" in *The Person and the Human Mind*, Christopher Gill, ed. (Oxford: Clarendon Press, 1990): 83–107.

The Constitution View can provide truth conditions for 'x is an animal' and 'x is a person' that make sense of all our ordinary talk about persons and animals.

'x is an animal' is true if and only if: $\exists y[y$ is an animal nonderivatively & (either $x = y$ or x has constitution relations to $y)$].

Since there is something (my body) that is an animal nonderivatively and that thing constitutes me (the person), it follows that I (the person) am an animal after all. On the other hand,

'x is a person' is true if and only if: $\exists y[y$ is a person nonderivatively & (either $x = y$ or x has constitution relations to $y)$].

Since there is something (me) who is a person nonderivatively and H (the animal in question) constitutes me, it follows that H (the animal) is a person after all.

The Animalist may insist on an "identity" reading of premise (a):[16] Either H is *identical to* a person or H is *not identical to* a person. A Constitutionalist can accommodate this reading as well. According to the Constitution View, H is not identical to a person. But then, (b) begs the question against the Constitution View because on the Constitution View it is perfectly acceptable to deny that H – a being that can think, is self-conscious, can deliberate, hold moral opinions, and so on – is *identical to* a person. From the fact that H is not identical to a person, on the Constitution View, it does not follow that H is not a person: H has the property of being a person derivatively – in virtue of H's constituting a person. On the Constitution View, H most definitely is a person. So, reading 'is a person' as 'is identical to a person,' (b) is false on the Constitution View and (b)'s being false has no bad consequences. So on the "identity" reading, the argument makes no trouble for the Constitution View.

Again, the opponents of constitution seem to think that if x constitutes y at t, then x and y are two things that remarkably happen to coincide spatially – as if a constituted thing were separate from or independent of what constitutes it. But that is not the idea of constitution-without-identity at all. What stands before you when your spouse comes into the room is not a pair consisting of a person and an "associated" animal; it is a person constituted by an animal. A person and the

16 Snowden does so insist.

constituting animal are not two separate beings. When your body hurts, you hurt. It is a complete misinterpretation of the Constitution View (at least my version of it) to treat a person and her body as separate things. The constituting animal is no more separate from the person than the constituting piece of marble is separate from *David*.

Another rich vein of objection to the Constitution View comes from putative difficulties of using of the first-person pronoun, 'I.' As I mentioned earlier, on the Constitution View, 'I' always refers to the person using it. If a person is constituted at *t* by a particular animal and the person uses 'I' at *t*, then the person refers at *t* to a person constituted by the animal. When a person refers to herself, she does not fail to refer to the constituting animal: She refers to an embodied being constituted by that animal. Since you are constituted by a body, you refer to yourself, an embodied being, when you say, "I generally have good digestion." There are not two referents of 'I,' nor are there two digestive systems. There is a single digestive system that you have derivatively and that the animal that constitutes you has nonderivatively.

However, several opponents of constitution-without-identity see variations on the "how many" problem generated by the use of 'I.' One such putative problem derives from the observation that if I speak English, then "the animal [that constitutes me] speaks English, or at least a language homophonically indistinguishable from English."[17] If I speak English, I speak it nonderivatively; therefore, whatever constitutes me speaks English derivatively. Should we conclude that whenever I say anything, there are two speakers, the constituting animal and me? Of course not. The animal's speaking (normal) English is solely a matter of its constituting a person that speaks English; if it did not constitute a person, it would not be speaking English. This is so because normal English includes locutions like "I wish that I were in Detroit," and anything capable of uttering such locutions meaningfully is ipso facto a person. Therefore, the animal's uttering an English sentence is not a separate event from the person's uttering an English sentence.

A more extended charge of linguistic incoherence is mounted by Paul Snowden, who offers what he calls the 'reductio argument' against denying animalism, understood as (A).[18]

17 Olson, *The Human Animal*, p. 106.
18 Snowden, "Persons, Animals, and Ourselves." The argument that I shall discuss appears on p. 91.

(A) I am [identical to] an animal.[19]

Again, call the animal that constitutes me 'H.' Here is a version of Snowden's *reductio* argument:

(1) (A) is false, then on occasion O, when I say "I am [identical to] an animal," then that remark is false.
(2) Animals – and hence H – have evolved the capacity to use 'I.'
(3) If (2), then remarks using 'I' made through the mouth of H are remarks in which H speaks of itself.
∴(4) Remarks using 'I' made through the mouth of H are remarks in which H speaks of itself.
(5) If (4), then the remark on occasion O ("I am [identical to] an animal," made through the mouth of H) was true.
∴(6) (A) is true.[20]

Although this argument looks unassailable to its proponents, the Constitution View has the resources to counter it. According to the Constitution View (4) and the consequent of (3) are susceptible of two readings. If read as

(a) Remarks using 'I' made through the mouth of H are remarks in which H speaks of itself nonderivatively,

then (4) and the consequent of (3) are false. Assume reading (a). Now premise (2) is either true or false. If premise (2) is true, then premise (3) is false, in which case the argument for (6) is unsound. If premise (2) is false, then straightforwardly the argument for (6) is unsound. Either way, on reading (a), the argument for (6) is unsound. On the other hand, if (4) and the consequent of (3) are read as

(b) Remarks using 'I' made through the mouth of H are remarks in which H speaks of itself derivatively,

then (4) and the consequent of (3) are true. But in this case, (5) is false. This is so because 'I' in "I am [identical to] an animal" refers nonderivatively to the person whom H constitutes, and that person is not identical to an animal. That person is constituted by an animal, H, but

19 Snowden insists that (A) is to be "interpreted as identity." Of course, I would agree that "I am an animal" is true if we allow that 'is' of constitution. For on my view, I am an animal in virtue of being constituted by an animal. And it follows from the definition of 'constitution' that I am not identical to what constitutes me.
20 From 4,5 MP, 5★(the remark on occasion O ["I am an animal," made through the mouth of H] was true; from 1,5★ MT, 6.

is not identical to H. So, on reading (b), the remark on occasion O ("I am [identical to] an animal," made through the mouth of H) was not true. Thus, on reading (b), (5) is false, and the argument for (6) is unsound. So, on neither reading (a) nor reading (b) is the argument for (6) sound.

There are other arguments that would charge the Constitution View with linguistic incoherence. I shall mention two more. First: "Where I am, surely there is an animal – call that animal 'H' – and animals have evolved to use 'I.' So, H ought to be able to say things about herself; in particular, H ought to be able to say, "I am an animal," referring to herself and making a true statement. Now if I am not (identical to) that animal, H, and I say (via H's mouth), "I am an animal," referring to myself, then I make a false statement. But a single token of "I am an animal" cannot be both true and false. So, I had better not deny that I am (identical to) an animal."[21]

This argument is specious. We can agree that animals evolved to use 'I.' But when animals evolved to the point of being able to use 'I' comprehendingly – so that anything capable of asserting "I am F" is capable of wondering whether she* is F – they came to constitute persons. So, when "I am an animal" issues from H's mouth, there are not two statements – a true one by H and an false one by me. There is only one statement (a true one) made nonderivatively by me and deriv- atively by H. 'I' refers nonderivatively to the person constituted by H. Suppose that H constitutes me. When "I am an animal" issues from H's mouth, I refer to myself nonderivatively and say of myself that I am an animal. What I say is true since, as we have seen repeatedly, on the Constitution View, I am an animal derivatively. In this utterance, 'I' refers to H derivatively. But there are not two referents of 'I' – any more than there are two persons or two animals – where I am. There is simply no incoherence in the Constitution View of the sort charged by Animalists.

Second: Michael Ayers claims to detect a "peculiarly deep silliness in the distinction between the *person* and the *man*."[22] Since, according to Ayers, there is no reason to deny that the man (i.e., animal) talks about itself as often as the person does, the "uttered thought 'I shall survive' is therefore thought and uttered by the man and the person at once. If man and person are distinct, then one psychological or linguistic event

21 See Olson, *The Human Animal*, pp. 106–7.
22 Michael Ayers, *Locke: Ontology* (London: Routledge, 1991): 283.

202

manages to bear a dual propositional content with dual self-reference."[23]
On the Constitution View, there is no silliness here, deep or otherwise.
'I shall survive' is not a thought that could be entertained by an animal
that did not constitute a person. Nothing that lacked a first-person
perspective could entertain that thought; only persons can conceive of
their own survival. The event of entertaining the thought 'I shall survive'
belongs to the animal only in virtue of the fact that the animal constitutes
a person. So, there is a single psychological or linguistic event that
belongs nonderivatively to the person and derivatively to the animal that
constitutes him.

A better example against the Constitution View would be of a
thought that could be had both by a person and by an animal that did
not constitute a person – for example, 'I am hungry.' But even in this
case, the Constitution View has a gloss. As we saw in Chapter 3, 'I' in
the mouth of an animal that does not constitute a person (assuming that
such an animal could talk) is just a placeholder; such an animal is, in
effect, the center of its universe. Such an animal would have a perspective on the world without realizing that it had such a perspective. Out
of the mouth of an animal that did not constitute a person, 'I' would
have no more force than it would on a label on a bottle saying 'I am
poison.' But when an animal comes to constitute a person, 'I' out of its
mouth always refers nonderivatively to the person. Since the person is
hungry only in virtue of being constituted by an animal that is (nonderivatively) hungry, the person is derivatively hungry. So, when "I am
hungry" is an assertion out the mouth of a person-constituting animal,
then the 'I' refers nonderivatively to the person, who is attributing to
himself derivatively the property of being hungry.

I see no objection based on self-reference that is beyond the ability
of the Constitution View to meet. Suppose that you get on a very small
airplane, and seeing the size of your seat, you say, with chagrin, "I'll
never fit into that seat." The 'I' there still refers to you, the person, even
though your fitting into the seat or not depends on your body's being
of a certain size. Again, as discussed in Chapter 3, you have a unique
relation to your body (i.e., to the animal that constitutes you) that you
have to no other body. You can speak of your body in a first-person
way, and when you do, you are speaking of yourself. The Constitution
View does not need to postulate any ambiguity in the referent of 'I.' If
a person asserts something by means of 'I,' the referent of 'I' is always

23 Ayers, *Locke: Ontology*, p. 283.

203

that person, even if what the person says is, "I am an animal." And indeed, if the person is a human person, then what she says is true. If a person insists, "I am identical to an animal," then, according to the Constitution View, she is still referring to herself (the person) nonderivatively and what she says is necessarily false. In any case, there is not in addition to the person speaking an animal that is not a person and is "associated with" the person and is also speaking. As Olson insists, this would be absurd. But it does not follow from the Constitution View.

IS THERE A "FETUS PROBLEM"?

On the Constitution View, the persistence condition for persons involves reference to first-person perspectives; the persistence conditions for human organisms, all sides agree, do not. So, if the Constitution View is correct, the persistence conditions for persons are different from the persistence conditions of human organisms. According to Olson, however, any view that denies that persons have the persistence conditions of human organisms has the consequence that I was never a fetus – a consequence that Olson labels the 'fetus problem.'[24] Why is this consequence supposed to be a problem? Because, Olson thinks, denial of my identity with something that was a fetus leaves no possibility of a coherent account of the relation between a certain fetus and me now. I want to show that for the Constitution View, Olson's so-called fetus problem is no problem at all.

If, as the Constitution View holds, I am not identical to my body, then from the fact that the organism that came to constitute me was once an early-term fetus, I need not – and do not – conclude that I was ever identical to an early-term fetus. Indeed, on the Constitution View, if my mother had miscarried when she was five months pregnant with the fetus that came to constitute me, I would never have existed. It's not that I would have had a very brief life; rather, there would have been no *me* at all.

It is no secret that the Constitution View does hold that I was never identical to an early-term fetus. On the Constitution View, I did not exist before having the capacity for a first-person perspective. The fetus that came to constitute me existed before it had the capacity for a first-

---

24 This appellation is a prime example of what is called the 'fallacy of persuasive labeling' in courses on critical thinking.

person perspective (and thus before it came to constitute me). Therefore, I was never (identical to) that fetus.

Olson calls this consequence the 'fetus problem.' I see no problem. Why does Olson? He thinks it incoherent to deny that I am identical to (not just constituted by) something that was once a fetus. He gives a series of arguments to back up his charge of incoherence: an argument from embryology, an argument from common sense, and an argument from "serious philosophical problems" with the view that I am not identical to something that was ever an embryo. Let me show that none of these is persuasive.

The Argument from Embryology

According to Olson, we learn from embryology that I once had gill slits, which "entails that there was once something with gill slits and that I am [identical to] that thing."[25] Does embryology have any implications at all concerning the identity of a person with something that once had gill slits? I do not think so. The domain of embryology is the organism before birth; embryology says nothing about persons and entails nothing about the identity of an embryo and me. It is just as consistent with embryology for me to be constituted by a human organism as it is for me to be identical to a human organism. Indeed, even substance dualism, which would agree with the Constitution View that I was never identical to a fetus, is consistent with embryology. Embryology is no help with the philosophical issue at hand.

The Argument from Common Sense

According to Olson, common sense "tell[s] us quite plainly" that I am identical to a fetus.[26] Of course it doesn't. Common sense is not fine-grained enough to distinguish between x's being identical to y and x's being constituted by y. Olson goes on to say that "there does not appear to be any deep logical difference" between saying in the ordinary course of life that I was once an adolescent and saying in the ordinary course of life that I was once a fetus.[27] This assertion seems plainly false. We do,

25 Olson, "Was I Ever a Fetus?" p. 100.
26 Olson, "Was I Ever a Fetus?" p. 100.
27 Olson, "Was I Ever a Fetus?" pp. 99–100.

in the ordinary course of life, regard fetuses and adolescents as different kinds of things. For example, in the late seventeenth century, Mary, the Protestant wife of William of Orange, daughter of James II of England, a Catholic, and heir to the English throne, became pregnant. Many nonCatholics feared that she would finally have a son, who would be brought up as a Catholic. The birth of a son would have altered the order of succession, and the temporary Catholic rule (of James II) might have become permanent. Any male person of whom Mary was the mother would be a new heir. When Mary was five months pregnant, there was no new heir because there was at that time no new person. But if at that time, instead of there being a five-month fetus, there had been an adolescent son, there would have been a new person and a new heir. So, I think that from the perspective of common sense, we do in fact regard a fetus as a different sort of entity from an adolescent.

The Argument from "Serious Philosophical Problems"

I responded to most of Olson's "serious philosophical problems" earlier when I canvassed his arguments against "coincidence." If those arguments were directed to the Constitution View, they would miss it altogether, for they would seriously mischaracterize the Constitution View. I see one remaining argument for the incoherence of the Constitution View. Olson notes that there was an early-term fetus and there is me now. What happened to the early-term fetus, he asks, when I came along? This question is no embarrassment to the Constitution View. Its straightforward answer is: nothing. Nothing happened to the fetus when I came along; the organism continued to develop (and subsequently to decline) after it came to constitute a person. There is absolutely no mystery on the Constitution View about the relation between me and now and a certain embryo earlier. Whereas Olson holds (I):

(I) There is an x such that at t, x was an early-term fetus, and now x is a developed human being, and *I am identical to x;*

the Constitution View, by contrast, holds (II):

(II) There is an x such that at t, x was an early-term fetus, and now x is a developed human being, and *I am now constituted by x,*

where there is a detailed account of what constitution is. The Constitution View has no "fetus problem" because it is perfectly clear what, on the Constitution View, the relation between a certain embryo and me is: I am constituted by something that was once an embryo.

In sum: Questions of personal identity presuppose that the individuals whose identity is under consideration are persons. Since, on the Constitution View, fetuses are not persons, the question of personal identity cannot arise for fetuses. But there is no mystery on the Constitution View about the relation between a human person and a fetus. That relation is clearly explicated: For any human person x, there is a y such that (a) at an earlier stage in y's career, y was a fetus, and (b) now y is an independent human being in organismic and environmental conditions conducive to the development and maintenance of a first-person perspective, and (c) y constitutes x now, where 'constitution' is explicitly defined in Chapter 2.

Now it is time to turn the tables. While Olson accuses others of having a fetus problem, he himself has a "corpse problem." To see that he has a "corpse problem," ask: On Olson's view, what happens to the organism at death? Does it still exist as a corpse?[28] On the one hand, if Olson says yes, then he must abandon his view that an animal "persists just in case its capacity to direct those vital functions that keep it biologically alive is not disrupted."[29] But this view is central to Olson's entire program.[30] On the other hand, if Olson says no (on pain of undermining his whole view), then what happens to the animal, and where does the corpse come from? Olson asked proponents of "coincidence" analogues of these questions regarding fetuses. He supposed that they had no answer. I showed that the Constitution View had clear and coherent answers. Now, I charge, Olson is the one who has no answers to parallel questions about corpses. So, whereas I have rebutted the charge that the what the Constitution View has to say about fetuses is a problem, I believe that Olson has a problem about corpses – a problem that I see no way to solve without undermining his own view. In short, I believe that (I), which Olson would endorse, has an analogue for corpses:

(III) There is an x such that at t, x will be a corpse, and now x is a developed human being and I am identical to x.

28 Sydney Shoemaker exposed this problem in a rather different way in "Self, Body and Coincidence," presented at a symposium honoring Helen Cartwright at Tufts University on September 25, 1998.
29 Olson, *The Human Animal*, p. 135.
30 See Olson, *The Human Animal*, pp. 135–40.

And Olson cannot coherently affirm or deny (III).

Incidentally, the Constitution View can make sense of corpses, just as it can make sense of fetuses. When I die, assuming normal circumstances, there will be a corpse. And that corpse will no longer constitute me, but it will still be an animal, a member of the species *Homo sapiens*. (How could it be anything else?) So, according to the Constitution View,

(IV) There is an *x* such that at *t*, *x* will be a corpse, and now *x* is a developed human being and I am now constituted by *x*.

The early-term fetus that came to constitute me, the adult human animal that constitutes me now, and the corpse that will remain when I die are all phases of one and the same thing: an organism. This is clearly as it should be: A single human organism goes through stages, first as embryo, then as mature animal, finally as corpse. But this satisfying picture is not available to Olson. So, while I can endorse (IV), which is the analogue of (II), it appears that Olson can neither endorse nor deny (III), which is the analogue of (I).

I conclude that the Constitution View has no fetus problem but that the Animalist View, at least Olson's version of it, does have a corpse problem. This completes my defense of the Constitution View against the Animalists' charges of incoherence. Let me turn now to a purported counterexample to the Constitution View of human persons.

A COUNTEREXAMPLE ON OFFER

The putative counterexample that I want to consider invites a quick and decisive response. I could say that 'constitution' is defined only for worlds in which the natural laws are like ours. However, I think that the alleged counterexample is sufficiently interesting to deserve a direct reply without restricting constitution to nomologically possible worlds.

Here is the putative counterexample: Suppose that there are ghosts made out of ectoplasm. Whatever ectoplasm is, it is not made up of particles that make up animals and rocks, tables and chairs; it is some kind of nonphysical stuff. Ectoplasmic ghosts are spatially located, and they have shape and weight that are determined by the intrinsic properties of the ectoplasm that makes them up; so, the weight and shape of an ectoplasmic ghost are different from the weight and shape of the body that produces the ectoplasm. Further, suppose that there are natural laws that govern the emergence of these ghosts from organisms that are in certain states. Now, the counterexample continues, assuming that any such ghost is spatially coincident with the body that produces it, the definition of 'constitution,' (C), is satisfied by a body/ghost pair. Check (C):

(a) Body and Ghost are spatially coincident at t.
(b) Body is in ghost-favorable circumstances at t.
(c) Necessarily, for anything that has *being a (right sort of) body* as its primary-kind property and is in ghost-favorable circumstances at t, there is a spatially coincident thing at t that has *being a ghost* as its primary property.
(d) Possibly Body exists at t, and there is no spatially coincident thing at t that has *being a ghost* as its primary property.
(e) Neither Body nor Ghost is immaterial.

Therefore, the example goes, according to (C), Body constitutes Ghost at t. But surely it would be wrong to say that Body constitutes Ghost at t.[31]

Yes, I agree, it would be wrong to say that Body constitutes Ghost at t. So, let me try to show that this example does not really satisfy (C). My argument is this: On the one hand, since Body and Ghost are both material things, made of entirely different kinds of matter, they are not, strictly speaking, spatially coincident. In that case, (C) is not satisfied by Body and Ghost. On the other hand, if spatial coincidence is interpreted in a looser way, according to which Body and Ghost are spatially coincident, then we should refine the 'spatial coincidence' clause to ensure that any spatially coincident x and y are such that it is possible that they are, strictly speaking, spatially coincident. In that case, (C) is still not satisfied by Body and Ghost.

My strategy is thus to challenge the assumption that Body and Ghost are spatially coincident, as they must be if they are to satisfy (a). In order to satisfy clause (e) of the definition, the ectoplasmic ghost must be material. One point of clause (a) is to preclude the possibility that if x constitutes y, then x and y could be made of different kinds of matter. (A number of objections to constitution-without-identity take issue with the following claim that I accept: that if x constitutes y, then x and y share all the same atoms.) In general, it is not obvious how to reconcile (i)

(i) x and y are spatially coincident

with (ii) and (iii)

31   Dean Zimmerman suggested an example like this to me in private correspondence.

(ii) x is made out of the kinds of particles that make up animals, and so on.

(iii) y is not made out of the kinds of particles that make up animals, and so on,
but y has weight and shape.

If the ectoplasmic ghost has a shape, then it takes up space. The shape of the ghost is determined by the intrinsic properties of the ectoplasm, not by the body that generates the ghost. So, the shape of the ghost is different from the shape of the body. Therefore, it would seem that the space that the ghost takes up is not identical to the space that the body takes up. In that case, it is entirely unclear how an ectoplasmic ghost could spatially coincide with a physical body.

Perhaps the idea is that the ectoplasm occupies the space between the nuclei and the electron orbits of the atoms that make up the physical body. If so, then (C) seems unsatisfied by the example. For, at this micro level, 'spatial coincidence' is plausibly taken as follows:

(SC₁) x and y coincide spatially if and only if: all and only those spatial points occupied by x are occupied by y.

If the ectoplasm occupies the space between the nuclei and electron orbits of atoms that make up the physical body, then the spatial points occupied by the ectoplasm are not the same spatial points occupied by the atoms that make up the physical body. In that case, given (SC₁), the ectoplasmic ghost and the physical body are not spatially coincident. Hence, (C) would not be satisfied.

But there is another way to look at spatial coincidence, more in keeping with how we use the idea at the macro level. Intuitively, I think, we count all the spatial points bounded by the outside of your skin as occupied by your body – even though many of those points are between nuclei and electron orbits and are hence unoccupied. This suggests a different construal of 'spatial coincidence' (one that reconciles (i)–(iii)):

(SC₂) x and y coincide spatially if and only if: x and y have the same closed outer boundary.[32]

Now, perhaps (SC₂) could be enlisted to press the alleged counter-example: If we understand 'spatial coincidence' as (SC₂), then, it may be claimed, Body and Ghost satisfy (a).

But even though (SC₂) is closer to ordinary judgments of spatial

32 *Modulo,* "the problem of the many."

coincidence than is (SC_1), it must be *possible* that x and y spatially coincide in the strict sense of (SC_1). Not only do Body and Ghost fail to coincide spatially on (SC_1), but also as the story was told, it is not possible that Body and Ghost coincide spatially on (SC_1). If we accepted (SC_2), then we would have to divide clause (a) into two subclauses:

(a$_1$) x and y have the same closed outer boundary, and
(a$_2$) it is possible that x and y occupy exactly the same spatial points.

With this elaboration of 'spatial coincidence,' Body and Ghost still do not spatially coincide. So, either we leave the definition of 'constitution' as it is and interpret 'spatial coincidence' as (SC_1) or we elaborate the 'spatial coincidence' clause of (C) as the conjunction of (a$_1$) and (a$_2$). Either way – since replacement of clause (a) by the conjunction of (a$_1$) and (a$_2$) is just a refinement of what was already there – the definition withstands the putative counterexample.

If, according to (C), Ghost is not an entity constituted by Body, then how should the Body/Ghost story be understood on the Constitution View? When Body generates the ectoplasmic stuff, it is not producing a new thing distinct from Body; rather, it is producing a new kind of constituent of itself. Body has one kind of ultimate constituent at the beginning of the story (ordinary atoms) and two kinds of ultimate constituent at the end of the story (an aggregate of ordinary atoms plus a quantity of ectoplasm). Here is an analogy that is a little closer to the actual world: Suppose that there is a cancerlike disease brought on when ordinary cells start producing bizarre cells. Even if the bizarre cells were distributed throughout the skin, so that they had the same outer boundary as the body's normal cells, collectively they still would not satisfy the spatial coincidence requirement: It is impossible that the collection of bizarre cells occupy exactly the same spatial points as the body (or as the ordinary cells in the body). So, according to (C), this bizarre cell case is not one of constitution.

This is as it should be. No matter how bizarre these mutant cells are, and no matter how unlike normal cells, we would (and do!) count them as cells of the body. They are new and unwelcome constituents of the body. On the definition of 'constitution,' they do not constitute a new thing that is spatially coincident with yet distinct from the body. I submit that the case of the ectoplasmic ghost should be treated the same way. Ghost is not a new thing that is spatially coincident with and yet distinct from Body. Rather, what the proponent of the counterexample regards as the generation of Ghost is simply the production of a new kind of constituent of Body. If Body generated nonphysical ectoplasmic stuff in its interstices, then Body would simply no longer be wholly physical. In short, the story of Body and Ghost does not unseat constitution-without-identity as defined by (C).

CONCLUSION

I have canvassed all the objections to the Constitution View of persons and bodies that are known to me. The Constitution View has the resources to meet each of them. Having tried to clear the deck of objections, I shall consider positive reasons to endorse the Constitution view in the next chapter.[33]

33 Portions of this chapter appear in "What Am I?" *Philosophy and Phenomenological Research* 59 (1999): 151–9.

9

In Favor of the Constitution View

Throughout, I have been giving reasons to accept the Constitution View of human persons. In this final chapter, I want to assemble those reasons, expand on some of them, and add others. The aim of this chapter is to emphasize the strengths of the Constitution View and to argue for its superiority to the rival views of persons and bodies.

YES, MATERIALISM

One of the virtues of the Constitution View that I have touted is that it is a form of materialism: The Constitution View shows what is special about human persons without supposing that they are anything but material beings. But does it, really?

Mind/body dualists sometimes weigh in with the charge that the Constitution View is not really a materialist view, but rather leads to immaterialism.[1] They argue as follows:

(1) If I am a material object, then there is some material object to which I am identical.
(2) If I am identical to any material object, then I am identical to my body or some part of it.
(3) It is possible that I exist when neither my body nor any of its parts exist.

Therefore,

(4) I am not identical to my body or any part of it.

---

1 Alvin Plantinga offered this argument (or something like it) at the Notre Dame Conference on the Mind/Body Problem in 1994.

Therefore,

(5) I am not identical to any material object (by (4) and (2)).

Therefore,

(6) I am an immaterial object.

Of course, we should resist drawing this conclusion, for premise (2) should be rejected outright. It would just beg the question against the Constitution View to suppose that if I am identical to a material object, then I am identical to my body or some part of it. I am identical to myself and not another thing. This is true whether I am a material being or not. Whether the *only* way for me to be a material being is for me to be identical to my body or some part of it is what is at issue and cannot be assumed in a premise against the Constitution View. For if the Constitution View is correct, then I am a material being, and I am not identical to my body or to any part of my body.

As we saw in Chapter 4, although human persons are not essentially human (they may have inorganic bodies), anything that begins existence as a human person is essentially embodied: If x is a human person at the beginning of x's existence, then at all times of x's existence there is some body that constitutes x. An essentially embodied being is a material being. (I pointed out in Chapter 5 that, according to the Constitution View, *human person* is just as much a material-object category as is *marble statue*.) The material object to which a human person S is identical is S. It is no surprise that we cannot find some *other* material objects with which to identify ourselves. Van Inwagen asks the proponent of the psychological-continuity view, "Just what material objects are we?" That may be a hard question for a proponent of the psychological-continuity view of personal identity to answer, but it is not a hard question for a proponent of the Constitution View to answer.

Despite the fact that it denies that persons are identical to bodies, the Constitution View steers clear of substance dualism. Substance dualism is the view that there are basically two kinds of things: material and immaterial. According to the Constitution View, there are basically indefinitely many kinds of things, not just two. (I have heard people respond by saying that dualism is the view that there are *at least two kinds* of things and that, on this criterion, the Constitution View is clearly dualistic. I am unmoved because an analogue of the proposed criterion of dualism (that there are at least two kinds of things) would also make the Constitution View come out monistic. For the Constitution View recognizes *at least one kind* of thing!)

Indeed, the Constitution View brings with it a general account of material beings,[2] for the notion of 'constitution' allows us to define 'a material thing.' Recall from Chapter 2 that x is constitutionally linked to y if and only if: Either [y constitutes x or $\exists z_1, \ldots, z_n$(y constitutes z_1 & z_1 constitutes z_2 & ... & z_n constitutes x)] or [x constitutes y or $\exists z_1,$ ... z_m(x constitutes z_1 & z_1 constitutes z_2 & ... & z_m constitutes y)]. If x is constitutionally linked to some aggregate of particles, let us say that x is ultimately constituted by an aggregate of particles. Then:

(M) x is a material thing at t if and only if x is a fundamental particle or there is an aggregate of fundamental particles, such that the aggregate of particles ultimately constitutes x at t.

I use the term 'aggregate' to singularize a plurality of things. An aggregate of x's exists at t if and only if there are some xs – that $x_1, x_2 \ldots x_n$ – such that $x_1, x_2 \ldots x_n$ all exist at t; and aggregate$_1$ of xs is the same aggregate as aggregate$_2$ of ys if and only if the xs in aggregate$_1$ are identical to the ys in aggregate$_2$. An aggregate of xs (as opposed to the xs) can thus be a relatum of the constitution relation. If F is x's primary-kind property, then the primary-kind property of an aggregate of xs is also F. So, an aggregate of things of a certain primary kind, on my view, has the same primary-kind property as the things in the aggregate.

Although it is true that an aggregate of H_2O molecules does not have the property of being an H_2O molecule, the aggregate of H_2O molecules does have the property of being H_2O. So, Lake Lanier is a material thing at any time that it exists because at any time t that the lake exists, there is an aggregate of H_2O molecules that constitutes the lake at t, and hence there is an aggregate of fundamental particles that ultimately constitutes the lake at t. Now on the Constitution View of human persons, a human person at t is constituted at t by a human body, which in turn is constituted at t by an aggregate of organs, which in turn is constituted at t by an aggregate of cells, and so on, down to an aggregate of particles. So, on the Constitution View, a human person is clearly a material

2 Peter van Inwagen has said that a material object is "a thing that is at any given moment the mereological sum of certain quarks and electrons." ("Materialism and the Psychological-Continuity Account of Personal Identity," *Philosophical Perspectives, 11, Mind, Causation, and World, 1997*, James E. Tomberlin, ed. [Oxford: Basil Blackwell, 1997]: 317.) If we accepted that characterization, then constitution-without-identity would be ruled out from the outset, by definition.

thing. Moreover, even though something that is a human person at the beginning of her existence may cease to be a human person without ceasing to exist, she cannot cease to have a body altogether without ceasing to exist. So, if x is a human person at the beginning of her existence, then x is a material being.

With the definition of 'constitution,' we can formulate a weak thesis of materialism in general: Materialism is true if and only if every concrete thing is either a fundamental particle or is constituted by aggregates of fundamental particles.

(Weak Materialism) For any x and any t, if x exists at t, then either x is a fundamental particle or there is an aggregate of fundamental particles that ultimately constitutes x at t.

We can formulate a slightly stronger version of materialism, according to which every concrete thing is either a fundamental particle or is *essentially* constituted by aggregates of fundamental particles:

(Stronger Materialism) For any x and any t, if x exists at t, then either x is a fundamental particle or x is such that, at each moment t' of x's existence, there is an aggregate of fundamental particles that ultimately constitutes x at t'.

Indeed, we can formulate a still stronger version of materialism, according to which (Stronger Materialism) is true in every possible world. The Constitution View of human persons is obviously compatible with all three of these versions of materialism without entailing any of them. Not only is the Constitution View of human persons materialistic, but also it can deliver almost everything that the dualist wants from immaterialism, as we shall see next.

DUALISM AND ITS DESIDERATA

'Immaterialism,' as I shall use the term, is the view that a person is identical to an immaterial substance (a soul) or has an immaterial substance as a part.[3] (I count as immaterialist any view according to which there is a soul that can exist separately from all bodies. So, Thomas Aquinas would be an immaterialist as I am using the term.) Although a

---

3 Classical philosophers like Plato and Descartes, in addition to Thomas Aquinas, were immaterialists. Contemporary immaterialists include Roderick Chisholm in "On the Simplicity of the Soul" in *Philosophical Perspectives, 5: Philosophy of Religion, 1991*, James E. Tomberlin, ed. (Atascadero, CA: Ridgeview Publishing Company, 1991): 167–82; Richard Swinburne in *The Evolution of the Soul*, rev. ed. (Oxford: Clarendon Press, 1997); John

minority position these days, Immaterialism has some able proponents who see substance dualism (of body and soul) as solving problems that beset materialistic views – most prominently, the duplication problem discussed in Chapter 5. According to substance dualism, a person is an immaterial soul conjoined (perhaps temporarily) to a body. Dualism is supposed to be able to satisfy certain desiderata. For example:

(a) A human person is not identical to her body.

(b) A human person can survive a complete change of body.

(c) Not all truths about human persons are truths about bodies.

(d) A person has causal powers that a body would not have if it did not constitute a person.

(e) Identity matters for survival: Concerns about my survival are concerns about myself in the future, not just concerns about someone psychologically similar to me.

(f) My survival does not depend metaphysically on the nonexistence of someone else who fits a particular description (like 'is psychologically continuous with me now').

(g) There is a fact of the matter (perhaps not ascertainable by us) as to whether or not a particular person in the future is I.

Unlike many materialists, I share these desiderata. But unlike Immaterialists, I believe that these desiderata can be satisfied without appeal to anything immaterial. For each of the preceding desiderata is satisfied by the Constitution View – without requiring that human persons have immaterial souls. So, a materialist who espouses the Constitution View can also agree to many claims dear to dualists. Indeed, the Constitution View can deliver everything known to me that dualists want, with the exception of the possibility of disembodied existence for human persons. But as I have argued elsewhere, the possibility of life after death does not require the possibility of disembodied existence.[4] So the dualist would seem to lose nothing that he wants by becoming a constitutionalist.

In case it is not apparent, let me indicate how the Constitution View can accommodate the Immaterialist's desiderata (a)–(g).

Foster in *The Immaterial Self: A Defence of the Cartesian Dualist Conception of the Mind* (London: Routledge, 1991); and Charles Talliaferro in *Consciousness and the Mind of God* (Cambridge: Cambridge University Press, 1994).

4 "Need a Christian be a Mind–Body Dualist?" *Faith and Philosophy* 12 (1995): 489–504 and "Material Persons and Christian Doctrine," presented at the Society for Christian Philosophers, Pacific Regional Meeting, March 7–8, 1997, Whittier College.

(a') Since on the Constitution View my body may go out of existence and be replaced by, say, a bionic body while I continue to exist, I am not identical to my body. Indeed, it follows from the general definition of 'constitution' that if x constitutes y at any time, then x and y are not identical. (See Chapters 2 and 4.)

(b') Although it may be empirically impossible for me to have a complete change of body, the Constitution View raises no theoretical barrier to a human person's having a complete change of body. (See Chapters 4 and 5.)

(c') The Constitution View makes sense of the fact that the properties of our bodies (i.e., the properties that our bodies would have if they did not constitute persons) are irrelevant to many truths about us. 'Fran is divorced'; 'Sam speaks German'; 'Harry is in debt' – these and countless other truths attribute properties had by Fran, Sam, and Harry nonderivatively and had by their bodies only derivatively. (See Chapter 4.)

(d') The Constitution View allows that many of our causal powers are independent of the causal powers of our bodies (i.e., are independent of the causal powers that our bodies would have if they did not constitute persons). Dean Jones has the power to cut the departmental budget; twenty-one-year-old Smith has the power to buy beer; I have the power to send e-mail from home. (See Chapter 4.)

(e') On the Constitution View, we need settle for no less than (strict) identity of persons over time as the criterion of survival. If I survive, then I – not someone else similar to me – survives. (See Chapter 5.)

(f') On the Constitution View, it is impossible that my survival depends on the nonexistence of anyone else who fits a certain description (like 'is psychologically continuous with me now'). Whether some future person S is I does not depend on the absence of any other person S' who is related to me in the same way that S is. (See Chapter 5.)

(g') On the Constitution View, whether some future person S is I is determinate, although not reducible to any nonpersonal fact. (See Chapter 5.)

So the Constitutionalist can deliver just what the Immaterialist wants without having to defend Immaterialism. I take this result to be a clear advantage for the Constitution View. Another advantage of the Constitution View is that it takes persons seriously in the way that our concerns about ourselves warrant.

TAKING PERSONS SERIOUSLY

On the Constitution View, there really are persons, just as there really are statues and horses. The Constitution View takes persons seriously in

218

a way that its materialistic rivals do not. Generically speaking, there are two materialistic rivals of the Constitution View: the Mainstream Psychological View and the Animalist View. I want to begin by specifying ways in which a theory may fail to take persons seriously and then show that, although the Constitution View does take persons seriously, the Mainstream Psychological View and the Animalist View both fail to take persons seriously in the specified sense. The only rival of the Constitution View that takes persons seriously in the specified sense is Immaterialism; however, as we have seen, the Constitution View can achieve almost all of the Immaterialist's desiderata without postulating immaterial souls.

Now how might a theory fail to take persons seriously? In either of two ways:

(I) Construe persons in such a way that the property of being a person is a contingent property that essentially nonpersonal beings have; we (the individuals who are persons) could exist without being persons at all. Or:

(II) Construe persons in such a way that that the property of being a person does not entail any mental properties whatever; we (the individuals who are persons) could exist and could be persons without having any psychological properties – no hopes, desires, plans, concerns; no character traits; no thoughts or inner life – throughout our entire existence.

Here is a thought experiment that illustrates both (I) and (II). Consider a possible world with exactly one inhabitant – your corpse. Would you exist in that world? If so, would you be a person? On the one hand, a view that holds that you exist in that world but are not a person is an example of failing to take persons seriously in sense (I); on such a view, although it is necessary (*de dicto*) that persons are psychological beings, you (this very individual) could have existed (as a corpse) without being a person. That is, a particular individual that never instantiated any psychological properties whatever could be you. On the other hand, a view that holds that you exist in that world and are a person is an example of failing to take persons seriously in sense (II); on such a view, although it is necessary that you are a person, you (this very individual) could have existed (as a corpse) without ever instantiating any psychological properties.

As another illustration of (I) and (II), consider the following pair of questions:

(a) What is a person?
(b) What am I?

Question (b) is to be interpreted as asking what I am essentially or most fundamentally. Of course, I am a lot of things: a teacher, a writer, a voter, a wife, and so on. But these are not relevant answers to question (b) in the intended sense. Any view that answers (b) by citing something that could exist without being a person is an example of (I); any view that answers (a) by citing something that could exist without any psychological properties is an example of (II). Any view that takes what I essentially am to be something that could exist even if no persons existed, or any view that understands persons in such a way that being a person has nothing essentially to do with having any psychological properties whatever, fails to take persons seriously.

Why is it that (I) and (II) are failures to take persons seriously? Consider (I). Any view of type (I), according to which being a person is a contingent property of essentially nonpersonal things, has these consequences:

(1) Being a person is irrelevant to the kind of individual that one is.

What makes one the kind of individual that one is depends on the essential properties of the individual in question. If a person is not a person essentially, then the individual would be of the same basic kind whether that individual was a person or not. In that case,

(2) Every person in the world could be eliminated without eliminating a single individual.

Every person in the world would be eliminated if the property of being a person ceased to be instantiated. If the property of being a person is a contingent property of persons, then, logically speaking, that property could cease to be instantiated without loss of the individuals who had been persons. (Similarly, since the property of being a student is a contingent property of persons, then, logically speaking, that property could cease to be instantiated without loss of the individuals who had been students. For example, suppose that all schools were abolished.) If (2) is true, then there is a clear sense in which persons as such have no ontological significance.

Now consider (II). Any view of type (II), according to which something can be a person without ever having any mental properties, has this consequence:

(3) Having any mental states at all is irrelevant to what a person is.

It is just a contingent fact about persons that they have beliefs, hopes, fears, plans. On any view that construed persons in accordance with (II), what a person is has nothing to do with having an "inner life" or, more generally, with mentality at all. But if being a person has nothing to do with mentality in any sense, then there seems to be nothing that is distinctive of persons. (1) and (2), which follow from any view of type (I), and (3), which follows from any view of type (II), in my opinion, are clear and blatant instances of not taking persons seriously enough. So any theory of persons of type (I) or (II) is convicted out of hand of not taking persons seriously.

Let me begin by showing how the Constitution View does take persons seriously in the specified sense. On the Constitution View, what makes me a human person is that I am constituted by a human organism; what makes me a person at all is that I have a first-person perspective (this answers question (a)). And I am essentially a person (this answers question (b)). The Constitution View entails the negations of (1)–(3). Since person is a primary kind,

Not-(1) Being a person is relevant to the kind of individual that one is.

Since persons are essentially persons,

Not-(2) Elimination of any person would be elimination of an individual.[5]

Since personhood is defined in terms of a mentalistic first-person perspective,

Not-(3) Having mental states is relevant to what a person is.

So, in an obvious way, the Constitution View does take persons seriously: Persons qua persons are ontologically significant beings with mental properties.

Taking persons seriously is a signal advantage of the Constitution View. Pretheoretically, we do take persons seriously in the sense just specified. Moreover, we suppose that persons have a special value, a particular moral status, perhaps even inalienable rights. The Constitution View justifies our practices of taking persons seriously. For if the Constitution View is correct, it is not simply arbitrary that we feel a level of responsibility toward each other that we do not feel toward nonpersons, not even toward nonhuman animals. A person, unlike a nonhuman

---

5   I am speaking here of entities that are persons nonderivatively.

animal, has a dignity that would be violated by being treated as a pet, even a beloved pet. Pascal said somewhere in his *Pensées*, "Are you any less a slave by being loved and adored by your master?" The implied answer ("No") suggests the important contrast between persons and nonhuman animals. Persons are special, and their specialness derives from what makes them persons – namely, their first-person perspectives. By taking persons seriously in the sense just explained, the Constitution View makes sense of and justifies the ways that we feel obliged to regard and treat each other.

MATERIALISTIC COMPETITORS

Now consider the materialistic rivals of the Constitution View, beginning with the Mainstream Psychological View. (The reason for qualifying the first approach as 'mainstream' is that the Constitution View and Immaterialism could both be considered to be psychological approaches in a broader sense.)

The Mainstream Psychological View

Let's begin with the familiar psychological view. Locke is famous for originating this view: A person is "a thinking intelligent being that has reason and reflection and can consider itself as itself, the same thinking thing in different times and places."[6] Many have followed Locke in taking psychological properties of one sort or another to be required to be a person. However the Psychological Criterion of persons is formulated, it entails this:

(DD) Necessarily, if x is a person, then x has psychological properties.

('(DD)' stands for '*de dicto*.') So understood, the Psychological View is an answer to question (a), "What is a person?" As an answer to question

6   John Locke, *Essay Concerning Human Understanding* II, xxvii, 9. The Psychological Approach is perhaps the dominant one today. Proponents – although they differ significantly from each other – include David Lewis in "Survival and Identity" in *The Identities of Persons*, Amelie O. Rorty, ed. (Berkeley: University of California Press, 1976): 17–40 and "Postscripts to 'Survival and Identity' " in his *Philosophical Papers*, Volume I (New York: Oxford University Press, 1983): 73–7; Robert Nozick in *Philosophical Explanations* (Cambridge, MA: Harvard University Press, 1981); Derek Parfit in *Reasons and Persons* (Oxford: Clarendon Press, 1984); Sydney Shoemaker in "Personal Identity: A Materialist's Account" in *Personal Identity*, written with Richard Swinburne (Oxford: Basil Blackwell, 1984): 67–133; Peter Unger in *Identity, Consciousness and Value* (New York: Oxford University Press, 1990).

(a), however, the Psychological View may remain silent about the answer to question (b), "What am I most fundamentally?" Indeed, Locke himself apparently did not take his Psychological Criterion to be an answer to question (b) at all. Persons, for Locke, were not (basic) substances. The basic substances are God, finite intelligences, and material atoms.[7] A complete inventory of the world, on Locke's view, need not mention persons.

(DD) is compatible with my now being a person, but my existing at some other time without any psychological properties – and hence my existing without being a person. To construe the Psychological View in this way is to take the property of being a person to be a contingent property – like the property of being a wife. Necessarily, if x is a wife, then x is married. I am a wife; but I could exist (in fact, for over two decades, I did so exist) without being a wife. I can imagine my existence if I hadn't been a wife, but I can make no sense of the idea of my existence (whose existence?) if I hadn't been a person. Being a wife is a contingent property that I might not have had, but being a person is part of my basic identity. If we construe the Psychological View as no stronger than (DD), then being a person is on a par with being a wife. This construal of the Psychological View makes being a person a contingent property of something that is essentially nonpersonal. Indeed, this construal of the Psychological View entails (1) and (2), and hence does not take persons seriously in the sense that I specified.

However, the Psychological View may also be construed in another way – one that does take persons seriously and avoids (1)–(3).[8] One could take the Psychological View to provide an answer to question (b), as well as to question (a). Understood as an answer to question (b), the Psychological View entails this:

(DR) If x is a person, then, necessarily, x has psychological properties.

('(DR)' stands for 'de re.') If what I am most fundamentally is a person, and if being a person entails having psychological properties, then having psychological properties is essential to me. Construed this way, as imply-

<hr />

7 See William P. Alston and Jonathan Bennett, "Locke on People and Substances," *Philosophical Review* 97 (1988): 25–46.

8 In his argument against the Psychological View, Eric T. Olson construes the Psychological View as entailing (DR). Hence, I think that his argument misses his mainstream opponents. In any case, the Constitution View does entail (DR), but, as I argue elsewhere, it avoids Olson's criticisms. See my "What Am I?" in *Philosophy and Phenomenological Research*, 59 (1999): 151–9.

ing (DR), the Psychological View does take persons seriously. However, I believe that any detailed development of the Mainstream Psychological View as a materialistic theory that entails (DR) will be forced to adopt the idea of constitution-without-identity. [9] In any case, the Psychological Views that do not entail (DR) do not take persons seriously in the sense specified. [10]

The Animalist View

Eric T. Olson, author of *The Human Animal* (1997), is perhaps the most recent contemporary proponent of the Animalist View to personal identity. [11] Olson states his view this way: "So I started out as an unthinking embryo, and if things go badly I may end up as a human vegetable – as long as my biological life continues. We might call this the Biological View of personal identity." [12] Although he bills his view as one of personal identity, Olson is not really concerned with answering question (a) "What is a person?," but only with answering question (b), "What am I most fundamentally?" And his answer to question (b) – that I am an animal, whose persistence conditions are determined by continuation of biological functions like metabolism – has nothing whatever to do with being a person. [13]

9 In *The Human Animal: Personal Identity Without Psychology* (New York: Oxford University Press, 1997), Eric T. Olson's criticism of the Psychological View, construed as entailing (DR), makes it apparent that a version of the Psychological View that entails (DR) will be pushed toward constitution-without-identity.

10 I am continuing to assume that persons are three-dimensional entities that endure through time. A four-dimensionalist, like David Lewis, takes persons to be aggregates of momentary stages. See David Lewis, "Counterparts of Persons and Bodies," *Philosophical Papers*, Volume I (New York: Oxford University Press, 1983): 47–54. On Lewis's counterpart theory, (DR) may be interpreted in a way that makes it come out true. However, discussion of Lewis's four-dimensionalist counterpart theory – which, I think, fails to take persons seriously enough on other grounds – is beyond the scope of the present project.

11 But Aristotle, who did not have a concept of a person distinct from a human being, was perhaps the first proponent of this approach. Other contemporary advocates include Peter van Inwagen in *Material Beings* (Ithaca, NY: Cornell University Press, 1990); Fred Feldman in *Confrontations With the Reaper: A Philosophical Study of the Nature and Value of Death* (New York: Oxford University Press, 1992); and P. F. Snowden in "Persons, Animals and Ourselves," *The Person and the Human Mind*, Christopher Gill, ed. (Oxford: Clarendon Press, 1990): 83–107.

12 Eric T. Olson, "Was I Ever a Fetus?" *Philosophy and Phenomenological Research* 57 (1997): 106. Following Snowden and other of its proponents, I shall continue to call this the 'Animalist View.'

13 Olson uses the term 'personal identity' in more than one way. For example, he calls his view the 'Biological View *of personal identity*,' but he recognizes the possibility of nonbio-

As for his own view, it is difficult to know what Olson thinks about persons since he always speaks of them cavalierly; but here is one thing that he says:

Perhaps we cannot properly call that vegetating animal a *person* since it has none of those psychological features that distinguish people from non-people (rationality, the capacity for self-consciousness, or what have you). If so, that simply shows that you can continue to exist without being a person, just as you could continue to exist without being a philosopher, or a student or a fancier of fast cars.[14]

My being a person, on this view, is metaphysically on a par with my "being a philosopher, or a student or a fancier of fast cars."

Thus, on at least one version of the Animalist View, I am essentially an animal and only accidentally a person. Consider what follows from this. On the one hand, since on that view I am essentially an animal, I could not survive replacement of my organic parts with nonorganic parts. It is metaphysically impossible – not just physically impossible – that I survive the extinction of the organism that I am. On the other hand, since on that view I am accidentally a person, my being a person is simply a contingent property borne by an essentially nonpersonal entity. Hence, this version of the Animalist View entails (1) and (2). In short, this Animalist View fails to take persons seriously in the sense specified.

Of course, a human organism can exist without having any psychological properties at all. So, on any version of the Animalist View, I could have existed without ever having had any psychological properties (whether an Animalist would count such a being as a person or not). So, if the Animalist View is correct, either I could have existed without being a person or I could be a person without having any mental properties throughout my whole existence. An Animalist View that holds that I could have existed without being a person has consequence (1): Being a person is irrelevant to the kind of individual that one is. But an Animalist View that holds that I could be a person without any

logical persons. ("Was I Ever a Fetus?" p. 106). And although he explicitly says, "Psychology is irrelevant to personal identity" ("Was I Ever a Fetus?" p. 107), what he means by this is that we are essentially animals, whose psychological properties are irrelevant to our persistence conditions. Strictly speaking, on Olson's view, there is no such thing as personal identity – any more than there is such a thing as infant identity or philosopher identity" (*The Human Animal*, pp. 26–7).

14 Olson, *The Human Animal*, p. 17.

mental properties throughout my whole existence has consequence (3): Having mental states at all is irrelevant to what a person is. Either way, the Animalist View fails to take persons seriously in the specified sense.

This book is a strong dissent from those who think that the fact that we are persons is not an ontologically important fact about us. It argues that there would be no "us" at all if we were not persons. If there were no persons, there would be no *me* to consider my own persistence conditions. Here we have a bedrock clash of intuition. On the Animalist View, I am essentially an animal; my continued existence is nothing other than the continued existence of an organism. On the Constitution View, I am an animal (in that I am wholly constituted by an animal), but I am not essentially an animal (in that I could be constituted by an inorganic body). So on the Constitution View, it is not the case that my continued existence is nothing other than the continued existence of an organism. (I seem to be able to imagine my surviving replacement of my organic parts with nonorganic parts until my body was no longer the body of an organism.)

With the entrance of the first-person perspective in the world comes a new kind of thing – something that can ponder its own future, something that can imagine itself in different circumstances, something that can ask the question "What am I?", something that has an inner life. Only beings of such a kind produce the arts, the sciences, philosophy, civilization. It is obvious to me, although not to everyone, that a first-person perspective makes an ontological difference in the universe. However, I do not know how to adjudicate intuitions at this level. So, I shall not press my intuitions further. Still, there are at least two further reasons to favor the Constitution View over the Animal View.

First, the Constitution View avoids a problem that afflicts Animalists like Olson. On the Constitution View, not only am I constituted by something that was once an embryo, but also I am equally constituted by something that (barring my body's being blown to bits at my death) will be a corpse. Of course, when my body is a corpse, it will no longer constitute me. But the very same biological entity, a member of the species *Homo sapiens*, that was a fetus and that constitutes me now will continue to exist for a short time after I am gone. This plausible picture of the unity of an organism from embryo to corpse is not available to Olson, who holds that "there is no such thing as a dead animal, strictly so called."[15] Olson's view makes a mystery of what a corpse is, how it

---

15 Olson, *The Human Animal*, p. 136. See Chapters 5 and 8.

came into being, and what happened to the animal that died.[16] These are matters on which the Constitution View has clear and credible verdicts: The corpse is the animal in death; the corpse is not an entity distinct from the animal that died; the corpse did not just mysteriously appear at the animal's death; the animal simply died, without disappearing or ceasing to exist. This plausible picture is unavailable to proponents of the Animalist View, and there is no clear idea of what picture they would like to substitute.

Second, the Constitution View has a virtue that the Animalist View lacks. As we saw in Chapter 6, what is uniquely characteristic of us prominently includes the facts that we have ideals, that we reflect on values, and that we are rational and moral agents – all of which depend upon our being persons. On the Constitution View, what we most fundamentally are – persons, understood in terms of a first-person perspective – makes it possible that we have the features just mentioned that are uniquely characteristic of us. By contrast, on the Animalist View, what we most fundamentally are – human animals, understood in terms of organismic integrity – has nothing especially to do with the features just mentioned that are uniquely characteristic of us. For what is uniquely characteristic of us depends on our having first-person perspectives; but the existence and persistence of a human animal are independent of a first-person perspective. So, if we are most fundamentally human animals, then what is uniquely characteristic of us is severed from what we most fundamentally are.

Not only are the facts that we have ideals, that we reflect on values, and that we are rational and moral agents uniquely characteristic of us, but also these are facts that matter deeply to us. It matters to us not only what ideals and values we have, but also the fact that we are the kind of beings who have ideals and values and can reflect on them. And our having ideals and values depends on our having first-person perspectives. On the Constitution View, what we most fundamentally are coheres with these features that matter to us deeply. The link is the first-person perspective. On the Animalist View, what we most fundamentally are does not require a first-person perspective; as a consequence, what we most fundamentally are is severed from these features that matter deeply to us. It is an advantage of the Constitution View

16 This problem for Olson was also discussed by Sydney Shoemaker in "Self, Body and Coincidence" at the Symposium in Honor of Helen Morris Cartwright at Tufts University, on September 25, 1998.

that what is ontologically important about us grounds what we care about deeply.

To sum up this discussion of the competing views on persons: The Animalist View and versions of the Psychological View that entail (DD) but not (DR) are all committed to one or more of (1)–(3), and hence they all fail to take persons seriously in the specified sense. Versions of the Psychological View that entail (DR) will be untenable unless combined with a Constitution View. The Constitution View and Immaterialism are the only ones to take persons seriously in the sense specified. Since Constitutionalists can give Immaterialists (almost) everything that they want without postulating immaterial souls, the Constitution View is superior to its rivals.

CONCLUSION

According to the Constitution View, the relation between human persons and their bodies is the same kind of relation as that between marble sculptures and the pieces of marble that make them up. What distinguishes a marble sculpture from a mere piece of marble is its relation to an artworld; what distinguishes a human person from a mere human organisms is its first-person perspective (or, in the sense defined, its capacity for one). A marble sculpture has a physical nature in virtue of being constituted by a piece of marble and an aesthetic nature in virtue of being (nonderivatively) a sculpture. So, too, a human person has a biological nature in virtue of being constituted by a human organism and a psychological/moral nature in virtue of being (nonderivatively) a person.

Both the Constitution View itself and the underlying idea of constitution-without-identity, defined by (C), have much to recommend them. In Chapters 7 and 8, both the idea of constitution-without-identity and the Constitution View of human persons were shown to be coherent. But there is more in their favor. First, the Constitution View of human persons shows how human persons are related to their bodies without any special pleading for persons. The notion of constitution is entirely general and can be used to give a comprehensive definition of 'material thing.'

Second, the Constitution View is superior to its competitors in its assurance of realism and determinacy about persons and in its compatibility with deep-seated intuitions – such as those underlying Locke's story of the Prince and the Cobbler – without any immaterialism.

Third, the Constitution View grounds what is unique to us (moral agency, rational agency) in our ontological difference from other things. Our status as moral agents depends on our being the kind of beings that we are. This feature of the Constitution View distinguishes it from Animalism. According to Animalist views, the most significant fact about us ontologically is that we are animals; according to the Constitution View, the most significant fact about us ontologically is that we have first-person perspectives. Since the first-person perspective underwrites the possibility of moral and rational agency, the Constitution View ties what is morally and rationally important about us, and what matters to us, directly to what we basically are. The fact, if it is a fact, that the first-person perspective evolved naturally does not diminish its ontological significance: Beings with a capacity for a first-person perspective (in the sense defined in Chapter 3) are fundamentally different from other beings.

Finally, the Constitution View explains how it is that, although we are set apart by our first-person perspectives, we are still animals and straightforwardly part of nature. Constituted as we are by animals, we have animal natures – just as, Michelangelo's *David*, constituted as it is by a piece of marble, has a marble nature. So, the Constitution View locates human persons firmly in the material world while accommodating the specialness of persons – that is, the first-person perspective that sets us off from other animals.

In addition to the specific merits of the Constitution View, the general idea of constitution-without-identity that underlies this account of human persons has manifold virtues. I shall conclude by enumerating them. First, the idea of constitution-without-identity can be explicitly spelled out by means of (C) and can be further elaborated by defining the notion of 'having properties derivatively' in Chapter 2. Second, the idea of constitution-without-identity achieves what proponents of contingent identity, relative identity, and temporary identity want without compromising the classical view of identity (and without using the word 'identity' to mean something other than 'identity'). Third, the idea of constitution-without-identity allows for a metaphysics that is nonreductive without being antimaterialistic: A metaphysics based on the idea of constitution-without-identity is compatible with global supervenience of all properties on fundamental physical properties (and hence is not antimaterialistic), but it eschews an "intrinsicalism" that holds that the nature and identity of a particular object are determined by the properties of the fundamental physical particles that constitute it (and hence is nonreductive). Fourth, and perhaps most important, this view of constitution supports an ontological pluralism that honors the genuine variety of kinds of individuals in the world.

Between the Big Bang and now, genuinely new things of genuinely new kinds have come into existence – some of our own making (e.g., tractors, computers, space shuttles), others created without human intervention (e.g., planets, continents, organisms). The Constitution View of human persons is comfortably situated in a general metaphysical view that is, I believe, attractive independently of the light that it sheds on human persons.

Index